ROYAL FAMILY
YEARBOOK
Volume II

First published in Great Britain by Colour Library Books Ltd.
© 1983 Illustrations: Keystone Press Agency, London.
© 1983 Text: Colour Library Books Ltd., Guildford, Surrey, England.
Colour separations by Llovet, Barcelona, Spain.
Display and text filmsetting by Acesetters Ltd., Richmond, Surrey, England.
Printed and bound in Barcelona, Spain by Rieusset and Eurobinder.
All rights reserved
ISBN 0 86283 065 6
COLOUR LIBRARY BOOKS.

ROYAL FAMILY
YEARBOOK
Volume II

FOREWORD BY
THE EARL OF LICHFIELD

TEXT BY
TREVOR HALL

PRODUCED BY
TED SMART & DAVID GIBBON

COLOUR LIBRARY BOOKS

Leafing through this superb record of the Royal Year, I found myself forcibly reminded of another, rather different collection of pictures that I recently unearthed at the bottom of a long neglected cupboard. In very clear contrast to the fine informal photographs found here, that ancient copy of the Jubilee Issue of the Illustrated London News displayed a distinctly rose-tinted view of Royalty. Or perhaps not so much rose-tinted as gold-plated, for the rather fuzzy quality of the engraved illustrations was more than made up for by the splendour of the mock-Gothic illuminations, a half acre of highly-coloured border per print, laboriously worked in gold and silver inks, all of it testifying to the seriousness of the Head of State.

What a very different view of our Sovereign we had in 1897. Queen Victoria, when she can be spotted amidst the thicket of supporting Peers and Prelates, appears as a symbol, not a woman. She frowns, as does everyone around her, engrossed in the awesome task of personifying the Majesty of Monarchy.

What a contrast to this current volume. Here, on almost every page, there is a positive riot of smiles. As a professional portrait photographer I flatter myself that I can identify a phoney smile instantly. There are none here. Amongst the memorable pictures in this book you will find Prince Philip laughing at the conversation of Australian surfers, Captain Mark Phillips chuckling at the antics of his son, the Princess of Wales beaming down on yet another small child presenting yet another huge bouquet and, of course, Prince Andrew on his return from the South Atlantic, grinning a characteristic grin, a single red rose gripped merrily between his teeth.

And what of the Sovereign herself? What would Queen Victoria make of the way her great great grand-daughter is presented to the world? She would, I'm sure, wholeheartedly approve of the solemn air with which her successor graces serious State occasions. And one likes to think of her quietly chuckling (in private of course) at the sight of the Head of the Commonwealth bravely downing yet another exotic potion from the South Pacific. But, best of all surely, she would be delighted to see, so often, the Monarch smiling.

Our circumstances have changed substantially since the Victorian era. Nowadays no member of the Royal Family can travel anywhere without a posse of press photographers hot on their heels. And, predictably, boundaries are sometimes overstepped, unspoken contracts broken. When the results of legitimate media attention are as charming as the ones seen here, however, nobody objects. Relaxing a little, Royalty smiles, a genuine human response to the extraordinary positions in which they find themselves. And we, seeing them smile, smile with them, happy in the knowledge that this Royal Yearbook shows us, not an empty array of symbols, but a genuinely happy family album.

RT. HON. THE EARL OF LICHFIELD F.I.I.P., F.R.P.S.

In essence, and if you don't look at things in too much detail, one year in the life of the Royal Family is much like another. Each of its adult members has a set programme of engagements to undertake, each twelve-month period ending with a long summer holiday after July, which is punctuated with repetitive festivals – Remembrance in November, Maunday in April, Trooping the Colour in June, Ascot, the Garter, the Royal Tournament, the State Opening of Parliament – and filled with more mundane duties in between. Only the particular impact of a major celebration like the Silver Jubilee, or the Royal Wedding, will distinguish the memory of any one year.

The disadvantage of major distinguishing features is that the big events that mark them out as such tend to distort or conceal the other events of the year, and drive into the shade public personalities who would otherwise deserve greater recognition for a job well done. The Mountbatten assassination in 1979, the Queen Mother's eightieth birthday celebrations in 1980, the Prince of Wales' wedding in 1981 and the birth of Prince William in 1982 all took the headlines so effectively that it is difficult to think of those respective years in any other terms. The twelve-month period beginning in July 1982 was comparatively free from such overwhelming events, and was consequently one in which the contribution of each member of the Royal Family to the institution and to the nation and Commonwealth it serves can be more clearly seen, more easily assessed, and the year as a whole more readily regarded as typical – at least in outline – of any.

It was however untypical in the detailed sense that July saw the unfolding of the legacy of the extraordinary episode of the Falklands crisis. For the Queen, head of a nation effectively at war with another, the South Atlantic campaign was a serious anxiety, the more so as her second son Prince Andrew was away fighting for the liberation of the Falkland Islands. The Argentinian surrender in mid-June had of course also seen the cessation of hostilities, but for almost a year afterwards the Queen and her family were reminded again and again of the war and its consequences. At the end of July, she led a nation's homage at the Service of Thanksgiving and Commemoration at St Paul's Cathedral – itself a controversial event as pro- and anti-conflict groups vied with each other to attach their own brand of significance to the service. Two months later, the Queen joined a much more evident celebration as she welcomed Prince Andrew back from the South Atlantic on his submarine-hunter, the 19,500 ton *HMS Invincible*. Portsmouth seethed with the bustle and noise of almost 60,000 relatives anticipating the first sight of their loved ones, just as the Queen looked forward to her very private meeting with her own son. Prince Philip and Princess Anne accompanied her, and for once the intensity of the celebrations induced the Queen to relax and show something of her usually very private feelings. They certainly showed two days later when, back at Balmoral, she beamed as she rarely has before while driving with Prince Andrew to Crathie Church. That evening she threw a champagne party to celebrate his return among the family.

No member of the Royal Family was invited to the great Victory Parade which took place in London on 12th October, even though a City of London spokesman had said that it was expected that one or other of them would be there. But in fact, most of the family were abroad at the time, including the Queen and Prince Philip, then in Australia. The following month, however, the Queen was inevitably thrown back into the continuing Falklands debate when she opened Parliament with a speech – nominally her's, but actually written by the Prime Minister – promising to "encourage the economic development of the Falkland Islands" and to maintain "an appropriate defence force there". Less than a fortnight later the Queen led her family at the Festival of Remembrance in the Albert Hall, and the Remembrance Service at the Cenotaph – both occasions haunted by the memory of another 256 men recently added to the national Roll of Honour.

A more explicit controversy blew up over the content of the Queen's Christmas broadcast. At one stage, the only question surrounding it was whether Prince William would feature, though Buckingham Palace fielded any such enquiries with practised ease – "We never reveal anything about the Queen's broadcast in advance". But only a few days before Christmas, the Labour MP Tom Dalyell, a consistent and articulate spokesman for those who opposed the Falklands hostilities, wrote an open letter to the Queen, telling her that there were rumours of "considerable Falklands-orientated content" in her speech which went "some way to endorse Mrs Thatcher's view that the South Atlantic war put the Great into Great Britain again". He warned the Queen that such content would "land the Crown in the middle of a fierce controversy" and, although he was aware that the televised broadcast had in fact been recorded a fortnight earlier, added, "I beseech the Queen to think again before it is too late". In the event, the Queen mentioned the Falklands conflict only briefly, dwelling upon the issue of courage and dedication as part of a wider issue. Even that was too much for the left-wing newspaper *Tribune*. It asserted that "the Queen's pro-Falkland Christmas broadcast" showed that she must be a Conservative. "It may not be popular to say so", it added, "but it has to be said; a democratic society is not possible unless the Monarchy is abolished".

Tribune's was very much a lone voice, and deservedly so. When in January the Queen sent a message to the people of the Falkland Islands to celebrate the 150th anniversary of continuous British settlement, she played a strictly neutral hand, merely hoping "that we can now look forward to a peaceful and prosperous future for the Falklands". And, apart from the incident in April whenthe organiser of a voyage to the Islands by bereaved Argentinians sent a telegram to the Queen asking her, "as a mother of one of the war's soldiers" to intercede with the British Government to allow the relatives to set foot on the Falklands, the issue of the war no longer involved the Queen in the bitter controversies it had stirred up.

That was just as well, of course, in view of the deluge of alternative scandal and mayhem that had afflicted her back in July. In that month, Michael Fagan had not only repeated his earlier *tour de force* of getting into Buckingham Palace, but had actually entered the Queen's bedroom; in the wake of the uproar in Parliament, press and public, the Queen's senior detective, Commander Michael Trestrail, resigned after admitting a homosexual affair with a male prostitute; a detachment of the Queen's personal Household Brigade had been decimated by an IRA bomb in the centre of London; the Queen herself had gone into hospital for a painful operation on a wisdom tooth; and she had lost a close friend in Lord Rupert Nevill, Prince Philip's former Private Secretary, after a long and debilitating illness.

"God Save The Queen From Another Year Like This" ran one newspaper headline, and for once the Queen may have been inclined to agree. It is a powerful disaster that keeps her from her horses, but by the end of July the accumulated strain was so great that she cancelled her annual visit to Goodwood Races, even though she already had an official engagement at Chichester the same day. "She is trying to take things a little easier," said a member of her staff, and indeed she spent a few days at Sandringham before coming to London again for Prince William's christening on 4th August. The journey to Balmoral the following day must have been sweet, and when she was presented with two boxes of freshly caught salmon, sea-trout and halibut in Aberdeen on the way, she must have already felt in quite a different world.

The two month holiday at Balmoral was a pretty miserable one from the point of view of weather, but none-the-less restful. Royal engagements were, as always, kept to a minimum and by the time the Queen appeared at the Braemar Games early in September she was her usual lively self, and in good humour as she presented prizes. One prize-winner was Geoff Capes, the caber-tossing champion; he won a bronze and granite statuette. "It's much heavier than I expected", said the Queen as she handed it to him, then threw her head back with laughter as he replied, : "Then I'll relieve you of it Ma'am". The Queen indulged in some antics of her own when Capes showed reluctance to shake her hand because of the sticky resin still on his palms. The Queen insisted, then pretended to prise her own hands apart as if they had become irrevocably glued together.

The Queen had been joined on holiday by most members of her family at one time or another – the Prince and Princess of Wales, Princess Anne, Prince Andrew (just for a fortnight), Princess Margaret and the Queen Mother. Prince Philip spent only a short time there because of commitments abroad, including a flight to Australia in advance of the Queen to open the 12th Commonwealth Games. The Queen followed him early in October for what was to prove one of the most colourful and imaginative of her many royal tours. The initial stage involved Australia, and was very much like any other tour of Australia, except that its emphasis was on the Games which the Queen, like Prince Philip, spent much of her time watching. In between times, Brisbane played host to her in the only way Brisbane knows, with massive welcomes everywhere and a succession of interesting, memorable engagements – one of them, a reception at the Queensland Cultural Centre, prefaced by a magnificent firework display as the Queen arrived by barge down the Brisbane river. She stayed on to close the Commonwealth Games, which came to a superb conclusion with a neck-and-neck finish for medal superiority and festivities which were as much a celebration of sheer enjoyment as of sport, and which the Queen truly relished. The Canberra leg of the Queen's Australian visit was less festive, but the walkabouts which she initiated in that part of the world twelve years earlier proved as popular as ever, and hundreds of children realised the ambition of their young lives as they spoke or gave flowers to their Queen.

Things were, however, much different for the next fortnight. In that period the Queen and Prince Philip visited six South Pacific Commonwealth countries – mostly those they had not visited since the gaining of Independence. Some of them, like Tuvalu and Fiji, had chosen to remain monarchies with the Queen as Head of State; others, like Papua New Guinea and Nauru, have their own President. But all lie within the same equitorial-tropical range geographically, and the potentially busy schedule in visiting them all was made lighter by the use of *Britannia*, which gave the Queen and Prince Philip the agreeable bonus of two or three days rest at a time as they sailed from one remote country to another. Their presence in each brought out the best in local customs. Tribal dancing in Papua, Warrior Challenges in the Solomon Islands, the giving of ceremonial necklaces in Kiribati and Tuvalu, the drinking of *kava* in Fiji. Colossal feasts awaited the royal visitors in Kiribati and Tuvalu, where the sight of the Queen drinking coconut water straight from the shell was a common one. And everywhere, from Papua to Fiji, there was an eerie silence:

cheering is almost unknown, and the obligation to greet is acquitted by a single, respectful wave, perhaps a smile or a flag, or the beat of a drum. Otherwise it is all noiseless. And in Fiji, every formal greeting was accompanied by a courteous half-kneel and the clapping of cupped hands. Only in Tuvalu was it different: the islanders of this friendliest of countries brought the Queen and Prince Philip ashore in canoes, and carried them through the streets to the centre of Funafuti to the accompaniment of exquisitely harmonised singing.

Their fond memories of that tour must have been enhanced by the somewhat less successful – though potentially monumental – trip they made to the Western Atlantic in February and March. Conceived as the most extensive ever undertaken since the 1953/4 Commonwealth Tour, it worked well enough during the stages which took them to Jamaica, the Cayman Islands and Mexico, where three quite distinct ethnic communities showed how universally similar the admiration for the Queen is, no matter how different their ways of expressing it. But the high point of the journey – the tour of the West Coast of the United States – proved disastrous. Rain fell practically every day and in quantity. Waiting crowds everywhere were soaked, welcoming ceremonies curtailed, whole engagements excised from the schedule, and the much publicised invitation by President Reagan for the Queen to go horse riding with him at Santa Barbara was cancelled. Natural disasters along the coast, with property flooded, boats smashed and lives lost, seemed to follow the Queen's progress. One of her escort cars crashed in appalling weather and at high speed, and a bodyguard was killed. *Britannia* was unable to keep to schedule because of impossible conditions in harbours, and the Queen and Prince Philip actually had to spend a night at an hotel rather than on their yacht. For all that, the Americans put on a show which only they could – spectacular, outsized and unmistakeably adoring of their distinguished visitors. It did not go unnoticed, meanwhile, that the numerous contacts between the Queen and the President were clearly as personal as they were official.

The quality of these visits abroad may make the Queen's official duties back home seem comparatively ordinary, but that is a relative judgement. There was plenty of pageantry during the year, not least by reason of two State Openings of Parliament – one in November, attended by many members of the Royal Family including, for the second time, the Princess of Wales, and one in June when, owing to the comparative suddenness of the General Election, only five members of the Royal Family could attend. There were two State Visits to Britain – one by the Queen of the Netherlands in November, the other by the President of Zambia in March. The former was very much a family occasion, even though Queen Beatrix is one of the more distantly related European monarchs, and boasted two elements distinguishing it from most other State Visits to London. One was that the visitors arrived by sea and were greeted at Greenwich (rather than travelling by air and being welcomed at Gatwick); the other was that Queen Beatrix gave her reciprocal State banquet not at Claridges, but at Hampton Court Palace, whose inner courtyard owes much to the influence of her ancestral kinsman, our own King William III.

Only one – less celebrated but none-the-less official – visit threatened to involve the Queen in politics again, and that was the courtesy call at Buckingham Palace of the Arab League Peace Mission in March. This was to have included a representative of the Palestine Liberation Organisation, but the Prime Minister had refused to sanction such a visit for a previous delegation, and there was speculation whether she would do so again, thus effectively intervening in the Queen's official schedule of engagements. Eventually, a member of the Palestinian National Council – Professor Walir al Khalidi – was chosen to represent the Palestinian interest, and the visit to Buckingham Palace went ahead, lead by King Hussein of Jordan.

The year's other ceremonial occasions took place very much as they always do. The Queen's official Birthday Parade in June lacked the drama of the 1981 ceremony, as well as the vile weather of 1982, and Prince William did not appear on the balcony of Buckingham Palace afterwards. The Queen's personal birthday, on 21st April, was marked – whether by design or coincidence has not been officially explained yet – by the issue of the new £1 coins, which have certainly proved less popular than the Queen herself. It was her 57th birthday, so there were 57 male and 57 female recipients of the Royal Maunday ten days earlier, when the Queen went to Exeter for that other annual and delightful ceremony.

It was mercifully not overshadowed by the peculiar little incident involving the scarlet cassocks, to the wearing of which the Queen had taken exception during the previous year. Scarlet cassocks are strictly the privilege of the Royal Chaplains and the clergy of Westminster Abbey and Canterbury Cathedral, and when the Queen realised that the clergy of Exeter, Ripon, Winchester and Leicester Cathedrals were wearing them, she insisted that they be changed. So much so that she gave the Deans and Chapters of those cathedrals a total of £3,000 so that new cassocks in different shades of red – though not maroon, because that was special to St George's Chapel, Windsor – could be bought. By May the scarlet garb was duly being phased out, and the Queen had won what seemed to be an easy skirmish. As one newspaper said, "Tough on the would-be scarlet clergy who chance upon the Queen in her most royal mood".

The "royal mood" was, apparently, nothing new. June 1983 marked the thirtieth anniversary of the Queen's Coronation, and Cabinet papers published under the thirty-year rule showed that the decision to televise the Coronation ceremony in 1953 was opposed by almost everyone except the Queen. Churchill was unhappy about the strain it might impose upon her, the Duke of Norfolk saw no need for it, the Archbishop of Canterbury felt that film extracts could be seen after the event. Sir John Colville, Churchill's Private Secretary at the time, wrote a long and entertaining article describing how the Queen was wholly in favour of her subjects being given the chance to see the ceremony live, and how her will prevailed. "Thus it was", he concluded, "that the new 26-year-old sovereign personally routed the Earl Marshal, the Archbishop of Canterbury and Sir Winston Churchill".

Much of the Queen's energies are spent, if not routing the press, then at least attempting to keep their enthusiasm for royal stories under control. The advent of the Princess of Wales brought with it an enormous amount of press intrusion into the less public lives of members of the Royal Family, and the phenomenon continued long after the wedding. Despite a good-natured visit to the Press Club to celebrate its centenary in November – it was the Queen's first ever visit there, and they presented her with a replica of James II's Proclamation against "the spreading of false news" – the relations between press and Palace, which had deteriorated the previous year, remained at a low ebb. Press treatment of Prince Andrew's holiday with Koo Stark in October had been a major new contribution to the antipathy; a possible misunderstanding about the Palace Press Office's view on the coverage of Princess Anne's Save the Children Fund tour in November had not improved matters, and the appalling free-for-all to get pictures of the Princess of Wales skiing in Liechtenstein in January naturally made matters worse.

But when, in February, the *Sun* newspaper ran the first of an anticipated series of articles based on the revelation of a former Palace employee, Kieran Kenny, the Queen decided to sanction legal action, and a High Court injunction was applied for and granted immediately. The *Sun*, which had published Kenny's insight into Prince Andrew's and Koo Stark's alleged romps at Buckingham Palace while the Queen was away, and planned the following day to reveal "How Barefoot Di

Buttered My Toast," expressed its amazement at the Queen's action, under the dramatic headline "The Queen Gags The Sun". When things had settled down, however, an agreement was reached out of court, the *Sun* withdrawing its proposed publication and paying £4,000 to charity and legal costs to the Palace. It was effectively the use of the stick where the carrot had failed. As Michael Shea, the Queen's Press Secretary, told the Guild of British Newspaper Editors in Cardiff in May, "If Fleet Street does not look to its own ethics, then there are many who will be only too willing to do it for them".

The strains and preoccupations of such a busy, and at times rather worrying, year were undoubtedly offset by some worthwhile off-duty achievements. If the notion of the Queen at leisure conjures up anything, it is horses, and though her year on the Turf was a comparatively indifferent one, there was plenty to keep the Queen occupied and interested.

"Our aim", said her racing manager Lord Porchester in September, "is to make the risky game of breeding as much of a self-financing exercise as possible". Thus, when the 89-year-old Sir Michael Sobell decided to put his stables at West Ilsley in Berkshire up for sale, the Queen stepped in with an agreement to buy. The contract, announced that month, was completed three months later and the price, though undisclosed, was thought to be at least £750,000. The idea, which originated with the Queen personally, was an apt one, since the stables were already being run by Major Dick Hern, her principal trainer. Lord Porchester was quietly satisfied at his employer's decision. "The Queen has now added a sound investment in bricks and mortar to her horses", he said.

Another sound investment had already been realised around the same time. The Queen's best filly for four years, Height of Fashion, was sold to an Arab horse owner for the incredible figure of one and a quarter million pounds. That paid for the stables with change to spare, but the filly's new owner would soon rue his decision. Height of Fashion ran second to last in the King George VI and Queen Elizabeth Diamond Stakes in July and last in the Yorkshire Oaks subsequently. Meanwhile Dunfermline, the Queen's Jubilee Year Classics Champion, came good as a brood-mare after four barren seasons. The Canadian stallion Dance on Time succeeded where Nijinsky, Roberto and Relkino had failed, and the spring of 1983 saw Dunfermline, now nine years old, with her first born – a filly. As Shakespeare said, "Though Patience be a tired mare, yet will she plod".

The Queen is still being patient about her long looked-for Derby winner. This year's hope was her Mill Reef colt, Special Leave, who had won the Hyperion stakes at Ascot in October, and was placed twice in his only three races as a two-year-old. His trainer, Ian Balding, considered him in February as "the most exciting prospect I have trained for the Queen" and Lord Porchester believed a Derby win for Special Leave – the star of the Queen's string of over a score of racehorses – was in prospect. Then on 23rd April he failed to get into the placings at the Guardian Classic Trial at Sandown. Assessed as below his best, he awaited a second attempt but never got it. With heavy rainfall during the spring, and the near certainty that the ground at Epsom would not dry out sufficiently by the time of the Derby meeting, Special Leave was withdrawn from the entries in mid-May, with the even more disappointing news that there were no alternative plans for him. Almost immediately, the Queen struck lucky with three other horses: the two-year-old filly Reflection came second at Newbury, the three-year-old Castle Rising won there the same day, and the three-year-old colt Red Duster came second in his first race of the season at Goodwood. But when Derby Day came round, there was again nothing for the Queen to pick up. Her jockey, Willie Carson, was clearly right when he said, "You feel a bit different when you put the Royal colours on – a little more important – and your adrenalin gets going quicker. But it doesn't make the horses go any faster".

The Derby was somewhat overshadowed by the continuing mystery over Shergar, the 1981 winner kidnapped at gunpoint from his stud in Eire the previous February. His fate caused anxiety for hundreds of stallion owners including those of Shirley Heights, also a Derby winner, who stands at the Queen's stud near Sandringham. The Queen owns a quarter share in the stallion and an increased guard was placed upon the stud, as indeed around all of Sandringham, as part of ever increasing security measures. With the death of Cecil Boyd-Rochford in March at the age of 95, it was a gloomy time for the Queen. Boyd-Rochford had taken over the royal horses in 1943, had won the One Thousand Guineas for King George VI with Hypericum in 1946 and had provided the Queen with eight golden years of success on the Turf between 1952 and 1960 with horses like Aureole, Pall Mall and Doutelle. He retired in 1968.

But there were brighter moments. Great patron as she is of the sport of kings, the Queen made a major contribution in May to resolving the perennial problems of maintaining the Grand National at Aintree. With the £4 million appeal still short of its target by £750,000, the Queen arranged a special open day at the Royal Mews at which Burmese, the mare she has been riding at Trooping the Colour ceremonies for fifteen years, and the drum horse Coriolanus were on show, together with some of the State carriages. This was, according to Lord Derby, "entirely her Majesty's own idea", and Buckingham Palace confirmed that she "had felt she wanted to do something herself to save the Grand National".

The previous month, the Queen had loaned many of her driving carriages to a special exhibition at Harrods, to mark the fortieth anniversary of the Royal Windsor Horse Show. And at the end of April, she personally opened the country's only national horseracing museum at Newmarket, to which she had been one of the main contributors. Among the exhibits she loaned was an oil painting of the future King Edward VII's Derby winner, Diamond Jubilee, a menu card for the celebration dinner after Persimmon had won the Derby for him in 1896, the stuffed head of Persimmon himself, a letter sent to the future King George V and containing betting advice from his jockey, a water colour of Ascot dated 1756 and a silver cup presented to Florizel, the sire of the first Derby winner, Diomed.

They were not the only loans the Queen made during the year. Two hundred rare and unusual pieces by Carl Fabergé, all from the Queen's collection at Sandringham, were lent for an exhibition forming part of the *Britain Salutes New York* celebrations in the spring. Along with those went seventy drawings, from the Windsor Castle library, of Tudor royalty by Holbein. In January an exhibition of 140 works of art on the subject of Britain's Kings and Queens was opened at the Queen's Gallery at Buckingham Palace, and in April an exhibition of royal travel held at Wolferton Station Museum near Sandringham displayed a first class ticket costing 43/-, sold to the Queen for her journey to Windsor in 1958. Three members of her household went too – second class – for only 22/8d each! And the previous September, the Queen gave permission for a photograph of herself and Prince Philip to be used on the sleeve of a record produced by Seaford College, Sussex. The record was of the carol recital which they had given before the Queen at Fishmongers' Hall in December 1981.

The lending of personal possessions by the Queen is, of course, a well-established tradition and they do provide some insight into the otherwise very private life of the sovereign and her family. Yorkshire Television went one better in February and produced a seven-part documentary for children, dealing with many aspects of royal life – such as travel, food, pets, palaces and clothes – both as it was in the past and as it is now. From it we learned that the Queen reads the *Sporting Life* daily, begins work in her office at ten o'clock, does not enjoy travelling by helicopter, does not carry money in her handbag, and sports statuettes of St George and the Dragon on her five Rolls-Royces. And that the custom by which a small black carriage makes daily deliveries of papers and documents from government departments to Buckingham Palace is not only quaint, but also important because it gives horses and drivers the opportunity of travelling among traffic and crowds. Television personality Michael Aspel divulged a couple of gems, from his meeting with the Queen, illustrating her sense of humour. She deplored helicopters landing on the lawn because "it makes the windows so dirty", and she thought that the reptile house at Regent's Park was "a good place for an assignation".

But without a doubt the most popular revelations concerned royal food. There is nothing, it seems, more fascinating than to know what the Queen and her family actually consume within the four walls of their grand residences. Shortly after the television programme dealing with the Royal Family's diet, came a book written by Mrs Alma McKee – a cook at Buckingham Palace for twelve years – called *The Royal Cookery Book in Colour*. These two sources of information revealed that the Queen hates oysters, garlic and milk puddings, but enjoys banana caramel with plenty of syrup, and prefers vegetable omelettes to richer meat dishes. Prince Philip by contrast would sink his teeth into game-pie any day of the week, while Prince Charles prefers meatballs or goulash, banana sandwiches spread with jam, and bread and butter pudding laced with rum. Fish is served daily at the royal table and the whole family enjoys steak and kidney pie. What is more, "from now on", said the Secretary to the Royal Household Tradesmen's Warrants Committee in February, "supplies of free- range eggs will be purchased". It seemed unbelievable that this wasn't already established practice, but an organisation called Chickens' Lib discovered that battery-produced eggs were being served to the Queen, and they sent her a dozen of the free-range variety for her to taste in an effort to persuade her to release battery hens from their misery. It worked: Chickens' Lib immediately celebrated "the Royal seal of approval to our campaign".

Of course free-range eggs cost more, and cost was something the Queen had to be particularly careful about. The economy measures introduced throughout the royal residences the previous year seemed to have achieved their objective. What a Buckingham Palace spokesman termed as "successful economies in manpower levels and general housekeeping" involved a cut of about 10% in staff, mainly by natural wastage, and a corresponding increase in private contracting for cleaning and catering. Job descriptions of remaining staff were made more versatile, materials were re-cycled, first class post was more sparingly used. Cost-consciousness had increased amongst the staff, the switching off of lights no longer required being specifically cited as an example. Meanwhile, in the royal stables, old newspapers were being shredded to provide bedding for horses – an excellent use, someone said, for the troublesome tabloids – and considerably cheaper than straw.

The economies were prompted by the country's general financial crisis which resulted in a comparatively modest 8% rise in the Civil List in 1982. The increase was even more modest on Budget Day 1983 – around 5% – bringing the total government funding to £4.8 million, of which the Queen received £3.5 million – and three-quarters of that went on household salaries. Neither the Palace economies nor the limited Civil List increase satisfied MP Willie Hamilton, who thought the Treasury ought to be clawing back part of the 1982 increase, because the rise in inflation had not been as great as the 8% awarded. Nor was he impressed by the £15,000,000 profit earned by the Crown Estate Commissioners, according to their annual report published the following month, which goes straight back into the Government's coffers.

But for once he was not the most vociferous of the monarchy's critics. Another MP, Tony Benn, made much-publicised capital out of his desire to have the sovereign's constitutional powers taken away, with the theoretical right to choose the Prime Minister and to dissolve Parliament being transferred to the Speaker, as in Sweden. Although he seemed to be advising this course out of concern lest the Monarchy should be drawn into the heat of a political debate, Mr Benn found few overt supporters, while Norman St John Stevas, a parliamentary colleague at the other extreme of the political spectrum, regarded his proposals as "unconstitutional and dangerous". Meanwhile, Labour councillors in Leeds, criticised the Monarchy as "the pinnacle of the capitalist society", and called in February for a ban on hospitality to royal visitors, and Socialist members of Tyne and Wear Council were urged to refuse to attend garden parties at Buckingham Palace. The Young Socialists went even further at their Bridlington Conference in April. One of their resolutions stated bluntly that "the way forward for the working class is to sack the monarchy" which it called "an archaic institution symbolising the corrupt system of hereditary privilege".

In a democracy, of course, these are permissible, perhaps even healthy comments, but insofar as they appear destructive and insulting, the Queen can console herself with three undoubted truths. One is that sentiments such as these have been voiced, heard and debated many times before. The second is that the overwhelming majority of British people, however passive their support for the Crown, reject them. The third is that, three years from her sixtieth birthday, she is as dedicated as ever she was to the task she inherited thirty-one years ago, and is seen to be so. The year, with its blend of old experiences and new, duties and pleasures, ceremony and routine, celebration and anxiety, praise and criticism, is typical in that it shows that in a changing world the Queen has acquired the uncanny knack of seeming to remain, reassuringly, very much the same.

It is not far from the truth to say that Prince Philip has not changed much during his years as the Queen's consort either. At sixty-two he seems as busy, versatile, questing and outspoken as ever. If, in addition, his reputation for irascibility has increased, perhaps it can be put down to an understandable impatience with the follies of the world to which he has never failed to direct his ready criticism. But whether praising or despairing, his contribution to the Monarchy's relevance as the twenty-first century approaches is fundamental. He is no great admirer of the glamourous royal occasion and the meaningless sycophancies from which a person in his position is rarely free. He prefers the business-like existence of a man of many parts: the meetings where decisions are made, the projects where things get done, the conferences and symposiums where attitudes are changed. Consequently, his official diary reads like the engagement book of a high-powered executive, with three or four major meetings per day when his duties as the consort and companion to the Queen allow. More often than she would wish, perhaps, those engagements take him abroad: by the end of 1982 he had visited over thirty foreign countries; by the middle of 1983 another ten foreign visits had been completed.

His most frequent reason for foreign travel is as President of the World Wildlife Fund International, a cause which seems to take up more of his time and energies as the problems of conservation increase. In September he took on probably his biggest task as a persuader when he addressed a conference in Los Angeles. With a display of alligator skin products, ivory jewellery, and elephant's-foot stools behind him, he appealed to the Californian rich to forsake their trendy luxuries made from the hides and horn of endangered species. He recited a list of colossal numbers of imports to the USA which, he feared, resulted in death for the sake of chic. "The world's wildlife", he said, "cannot stand so much exploitation". Even importation which did not of itself involve killing, he thought questionable. Citing as an example that over a quarter of a million parrots were brought into the country, he said, incredulously and with belittling mockery, "Are there really so many people who see themselves as Long John Silver?"

Two months later he was in Japan – he left the Royal Tour of the South Pacific early to be there – telling the local World Wildlife Fund Committee that the £15,000 raised to assist conservation efforts was "a disappointment", though he was no doubt encouraged by the fact that a study prepared by the Fund had finally persuaded the Yemen Arab Republic to ban the import of African black rhino horn. The Duke was approached in February by North German conservationists wishing to preserve Luneberg Heath – rich in wildlife and historically important as the place of the German military surrender in 1945 – from the ravages it now suffers because of British tanks exercising there as part of the NATO commitment. That is a more delicate problem, and the Duke said he would enquire.

Politically controversial trips abroad have rarely been ducked by Prince Philip, and his short visit to Zimbabwe in May was no exception. He was due to attend the opening of a Royal Agricultural Society conference, but the arrangements, which were not confirmed until the last moment, were subject to pressures from two sides at least. On the one hand were security problems: in April three white farmers – very much the sort of people that the Duke would be likely to meet, were shot dead in Matabeleland, and the Foreign Office and Buckingham Palace watched events closely. They finally insisted that the Duke "will be mainly in Harare and security is not a factor in this case". On the other hand, many feared that the visit would be seen as lending royal support to the regime of Robert Mugabe, which was already being deplored as one of terror and coercion. One newspaper editorial hoped that the Duke "might have a few words with Mugabe and tell him to stop the killings". Another spared a thought for the white farmers, but appreciated that the Duke was his own man who "would not go as a belated and hand-wringing emissary of the Government. He goes as himself with his personal feelings and a clean political balance sheet, to people about whom his wife's Government never cared enough". The visit to Zimbabwe, following immediately on a five-day visit to Zambia, went ahead without incident or repercussion.

There were repercussions, predictably perhaps, from a speech made by Prince Philip when he opened a technology symposium in London in April. The theme of the speech was the relative importance of Man and the nuclear weapons invented by him. "Many people still seem fervently to believe", said the Duke, "that wars are created by weapons. What really matters are the scruples of their possessors. People are far more dangerous than inanimate objects". But his reference to "the successful deterrent effect of nuclear weapons, which have prevented escalation and appear to have discouraged armed conflict in Europe" brought howls of protest from many Labour MP's concerned that the Prince should be taking a pro-Government line against unilateralism. George Foulkes accused him of having breached the traditional neutrality of the Royal Family, while Leo Abse compared the Duke's stance badly with "the position taken by his uncle Lord Mountbatten, who saw the danger of nuclear weapons. He appears not to have the intellectual courage of his uncle." Doubtful, that: if anything, it's just a difference of opinion. Nor had the Duke breached royal neutrality. As a figure without any position in the Constitution, what he says is, as one legal expert put it, "in the same category as what sort of a hat the Queen choses to wear". Nevertheless the cartoonists had a field-day, showing the Duke pressing the nuclear button on everything from pheasants to Michael Fagan; one portrayed him as a missile, with a warning notice "Danger, leaking again".

As president, patron or chairman of hundreds of highly technical or learned bodies, the Duke tends not to lead a particularly colourful life in the eyes of the public. Darting from one London office to another as unceremoniously as possible does not make for the glamour and awe normally lavished on the Queen or his other female relations. Nevertheless he does have the opportunity of meeting the sort of people others would give their eye teeth to meet and he would probably count his meeting with Alexander Solzhenitsyn as the most fascinating of the year. They met in May, when the Duke awarded the Russian author the 1983 Templeton Prize for Progress in Religion. Prince Charles, who in an earlier interview admitted wanting to meet Solzhenitsyn above all others, missed the occasion.

The previous March, Prince Philip became the first member of the Royal Family to be invited to County Hall since the Labour Council took power in 1981. There were none of the upsets or verbal fireworks as expected when the event was announced, and the conversation over lunch was strictly official, turning on the desirability of the Kennet and Avon Canal being opened all the way from the Thames in London to the River Severn. The well-known GLC leader, Ken Livingstone, left before the lunch ended but that, Buckingham Palace assured everybody, was known in advance and there was no question of a royal snub. There was certainly none at the new Billingsgate Market in East London, which Prince Philip visited in February. It must have been one of the earliest official duties he had ever undertaken: he arrived there at seven in the morning as deliveries were being ferried about ready for the day's trade. His special efforts were rewarded with a box of oysters.

The Duke continued his efforts on behalf of international sport. In December he opened the Commonwealth Games in Brisbane and spent most of the following week watching the events, as and when he decided and without any pre-arranged schedule. In April he was at Windsor to present the leader's yellow jersey to the Dutchman Bert Wekema at the beginning of the third stage – Windsor to Bath – of the Sealink International Cycle Race. The following month he was castigating the changes in attitude assumed by political supporters of sport once they rose to power. Speaking at a Central Council for Physical Recreation meeting, he deplored the way in which politicians, pressed for tax relief for sports when they were in opposition, yet soft-pedalled on the issue when they "changed from poachers to gamekeepers". Meanwhile, the Duke had done his little bit for the National Playing Fields Association, of which he has been President for almost thirty years, by donating a bottle of port for auction in December. It was no ordinary port: it had been given to him in Oporto during the Queen's State Visit to Portugal in 1957.

The Duke's personal preference in sport – yachting and carriage driving – were not neglected. At Cowes in August, he came second in Yeoman XXI, thus apparently just missing winning the Queen's Cup – though in effect he was relegated to thirteenth after the handicaps were taken into account. In his much more active sport of four-in-hand carriage-driving, he was more fortunate. He drove a winning team of the Queen's horses in a competition at Smith's Lawn in April, came third in the National Driving Championships at Windsor the previous September, and fourth at the Royal Windsor Horse Show in May. The April event was especially successful for the Queen, whose pair of horses driven by the Crown Equerry Sir John Miller won their event, and for whom David Saunders drove four-in-hand into third place in the event won by the Duke. Indeed, David Saunders and the Duke make a good, close-knit team, according to the documentary *Royal Four in Hand* shown on ITV in March. Saunders, a former blacksmith who acts as the Duke's coachman, said, "We think the same way. The Prince has a mind like a computer, but I think I can match it". No wonder their partnership is rated number two in Britain, and number six in the world.

The documentary had been produced back in August; a month before the Duke was sporting enough to be featured in a BBC programme called *In at the Deep End*. In this he explained to the presenter Paul Heiney what four-in-hand carriage driving involved, and helped him to become "an expert" in only six months. "You need a prayer mat", was one of the Duke's recommendations. "I often used one when I was starting out on the sport". And, the Duke pointed out, it is not the done thing to ask a man whether he has ever had an accident. "You don't have to ask me", he added. "Everyone's seen me!"

———————

Everyone has now seen Prince Willian too – at least in photographs, but for what seemed an unconscionably long time after his birth, there was no sign of him. Eventually Lord Snowdon's exquisite portraits of the Prince and Princess of Wales with their son appeared on their first wedding anniversary, though any hint of goodness in the infant's nature was quickly dispelled that day by Prince Charles who said that his son was "getting angrier and noisier by the day". It is clearly his parents' policy to keep Prince William well out of the public eye, and the number of occasions on which he has been seen have been extremely limited. There was a photo call at Kensington Palace three days before Christmas, a set of official pictures, also taken at Kensington Palace, to mark the beginning of the Prince and Princess of Wales' Australasian tour in March, and another press photographic session in the grounds of the New Zealand Governor-General's residence on St George's Day. That apart, the young Prince has been spotted being carried on and off planes in Scotland, Alice Springs and Melbourne, and the odd snap has been stolen in Kensington Gardens as, wheeled in his pram by his nanny and guarded by detectives, he has been taken for afternoon constitutionals. But so far, save at his christening in August, there have been no official photographs of him with the Queen, or indeed with any other member of the Royal Family.

That is not to say that his progress has not been reported. Various casual comments, most of them from his mother, have charted his first year's growth. Two teeth, then four, then – by the time of the trip down-under – six teeth were reported: Princess Michael said he had red hair; the Princess of Wales put her right and confirmed it was blond: he was, she said in February, "quite a handful, fast taking everything over, but not crawling yet". By April he was crawling, indeed almost taking his first steps unassisted, and Prince Charles reported with evident amusement that he was dribbling a lot and liable to climb into things and tip them over.

Indeed there were times where everyone looked forward to an announcement that the Princess was expecting again. Her visit to Leatherhead in November was marked by the first of three indications to that effect. She commented approvingly to one spectator on the quality of married life; the following day, while attending a function in aid of the Pre-School Play Group Association, she talked of Prince William enjoying nursery life "with his brothers and sisters" and during the same week the Princess' gynaecologist, Mr George Pinker, was alleged to have paid several visits to Kensington Palace, though that was something which the royal spokesman dismissed as in the normal course of events for a woman coping with her first post-natal experience. A fortnight later, while talking to mothers about Prince William – then weighing sixteen pounds, learning to spit and being bathed constantly by Prince Charles – she assured them that she was not expecting another baby. "You must be joking", she said. "I'm not a production line, you know."

Clearly Prince William was beginning to creep into the news in his own right. When his mother toured the London headquarters of Capital Radio she received a book called *Tales for a Princess*, which contained stories written by children for children – in this case everyone thought they would do well for Prince William. The Princess responded by thanking the young contributors on his behalf, and by assuring Capital Radio's disc-jockey that she always listened to his programme while bathing her son. Only two days later, the issue of the colour of Prince William's hair blazed into the headlines. Princess Michael of Kent had just divulged that he had "little tufts of red hair all over his head...and absolutely gorgeous blue eyes". Buckingham Palace confirmed the information about the red hair, but the Princess of Wales contradicted it the next day. "William is blond", she said during a trip to Wales. "He has masses of blond hair". The confusion was ultimately put down to a trick of the light and, as official photographs the following month showed, blond was – if not conclusively accurate – the nearer of the two.

During the royal tour of Wales in November the Princess was irresistably drawn into more baby talk with excited and curious housewives. "We all know about that, don't we?" she joked as one baby's persistent cries interrupted one of her conversations. But it was Prince William they all wanted to know about, and she found herself repeating details of his bright blue eyes, his rate of growth – "he's getting very heavy" – and the fact that he was so active that she could not stop playing with him. At Wrexham she was asked whether she was experiencing any sleepless nights because of her son. She said not, and that the young Prince was being very good. He was not being allowed a dummy, though he had acquired the habit of sucking his fingers. Meanwhile, in another conversation, Prince Charles praised his son as "wonderful fun: he really makes you laugh. He is not at all shy. He is a great grinner, but he does dribble a lot". "Just like his father", chipped in the Princess, with a look of mock intolerance.

Prince William was, of course, everybody's baby, judging by the thousands and thousands of toys and gifts received both before and after his birth. The Royal Wedding gifts department at Buckingham Palace had to be resurrected for the new purpose, but even that must have been overwhelmed by the continuing deluge of presents – both those sent by post and those given to the Prince and Princess every time they set foot outside Kensington Palace. The more official gifts – Nancy Reagan's reproduction Chippendale chair, the gold jewellery from the Middle East Sheiks, the cases of claret, to be opened on Prince William's eighteenth birthday in the year 2000, from a French diplomat – were all retained of course, but even in September a Buckingham Palace spokesman was explaining that "many other gifts are duplicated, so lots will have to go to charity". There was one gift in the other direction: in December Prince Charles gave Kit Hill, a 1,000-foot high feature near Callington, to the people of Cornwall as a leisure site. The West Midland Metropolitan Borough Council named Dudley Street after Prince William, though it was explained that "the Queen didn't like this practice until members of her family are old enough to decide for themselves whether they want something to be named after them". And there was further disapproval for a baby-sitting agency which had adopted the name "Prince William Agency" in defiance of the convention that the names of living members of the Royal Family are not used for commercial purposes.

The Princess of Wales, who already seems to have influenced much of our daily lives, may have viewed with some satisfaction the Family Planning Association's opinion that "her popularity and the publicity over the Royal birth could encourage a lot of others to have their babies early", though she may not have relished the subsequent public discussion on the subject of whooping cough. By August the whooping cough scare – caused by an outbreak of the disease among those whose parents had decided against vaccination for fear of possible brain damage – was sufficiently severe for doctors to be publicly begging the Princess to have Prince William immunised, both for his own good and as an example to others. She may have relished even less the long drawn-out public discussion about whether her son would accompany his parents to Australia. For weeks after the tour had been announced, there was no shortage of press advice and opinion as to whether he would or would not, could or could not, should or should not go, and a rumoured but heavily denied difference of opinion between the Princess and the Queen was the least edifying aspect of the entire episode. The persistent public discussion may well have been responsible for the unusually early confirmation, coming in December, that for the first time, the second heir to the throne would accompany the heir apparent abroad.

It is always dangerous to appraise history from a position too close to the event, but from the Royal Family's point of view it is probably as safe as anything to say that 1983 will be remembered above all for the three enormously successful Commonwealth tours carried out by the Prince and Princess of Wales. The first two – of Australia and New Zealand in March and April – were combined in one six-week journey; the third, of Canada, covered the Maritime Provinces, Ottawa and Edmonton, and took eighteen days. In all three cases – especially the last, because the Canadian tour was expected to be a pale shadow of the first two – the result was an outstanding triumph for the royal couple personally, for the new Princess in particular, and for the projection of royalty to the public in an age when images fade more easily than they are created.

In all cases, the tours were described as gruelling, but this was not really the case by comparison with many others. In Australasia, the presence of Prince William gave the royal couple ample excuse to take days off at regular intervals, so that they could return to their home base at Woomargama and relax with their son. Here they would swim in the private pool, drive around the estate, go off in search of kangaroos or – in the all too frequent bad weather – stay indoors and simply unwind. This arrangement brought the added benefit of not exposing them – particularly the Princess, whose first foreign tour this was – to continuous public curiosity and the strain of activity under the relentless gaze of press and broadcasting media. Prince Charles was used to that of course, but everyone realised the dangers to his wife of a six-week tour devoid of frequent breaks and the opportunity to relax.

As it turned out, it almost seemed unnecessary to have bothered. The Princess took to Australia like a duck to water, and after a somewhat low-key visit to Northern Territory, she fairly sailed through the whole of the itinerary without a grumble, pout or sigh. For a while, press reporters tried the usual formula of inventing crises – she was suffering from sun burn one day, her tights were uncomfortable the next, she didn't like being prompted by Prince Charles, and so on – but even they evaporated when it became clear that the Princess was enjoying herself and was fully in command of every situation she faced. She answered children's questions during a broadcast to the outback directly and with simplicity; she showed sympathy with hundreds of families bereaved or impoverished by the recent southern Australian bush-fires; she chatted on equal terms with housewives and State premiers, children and workmen, freely offering them her impressions of Australia or the latest about Prince William. With the accent on youth, the Prince and Princess were placed most frequently in front of huge gatherings of schoolchildren – over 43,000 of them in Newcastle alone – and they all cheered, waved, sang and applauded. On walkabouts the Princess was the star attraction; people on each side of the street willed her to come and speak to them, but it was impossible for her to please both sides of the street at once. Every time she crossed over, the disappointment from the side she had left was as obvious as the elation on the side she was approaching. "It would have been easier to have brought two wives", said Prince Charles.

In New Zealand the story was the same, except that the weather was far worse and the demonstrations from Maori minorities and IRA supporters were much more frequent. One individual Maori even bared his backside to the royal couple as their car approached him. On the other hand, the Princess learned the art of nose-rubbing – the *hongy* – on her very first day in Auckland, and became a firm favourite when the following day she opted for an extended walkabout in torrential rain when the royal car failed to start for the journey back to base. And despite New Zealand's reputation for harbouring the occasional eccentric, she willingly dived into crowds to shake hands and receive flowers, crouching down to speak to toddlers, stooping to exchange a few words with chair-bound pensioners – giving everyone, it seemed, a few seconds of her time and justifying the hours and hours of waiting for a chance to see her.

When the six-week tour came to an end, the Princess was hailed as a triumph, and regarded as fully blooded, qualified for any job required by her royal position. In the froth of public ecstacy, Prince Charles received less public recognition for his role than he should have done, both for keeping a considerably lower profile than usual, to allow his wife's popularity to blossom and breathe, and for unobtrusively guiding her through the various parts of the tour. To those closely watching, the gentle pull of the elbow, the arm around the waist, the occasional nudge, nod and wink, the frown that indicated concern, the smile that confirmed all was well, showed that the Prince saw his role on the tour as introducing his wife not only to the towns and country areas they visited but to the way in which royal tours were carried out – protocol, tempo and style.

By the time the Canadian tour came round there was an uneasy feeling that what was about to be seen had all been seen before. But that opinion did not take into account the imaginative Canadian mind, nor the Prince and Princess' ability to react in kind to the effusive and sincere receptions they were given. The Princess made a tactful start by dressing in clothes matching the colours of the maple-leaf flag, and from the moment of their arrival the Canadians almost bayed for her night and day. "We want Di" became the universal shout outside every building she and Prince Charles were due to visit, and few occasions were so formal to her that she didn't stop for a quick chat or to receive a small child's tribute of a flower. Premier Trudeau, not a man normally bowled over by royalty, read his people's mind early, and fairly covered the Princess with glory at a State dinner in Halifax. Newfoundland's premier, Brian Peckford, was equally bedazzled by her effect, and babbled endlessly to the press about her afterwards. New Brunswick's premier went well overboard in a long rambling speech, almost embarrassingly fulsome in its praise of the Prince, the Princess and what he called "the triumph of love".

The Canadians put on a wonderful programme for them, and even the foggy, sometimes bleak weather of the Maritime Provinces failed to spoil it. The Empire Loyalists dressed up in their Colonial best, the Mic Mac Indians did war dances, the people of Newfoundland put on their finest St John's Day celebrations. The Prince and Princess responded to it all – Prince Charles was bibbed and tuckered at a lobster lunch in Bridgewater, his wife tucked into sweet corn and salmon at a barbecue near Ottawa, and both revelled in their Klondike-period costumes at a fancy dress entertainment at Edmonton towards the end of the tour. By the time it was all over, everyone realised that not only could the Princess manage a tour with ease but that she had brought a new style and informality to almost any royal occasion at home and abroad, and could show many of her in-laws how to appeal to the public without sacrificing dignity, and even gaining mystique in the process.

It had not always been thus. Only as recently as the previous October, the Princess was rumoured to be on the rampage again. Not that she had been before, but it was getting toward the end of a long holiday which she had been almost continuously out of the public eye, and the press seemed in desperate need of a story. So when the Princess suddenly flew from Balmoral to London for a shopping spree at Harrods, Harvey Nichols and – if some are to be believed – almost every other clothes shop in Knightsbridge, the story ran that she was bored with the weather and the company at Balmoral, and had left Prince Charles to complete any unfinished business at the castle – including that of bringing up little Prince William – before he went off to Mexico to open a college. In fact the Princess was in London to welcome her friend Madame Sadat for a three-day visit, but the rumours were not dispelled. In November, Prince Charles turned up at the Festival of Remembrance without his wife, explaining – according to one source – that she was ill, and would not be coming. Five minutes later, the Princess arrived "looking grumpy and not at all happy" and, as there was no official explanation for her lateness, a marital tiff was immediately guessed at. Suddenly her behaviour had become "increasingly unpredictable" – a phrase much used in the subsequent light of concern over her health.

Since Prince William's birth, the Princess had undoubtedly been slimming. Her strenuous efforts to get back into shape had been much applauded, and many young mothers seemed to be copying her example, thirsting for any chance information about her diet. By November, however, she had become disturbingly thin, rather angular and hollow-cheeked, and no matter how vivacious she appeared on any public occasion, there was considerable anxiety for her, even among those not in search of sensation. When, during a tour of the West Country, she refused a lunch of pork tenderloin in cider, stating a preference for salad on the grounds that "I'm minding my figure", she was rumoured to be having difficulty keeping food down, while details of the anorexia nervosa suffered by her sister Sarah a few years before settled it for some people that the Princess herself was in the grip of this disease. There was no shortage of diagnoses. She was suffering from post-natal depression, missing her sleep, had lost interest in food. An un-named member of her family was quoted as saying, "I am extremely worried about her. She has become frighteningly thin. But she won't take kindly to advice, however well-meant".

Buckingham Palace was naturally inundated with requests about the Princess' health, and lost no time in stressing that the Royal Family was "appalled" by these "groundless rumours". "I would have thought", said one spokesman, "that the fact that the Princess of Wales was in sparkling form on two public occasions yesterday for millions to see speaks for itself". Almost desperately, a few days later, he added, "We ask those responsible for these grossly exaggerated stories to leave her alone, for God's sake".

Miraculously it happened; the rumours stopped, the gossip writers and columnists took a more sympathetic line – though without necessarily admitting defeat – and when Nigel Dempster appeared on television in December accusing the Princess of being "a monster, a fiend who is ruling the roost and making Charles desperately unhappy", the Princess soon discovered who her friends really were. Those who only the previous month had asserted that she obviously did "not have the intellectual capacity to come to terms with what she so blithely took on" now praised her "inveterate good nature and cheerfulness", talked of her not putting a foot wrong and applauded the way she had charmed and inspired everybody – so much so that every charity was apparently falling over itself to engage her for their major fund-raising events. And when she was twice seen riding a horse at Sandringham in January – once in Prince Charles' company and once with the Queen – everything was forgiven. She was clearly back in the royal fold, contrite, obedient, conformist. Barring an unfortunate holiday in the Alps in mid-January, when she and the Prince were almost under siege by British and European photographers, the Princess ceased to be the butt of over-zealous press interest in her health, her temperament or her relations with Prince Charles and his family.

Her experience was something that Prince Charles had himself undergone in the past and was still finding somewhat annoying. "As I get older", he said in Mexico in October, "I find that less privacy becomes available and more and more people seem to be interested in every small and minute aspect of one's life". He was speaking at Montezuma where he opened another college for the United World Colleges organization, which had been inspired and nurtured by his great-uncle Lord Mountbatten. Mountbatten's grandson Lord Romsey was with the Prince, who defied an IRA bomb scare and some fairly hostile anti-British demonstrations in order to attend the opening ceremony. He referred openly to the Irish question, despairing of a solution so long as "each generation seems to become infected with what happened in the generation before". Two months later he was at Chester Cathedral, attending a memorial service for ten members of the Cheshire Regiment killed by an IRA bomb at Ballykelly. It was almost three years to the day since he had spoken in Westminster Abbey at Lord Mountbatten's memorial service, and he referred to the Earl's assassination when he spoke to the soldiers' relatives at Chester: "When my uncle was killed, I felt a deep sense of loss. I can understand your grief and my sympathy goes out to you".

By that time he had expressed his sympathy – and his congratulations – several times in connection with the Falklands campaign. There was sympathy for the wounded troops he visited early in July at the Royal Navy's Hasler Hospital at Portsmouth, and again a fortnight later for the relatives of thirty-eight Welsh Guards killed at Bluff Cove. On that occasion, as Colonel of the Welsh Guards, he attended a memorial service at Llandaff Cathedral and held a private meeting with the bereaved families afterwards.

As Colonel-in-Chief of the Parachute Regiment, he was at another memorial service at Aldershot in October, and at the beginning of December he took part with his father and the Duke of Kent in the distribution of South Atlantic Medals to 942 members of the forces, on the lawns of Buckingham Palace. Some of them, including Welsh Guardsman Simon Weston, were badly mutilated by the fire which destroyed the *Sir Galahad*, but nevertheless stood bravely in line with their colleagues for the presentations.

The happier times merged with these more personal and moving occasions; Prince Charles was at RAF Brize Norton to see 600 of the Parachute Regiment home in early July, and again on his first wedding anniversary to welcome 450 Welsh Guardsmen back to British soil. On each occasion he shook hands with every man as he disembarked, and filled in the time between his arrival and theirs by talking to the families awaiting their return. He even held a baby of one soldier who was in the South Atlantic at the time of its birth. In mid-July Prince Charles had flown a Wessex helicopter onto the deck of the *Canberra* to add his personal welcome to homecoming troops as they approached Southampton. "I am delighted", he said, "to be able to do something towards welcoming these people back. They have done the most fantastic job". And a week later he attended the hastily arranged but glittering and successful entertainment *Salute to the Task Force* at the London Coliseum, where a cast of a hundred, plus two hundred dancers, entertained an audience of 2,500 and raised over half a million pounds for the newly-founded South Atlantic Fund. Well patronised by the Prince from that point, the fund stood at over £14 million by the following February. And there was a final royal tribute to the Parachute Regiment. Prince Charles expressed his appreciation of them at the beginning of a television series in March called *The Paras*. He called them "an extraordinary bunch of people, with a peculiar kind of determination and dedication. I am not surprised that they did achieve what they achieved out there because they were so utterly determined to give a good account of themselves".

Three appeals with which Prince Charles has been closely connected came to fruition during the year. One was the United World Colleges Appeal, which by the beginning of 1983 had accumulated sufficient funds for the Prince to be able to bow out and devote his energies to other causes where money was badly needed. Another was the Trans-Globe Expedition, for which he had helped to raise £10 million in the late 1970's, and which he saw off on the 35,000-mile trip shortly after the death of Lord Mountbatten in August 1979. In August 1982 he welcomed the team home again from its successful journey, proud that he had been able "to play a small part in getting the expedition going".

Two months later the *Mary Rose*, for the raising of which Prince Charles had helped to raise £4 million, was ready for bringing to the surface of the waters off Southsea. He personally attended the lifting, despite successive delays because of bad weather, and stayed nights at Lord Romsey's house, Broadlands, for the duration. The operation failed on the day fixed for the lift, so Prince Charles made his tenth – and final – dive below to see the work in progress. He promised to stay till the end. "We've got to get her up", he said, "and I'm determined to be here when we do". The team leader, Colonel Peter Chittey, responded in the same spirit after Prince Charles had inspected the submerged wreck: "When a Prince tells you to get the ship up, you get it up". Eventually, and despite a last-minute hitch when the lifting gear collapsed onto the hull, the ship was brought above water. The Prince confessed "great elation" and admiration for the work of the team. "They have given up a hell of a lot of their time, and sacrificed their family life", he complimented. He even persuaded the Princess of Wales to visit the ship at Portsmouth the following month – she inspected it from a covered cage hoisted above – before they both attended a celebration dinner on board *HMS Victory* at Portsmouth. The enterprise effectively accomplished, the Mary Rose Trust, of which he was President could now afford to allow the Prince to assist other good causes.

They were not slow in presenting themselves. In July, Prince Charles had opened an extension to the Royal Opera House, Covent Garden following the raising of £9 million to pay for it. He played a part in that too, selling his famous old 'cello – "I never play it at all now" – and giving half the proceeds of his book *The Old Man of Lochnagar* – a total of £50,000 – to the appeal fund as well. He has also helped to provide the Stoke Mandeville Hospital with funds to help the disabled, and saw a spinal injuries centre opened there, marvelling at the way in which £10 million had been raised at a time of severe economic crisis.

Indeed, medicine seemed to play a great part in the lives of both the Prince and Princess of Wales. Prince Charles was discovered to have taken to carrying a donor card with him so that, in the event of his sudden death, any part of his body could be used for transplant surgery. The Princess became Patron of the Royal College of Physicians and Surgeons in Glasgow in February, and in the same month founded a new fund – the Princess of Wales' Charities Trust Fund – which expects to distribute £50,000 a year to worthy causes. The previous month, a total of £11,500 raised by successive countrywide exhibitions of the Princess of Wales' wedding dress were distributed to charities for sick children. And, speaking at a British Medical Association dinner in December, Prince Charles had made one of his most forthright speeches of the year, when he deplored the "edifice of modern medicine" as "like the tower of Pisa, slightly off-balance". He attacked the present-day fascination for the "objective, statistical and computerised approach to the healing of the sick", and warned that medicine must not lose sight of the patient as "a whole human being".

Two instances of Prince Charles' own capacity for treating people as human beings came to light around the same time. One 17-year-old boy managed to get into the Army after the Prince had personally intervened to recommend him. The lad had written to him to explain that he was unemployed, had been a truant at school, and had spent time in a reformed school. Prince Charles passed the letter on, and the Army accepted him in October. "I'm thrilled that I have done something to help", said the Prince. Two months later a pensioner who had been mugged and robbed of over £150 was surprised to receive a cheque from Prince Charles, together with a sympathetic letter saying that he was "appalled" by the attack, and found it "impossible to understand how anyone could do such a thing".

Another of Prince Charles' interests which seemed particularly to absorb him during the year was farming. As Duke of Cornwall, he is the owner of the freehold of several thousands of acres of farmland in the West Country, and in February he spent a week working as a farmer on farms in Dartmoor. He worked a twelve-hour day, mainly looking after cattle and sheep, but also supervising the movement of foodstuffs, the preparation of crops, and taking part in the general administration of the farms. Buckingham Palace, who divulged nothing of the experiment until it was over, explained that the Prince had "wanted first-hand experience of what life is like on a Duchy farm. He found it most rewarding, and feels it has enabled him to get a better understanding of the points of view of the Duchy's farm tenants". Prince Charles himself was a little more direct: "I think being down here for a week has returned my sanity", he said wryly. The Palace assured everyone that it was a coincidence, but a fortnight later Prince Charles had paid £1.5 million for a 700-acre farm near Llantwit Major in Glamorganshire, which he will farm jointly with a young Welsh farmer.

Perhaps Prince Charles will be somehow relieved by the realisation that, with his wife now able to play her full part in the endless round of royal duties which fall to the heir apparent, he can keep a comparatively low profile and continue to involve himself in the less glamorous, more positively useful side of the monarchy's functions. For there is no doubt that the Princess of Wales has found her feet – remarkably so in only two years, of which one was effectively consumed with her pregnancy and the birth of her son. She has travelled not only to the old dominions but also the length and breadth of Britain, accomplishing a complete year's engagements. Many of these have been undertaken on her own, and she is now as confident as ever she will be. She has brought to an institution where conservatism creeps in at all corners a freshness and simplicity which appeals to everyone, and she is available for everyone to express their appreciation of her. When she sits on a young patient's hospital bed, as she did at the Great Ormond Street Hospital for Sick Children, or allows children to be specially photographed with her, as she did at Thornton Heath, or chats about playing bridge to a group of pensioners, as she did at a Wandsworth home for elderly Jews, she is forging links between the Crown and its subjects which will last well into the reign of her husband, when she will be Queen Consort. It is an attitude which has already had an effect on other members of the Royal Family – notably the Duchess of Kent, certainly the Queen Mother, even the Queen who seems increasingly more relaxed on her walkabouts no matter how many children swarm around her with their gifts and bouquets. After the Maundy Service at Exeter, Prince Philip actually lifted a child up from behind a barrier and directed her, flowers in hands, towards the Queen. One feels that a couple of years ago that would not have been contemplated. Prince Charles is plainly proud of his wife, and has never spared her blushes by not saying so in public.

She has given an enormous boost to the British fashion industry, and stunned her public, with the variety and flair of many of her outfits and evening dresses. Though she would doubtless confess to being influenced by her designers, she is very much her own creature when it comes to choosing clothes and has never conformed to any standard royal look. The slinky blue off-the-shoulder evening gown she wore for the Birthright fashion show in December, and the figure hugging dress she wore at Melbourne evidence her confident and original quest for the dramatic.

Prince Andrew came home, with a thousand fellow Falklands campaigners, on 17th September, and his ship *HMS Invincible* was cheered rapturously into harbour at Portsmouth. One of his first comments was to express the desire for a pint of milk, but within three weeks his cup was beginning to overflow. Not with milk, unfortunately, but with the unenviable, sometimes rather polluted blend of curiosity and scandal which the world's press inevitably brought to bear on his liaison with Miss Kathleen Norris Stark – soon to be known universally as "Koo".

The Prince flew with her from London early in October to spend a fortnight as part of a small party based at Princess Margaret's holiday home *Les Jolies Eaux* on the island of Mustique. The press lost little time picking the story up, though initially it was not quite as newsworthy as Miss Stark's past. As a twenty-eight-year-old actress, she had under her belt a *curriculum vitae* involving nude photography, pornographic films and, according to some sources, wild goings-on in South Africa where alcohol and marijuana were in ample supply. Much of the past was evidenced by photographs, reproduced large and often in newspapers and magazines during that fortnight, and culled from personal albums or film still archives. One of her most recent films, *Emily*, contained lesbian scenes in which she featured prominently, and an American television station showed it during the currency of the story. Before long, a photograph of her in bed with the actor Anthony Andrews, for another film, *The Adolescents* was also made available.

Within days, an army of press-men had besieged Mustique, and the local police began to get tough. Plane-loads of journalists arriving from Antigua were turned back; two photographers were jailed on a charge of attempting to take pictures of the Prince and his girlfriend; another was threatened at gunpoint; yet another claimed to have been knocked off his motor-bike by a police jeep. Meanwhile, the royal party attempted to continue what everyone was assured was an innocent holiday, comprising underwater swimming, catching crabs, inspecting dead sharks and throwing parties – until one of the group, Elizabeth Salomon, leaked tales of Prince Andrew ripping off his bathing shorts, frolicking around in the buff, and enjoying a spot of more original fun, like trying to jam live lobsters in Miss Stark's bikini. That of course increased the interest of the media, whose presence prompted the Prince to consider cutting short his holiday. Indeed, he arrived back in London, minus his companion, on 13th October, five days before his leave expired.

The invasion of privacy – his detective, Inspector Geoffrey Padgham, had complained that the Prince had been unable to water-ski, swim or scuba-dive without being photographed – was clearly a factor, but whether the holiday had been curtailed, or had come to its arranged end was just one of a number of unresolved questions in a whole chapter of rumour and denial. Hardly any fact or allegation about the affair went unchallenged. Some reports said that the Queen, helplessly distant on her visit to Australia, was very angry at the news; others that she had given the holiday her full blessing, and had even paid the Prince's air fares. Buckingham Palace was quoted one day as saying the Queen would be very unhappy about the trip, because of Miss Stark's earlier involvement with films; the next day they denied that the Queen would know the background of any of Prince Andrew's friends, and would not question his judgement anyway. Another report alleged that Miss Stark had met the Queen during a recent three-day trip to Balmoral: Buckingham

Palace denied knowledge. When Miss Stark's mother was discovered to be on the island, the story went around that the Queen had insisted upon this so that the daughter should be properly chaperoned; again Buckingham Palace denied that the Queen had made any such demands. Similarly the story that the Queen had ordered the Prince to return to London, or had drawn up new rules concerning the people whom Prince Andrew could take into Buckingham Palace with him, were refuted. There was no doubt, however, that the Queen was upset – if not positively annoyed – by the enormous publicity. One of her spokesmen denounced the press coverage as "very excessive" and said simply, "Prince Andrew is on a private holiday. We wish it could stay that way." And she was particularly put out when the BBC showed a clip from one of Miss Stark's films during a news bulletin when the story was at its height.

The British public seemed to recover from the initial shock of the publicity explosion quite well. When Prince Andrew arrived back to Heathrow Airport, it was to a chorus of "Nice One, Andy" from a crowd of airport staff. All the newspapers who bothered to conduct their so-called polls on the issue, found that well over 80%, and on occasion up to 93%, approved of Prince Andrew's "fling", though almost as many disapproved of the prospect of the lady becoming his wife. Princess Margaret herself seemed to lend her support when she asserted that her nephew had had "a smashing time on Mustique" and deserved it. From his school in New Zealand, Prince Edward denounced the press's intrusion, without comment on his brother's choice of company. There seemed plenty of additional support for the Prince from the history books: royalty's penchant for actresses and other unlikely candidates – from Nell Gwynn to Lily Langtry – was handsomely aired in print that month.

Prince Andrew's senior officers denied that he had been the butt of his squadron's jokes when he arrived back at RNAS Culdrose, though that would have been preferable to the more sinister events of the following week. A newspaper ran a story purporting to explain Koo Stark's philosophy on love, sex and marriage; Elizabeth Salomon was already said to be negotiating for the sale of her account of the holiday with newspapers throughout the world; and police began to investigate the reported loss of letters and home movies belonging to Miss Stark, who returned to London at the end of October.

Within a few days, the general impression had been gained that any romance there was had ended, after an alleged meeting between the Prince and Miss Stark at Buckingham Palace. Only the Italian press was reporting that they had wed at Gretna Green: more local sources talked of the couple drifting apart, and the liaison being in its death-throes. In the process Miss Stark was said to have sacked her manager for his handling of the story, and shunned her own father for having introduced her to films at too early an age. For a month, the steam went out of the story. Desultory tales of candle-lit dinners between the Prince and Miss Stark at Buckingham Palace lost credit when her much anticipated visit to Sandringham for the New Year failed to materialise, and she left London for St Moritz on a skiing holiday without Prince Andrew.

Her return in mid-January was noted for the fact that she was wearing the Prince's service identity tag as a pendant; this gave some journalists the confidence to announce that "their love will not die." But apart from the occasional and often unauthenticated reports of rendezvous at nightclubs, the affair either lost ground or became successfully covert, its death-knell sounding, to all intents and purposes, when the couple were not seen to meet again during *Invincible's* stay only ten miles from Miss Stark's mother's home in Florida in February.

At that point another, somewhat avaricious female hove into the public view. During *Invincible's* docking at Barbados in mid-March, Vicki Hodge was entertained by Prince Andrew, along with two of her friends, Tracie Lamb and Lucy Windom. Miss Hodge lost no time in telling how they had enjoyed beach parties which included near nude romps in the surf, and the now rather old hat practice of removing swimming trunks. Photographs of the royal posterior rising from the waves were said to exist, and though they never materialised, Miss Hodge freely admitted setting Prince Andrew up so that she could sell what turned out to be some rather ordinary photographs of a brief holiday for £40,000. In the wake of that episode, Prince Andrew was said to have had a violent argument with his detective, Inspector Steve Burgess who – coincidentally, it was officially explained – was recalled to London.

The combination of royal Romeo and member of the armed forces is one many young men would envy, and Prince Andrew's naval career progressed in keeping with the Royal Family's traditions during the year. His homecoming on *Invincible* was the focal point of a whole day of celebration, and shortly afterwards he was promoted from second to first pilot, qualified after four hundred flying hours to captain his own helicopter. Two hundred of those hours had been completed during the Falklands campaign alone.

The memory of the Falklands kept cropping up. Six days after his return, he donated a pair of his kid flying gloves to a charity auction at the RAC Club in Pall Mall, the proceeds of which went to the South Atlantic Fund and the Falklands Appeal. The gloves, autographed by him and accompanied by a letter of authenticity, comprised one of 400 lots, among which was a Royal Doulton bone china plate given by the Prince of Wales.

Mid-November brought more Falklands reminders. On the 12th, Prince Andrew put on his flying gear to pilot a Sea King helicopter in a fly-past which was part of a parade organised by the citizens of Plymouth to welcome home their Falklands campaigners. The following day, the Prince wore his South Atlantic Medal next to his Royal Victorian Order at the Festival of Remembrance at the Albert Hall; and the day after that he laid a wreath for the first time at the Cenotaph. Whereas most other wreaths, royal or otherwise, were laid in memory of the dead of two world wars, Prince Andrew's bore a message with the words, "In memory of those who died in the South Atlantic – Andrew."

Invincible, now fitted with a rapid fire Phalanx anti-missile system, put to sea at the beginning of February on a three month tour of duty in the Atlantic, though not in the best of circumstances. Storms delayed her leaving, and three days after she sailed one of Prince Andrew's close friends, 34-year-old Malcolm Kelham, was killed when his Sea King helicopter crashed into the sea off Portugal. The Prince was not involved in the unsuccessful rescue operation, but was said to be "very upset" about the accident – an ironic occurrence after all *Invincible* had been through. *Invincible* reached Florida on 18th February, and the few days' courtesy visit became famous for the celebration of Prince Andrew's 23rd birthday with a party of eighteen at a steak-house in Jacksonville. Here he blew out a single candle on a coconut layer cake, though his 24th year started badly when he injured his hand during a game of deck hockey back on board, and had to have four stitches.

There were other stops during the tour. In mid-March, a weekend call at Barbados gave the Prince time to be hosted in style, with some of his shipmates, at a reception at Government House. *Invincible* called at Montego Bay a month or so after the Queen and Prince Philip had been there during their Western Atlantic tour, and Puerto Rico became host to the ship a week later. A more controversial stop was that at Gibraltar in mid-April. Spain, still with an eye to her oft-claimed sovereignty over the Rock, issued no fewer than four official protests against *Invincible's* proposed training exercises from there, and Prince Andrew's presence – mirroring as it did the brief visit of the Prince and Princess of Wales *en route* for their honeymoon cruise in August 1981 – became a source of diplomatic embarrassment. The Queen was said to have assured the King of Spain that there was no significance in Prince Andrew's being there, as indeed he was when *Invincible* called in on her way to the Falklands conflict a year earlier. All the same, the Prince was grounded and kept off flying duties while his ship was at Gibraltar, and he went ashore only a couple of times.

In the meantime he had apparently lost his identity card – his only reported lapse during his time with *Invincible* – but he sailed home on her on 28th April for a fortnight's leave, with a good report. A senior officer Captain Nicholas Hill-Norton described him as "a very fine pilot, and a very popular and cheerful chap to have on board." A month later it was announced that he would be joining 702 squadron at Portland the following September, training to fly Lynx helicopters. So with three of his twelve years service over, Prince Andrew had acquitted himself with credit, and looked set to find his own way up the rankings by virtue solely of his own performance.

His links with his family appeared as strong as ever, and his absences from home on naval service seemed only to strengthen his wish to be with them as often as possible during leave. The celebratory return in mid-September 1982 was a case in point – the Queen, Prince Philip and Princess Anne all being at Portsmouth to greet him. He joined the Queen at Balmoral shortly afterwards, returning with her to London two weeks later – and experiencing trouble getting some of the royal corgis on and off the plane. He was back with the family at Windsor for Christmas, and at Sandringham afterwards, spending over a month there, and trying his hand at shooting pheasant. He killed several birds, though he attracted some criticism for being seen carrying his kill by the wings, rather than by the legs or neck. His social outings were either few and far between, or kept very, very quiet. There was a little-publicised skiing holiday at the beginning of December with the Liechtenstein Royal Family, and the occasional night out at Annabels or the Embassy Club in London. And he did not forget his old school Gordonstoun: in mid-November he attended a reunion, spending, it was said, £50 on an eighty-year-old bottle of whisky, to assist the school's attempt to raise half a million pounds for scholarships.

Despite all the fun and the hard work, Prince Andrew could not forget he was a member of the Royal Family. Official duties began to claim some – though *only* some – of his time. Five engagements, from switching on the Regent Street illuminations to opening the Fleet Air Arm Museum, were arranged between November and July, the month when he went to Rhode Island to attend functions in connection with the British challenger for the America's Cup – *Victory 83*. In this connection it was significant that, for the first time, Prince Andrew retained the whole of his £20,000 Civil List payments, and that it was announced in May that, as from late in 1983, he would be allocated a Private Secretary in the shape of Squadron-Leader Adam Wise, whose term of duty as Equerry to the Queen was due to expire.

––––––––––––––––––––

Squadron-Leader Wise will also act as Private Secretary to Prince Edward, most of whose year was spent in the comparative quiet of New Zealand.

"It's not quite the same as Britain, where everything is go, go, go. You can actually stop to think for a while", he said after six months there. He had left Britain early in September, one of 308 passengers on a scheduled flight from Gatwick, to begin a two-term spell as a junior tutor and housemaster at Wanganui Collegiate near Wellington, regarded by some as "the Eton of New Zealand". The Collegiate is one of several Commonwealth schools operating a reciprocal arrangement with Gordonstoun School, which the Prince had just left, and both Prince Charles, who spent a year at Geelong School in Australia, and Prince Andrew, who went to Lakefield College in Canada, have benefited from these exchanges in the past.

Life as a member of the Royal Family, according to Prince Edward "is not that hard, when people are ready to accept you. We try to live as normal a life as possible." He would no doubt have wished his stay at Wanganui to be as normal as any housemaster's, but with three bodyguards and an equerry, and a formal welcome by the Governor-General of New Zealand, Sir David Beattie, that might have been more easily hoped for than achieved. Nevertheless, within three weeks he had settled in to his self-contained flat on the College campus, and the headmaster, Mr Ian McKinnon, was able to confirm that "the boys think highly of him. He has successfully begun teaching English grammar and literature to a third form class." Academic teaching was, however, only part of his duties. He had to supervise his year from breakfast time to lights out, and participate in the heavy cross-country schedule which dominated the sports activities during the first term. On average he was out four times a week, even in the squally spring weather down-under, jogging or racing over a three or four mile endurance course. During his second term he organised camping expeditions in the hills, complete with camp-fire entertainments including, it is said, the Royal Family's favourite game of charades.

In the informal circumstances of his stay at Wanganui, he found himself the unwilling target of the attentions of the British press, and a few newspapers reported details of less than amicable conversations between their journalists and the Prince. In October an even less welcome taste of adventure presented itself when an earth tremor, registering over 5 on the Richter Scale, struck Wanganui and set the whole college onto a programme of emergency drill and civil defence exercises. But there were compensations. Prince Edward was able to continue his necessarily spasmodic flying career by continuing to train with the RNZAF's 42 Transport Squadron, only thirty miles from Wanganui. He spent Christmas in the comparative luxury of the Governor-General's residence in Auckland, and was able to spend a long weekend in Australia, visiting a former Gordonstoun schoolmaster, Jim Graham, at Armidale Private School near Sydney. He took the opportunity to bone up on his water-skiing at Nambucca Heads on the New South Wales coast, though he did not meet the Prince and Princess of Wales who were then coming to the end of their Australian visit.

That meeting occurred a few days later when he flew to Wellington with them, leaving immediately for Wanganui where he entertained them at the Collegiate a couple of days later. He greeted them wearing the highly colourful cloak of hide and kiwi feathers which he became entitled to wear as an honorary chieftain of the Ngati Awa tribe. Prince Charles was full of mischievous disbelief. "Good Lord!" he exclaimed, "It must be a fancy dress party. What have you come as? It looks like a blanket." Who needs enemies?

But perhaps the most exciting episode of Prince Edward's nine months stay at Wanganui was the week-long trip he made in December to the Antarctic region. He left Christchurch in an Air Force Hercules, with an official of the New Zealand Science and Industrial Research Department, and visited scientific posts and ice stations in much the same way as his father had done in 1956. But he managed more than Prince Philip had been able to. He actually reached the South Pole – and walked round it, visited huts used by Shackleton and Scott and, during a stop at Scott Base on

Ross Island, drank water which had fallen as snow during Amundsen's passage through in 1911. He explored a glacier crevasse on Mount Erebus, nine miles from Scott Base, lived in an igloo and, to cap it all, was made a member of the world's most southerly skiing club!

Perhaps excitement like this tended to make the ordinary life of a school teacher tame; perhaps life on the other side of the teacher's desk turned out to be not so glamorous as many pupils think it is. However that may be, Prince Edward did not find teaching much to his liking. "I'm not cut out to be a teacher", he had said as early as December. "There are times when it's been sheer hell." His opinion was reinforced during an interview he gave – some say he betrayed a discernible New Zealand accent in his voice – in March. "I don't agree that schooldays are the happiest days of your life. A school is a school." It was seemingly no more than a dispassionate evaluation, and not through the want of taking part. Even within less than a month of his departure, he was given the leading role in the play *Charley's Aunt*, which the school's dramatic society produced in late April. The headmaster had heard that Prince Edward liked acting – in the best traditions of the Royal Family – and applauded his witty, gifted and professional style – even in drag!

By the time he had left Wanganui in mid-May, Prince Edward's immediate future career had been mapped out. Initially he was to undergo a two-week course with the Royal Marines, training to qualify for the coveted green beret. He had already survived a three-day familiarisation course the previous year and had not been put off by its forbidding taste of the gruelling life to come. "They go through hell", said one officer. "Only the toughest survive." Confident of survival, Prince Edward thus hoped to be a Royal Marine Cadet by the time he began his university career at Jesus College, Cambridge in October.

Unfortunately the Prince was the continuing centre of controversy in connection with his transfer from school to university. His three A-level passes, published in August 1982, had been hailed as justifying his reputation as the most academically accomplished of the Queen's children. However, the unofficial publication of his grades – deplored by the joint secretary of the Oxford and Cambridge Schools Examination Board as a breach of confidence – caused dismay. A grade "C" in English Literature, and grade "D" in Politics/Economics and History, though boosted by a Grade 2 Special in History, were not only below what was generally expected, but also thought inadequate for the Cambridge place which had been taken for granted. Even on that showing, it was reckoned that if Prince Edward qualified for Cambridge, then well over five thousand other students who had taken A-levels that year would have qualified also.

When, the following month, rumours gained strength that Jesus College had given the Prince a place, there was something of an outcry. The National Union of Students deplored the implication that he would not be sitting an entrance exam like everyone else, and when this appeared to be borne out in November, 150 undergraduates signed a protest against his proposed admission. Prince Edward refused to comment, as did Palace spokesmen, on the grounds that his future had not been decided. In mid-January however, confirmation came through from the Master of Jesus that the Prince had satisfied the entrance requirements, and that he would therefore be taking his place as an undergraduate in the autumn, studying for a degree in Archaeology and Anthropology, with the option of changing to History in the second year. Another furore of protest, alleging that Prince Edward had got in by the back-door, and suspecting the influence of the Duke of Edinburgh as Chancellor of Cambridge University, made for an uncomfortable few days for all concerned. It may well do so again for the Prince in his first few weeks at Jesus College but perhaps, after having gone through hell with the Royal Marines, that won't present him with too many difficulties.

If ever there is any comfort to be taken from the strains of life in the glare of a sometimes hostile publicity, Princess Anne might take hers from the undoubted achievement of increased popularity during the year. The temperament which, like her father's, does not suffer fools gladly – and the press even less – has been dwelt upon too much and for too long, and it was refreshing to see that royal smiles in the right places were reflected in press reports and in the public reaction to them.

Not that her year began very promisingly. When she returned from a two-week tour in Canada in July 1982, someone noticed not only that she had been unaccompanied by her husband on trips abroad since October 1980, but also that Captain Phillips was not due to undertake any engagements with her – at home or abroad – until the following December at the earliest. Immediate speculation about the state of their marriage flared up, fanned by Captain Phillips' absence from a garden party at Buckingham Palace, and his remaining at Gatcombe as his wife and family accompanied the Queen to Balmoral two weeks later. The gossip became so widespread that Captain Phillips felt impelled to offer a personal explanation. "I am a full-time farmer and am too busy on the farm. I have to make the business pay like anybody else", he said. But neither this nor an official statement that, not being funded from the Civil List, "obviously he does not have to keep attending royal engagements", stemmed the torrent of questions, nor did the fact that he *had* accompanied Princess Anne to the Royal Tournament towards the end of July. Captain Phillips denounced the speculation as deeply hurtful. "This week has been one of the worst I have experienced", he complained.

Within less than a month any serious suggestion of a breakdown lost currency. The couple were together for a shooting match in North Wales early in August, and Princess Anne left Balmoral to rejoin her husband, who was busy harvesting at Gatcombe, for her 32nd birthday. Well-publicised anticipation of an encounter between Captain Phillips and Angela Rippon, the subject of an earlier and equally unwarranted sensation, at horse trials in Exeter fizzled out when they took pains not to be seen in each other's presence. And as the eventing season progressed, Princess Anne and her husband joined forces to compete or to watch, and were publicly seen to be very happy indeed. To confirm it, the unusual step was taken of issuing a set of official pictures of the couple to celebrate the birthday, not of Princess Anne or her children, but of Captain Phillips himself – his 34th on 22nd September. The photographs, taken at Gatcombe by Norman Parkinson in August, showed them informal, patently relaxed, happy, almost pointedly loving. Buckingham Palace played down the timing by explaining that as there had not been many official pictures of them since their marriage, "it was felt that this was an appropriate time to put the matter right", but the real purpose of releasing only part of a set, the remainder of which were duly issued on Peter Phillips' fifth birthday in November, was lost on no-one. Its contribution to allaying further fears when it was announced that Princess Anne was to undertake a three-week tour abroad, unaccompanied, and that her husband was to spend a solo equestrian month in Australia, was probably very significant indeed.

The rumours, which had depressed Captain Phillips, positively angered his wife, and her unprintable expletives against the intrusion of photographers during grouse shoots at Balmoral in August, and horse trials at Aldershot and Fontainebleau in September, set off the usual vicious circle of unedifying insult-swapping in the newspapers. Much was made of the Princess' alleged failure to speak to children waiting in the rain during her visit to Blandford in September, or to speak at all during a ceremony to open a runway at Manchester Airport. Unenviable comparisons were made between her, her brothers and her sister-in-law, and in December a former editor of *Burke's Peerage* castigated her casual use of four-letter words under the well-used and irrelevant cover of "What would Queen Victoria have thought?" One might as well have asked what Dr

Arnold would have thought of video games.

What turned the tide, effectively and enduringly, was Princess Anne's Save the Children Fund tour of no fewer than eight African and Middle East countries in three weeks from late-October to mid-November. From the day that the Princess received her first rabies innoculation, it was clear that this tour was going to be like no other. Pomp and ceremony were out, and a heart-rendering look at the realities of life in poverty-stricken and war-torn corners of the continent would replace them. In Swaziland she visited an immunisation centre where doctors worked from a table in a field to fight polio and typhoid. "I don't think people realise", said the Princess afterwards, "until they have an epidemic, what it means to keep it under control". She also visited Project Zondle which, incredibly, ensures that 14,000 people in one district alone receive a hot meal every day. In Zimbabwe she saw some dreadfully crippled children at a rehabilitation centre for the handicapped, was given a poem by a victim of cerebral palsy, and visited the Victoria Falls under the heavy guard necessary because of continuing terrorism in Matabeleland. Her visit to Malawi coincided with a rabies scare, and in Somalia she witnessed the harrowing experience of life in a tent city of 40,000 refugees from the long and bloody Ogaden war. The camp is only five miles from the Ethiopian border, disease is rife, medical aid is constantly under strain, and the hundreds who flee there every day rely totally on relief food.

Throughout the whole of her tour, she insisted on being spared nothing and, on the whole, nothing was spared. The personal discomforts – dust, climate, mosquitoes – which, perversely, would normally make news during a more bland royal schedule, paled into insignificance beside the tragedy and waste from which only hope can spring. Unusually, the very arrangements for the tour were fraught with successive last minute difficulties. A stop-over in Johannesburg was nearly called off because the South Africans threatened to treat it as a full-scale diplomatic visit showing royal approval of the apartheid system. The arrest of an RAF crew testing out landing strips in preparation for the Zimbabwe leg of the tour nearly caused a diplomatic incident, and the visit to Somalia was cancelled because of renewed fighting, much to Princess Anne's annoyance; then restored again at the very last minute, equally much to her delight.

But what earned the greatest degree of public applause was her courageous decision to spend a day in Beirut, a city still reeling after eight years of civil war and in particular after the massacre of over 200 people in a Palestinian camp two months previously. Even an explosion which the day before had flattened the Israeli military headquarters in Tyre, killing 62 people, did not deter her, and for ten hours she toured some of the worst-hit areas of the Lebanese capital. Passing collapsed houses and walls peppered by gunfire, she called in at a Moslem-run refugee camp school, a Palestinian medical clinic and the Presidential Palace for an audience with President Gemayel. Her visit was enormously appreciated – the floral garland she wore round her neck was evidence of that – and a Save the Children Fund official said simply, "We're very proud of her".

Britain seemed impressed with her too, and overtly so. An appreciative article about her in the *Daily Mirror* that October prompted hundreds of enthusiastic letters from its readers. "What a difference a smile makes", beamed the *Daily Express*, while the *Daily Mail* conceded that she was "softer than she is prepared to admit". Everyone seemed to fall over themselves to disprove what had been common ground for years, and one writer even referred to her as "a royal rose", comparable with the Princess of Wales. Progress indeed! She had even lost weight – a special treat, someone said, for Mark when they were reunited at Gatcombe for young Peter's birthday.

The Save the Children Fund has for many years claimed much of Princess Anne's official time and this year was no exception. At least a dozen of her engagements were connected with the Fund, from awarding prizes for a slimming competition organised by *Woman's Own*, which raised £55,000 in September, to attending the inauguration of the Dutch Save the Children Fund by Princess Juliana of the Netherlands the following March. And when, in April, seven fund workers were kidnapped in Ethiopia by the Tigrai People's Liberation Front, the Princess was quick off the mark to express her "extreme concern" publicly. On that occasion, she was in Japan, during a two-week tour of the Far East and Pakistan – and accompanied by Captain Mark Phillips to boot. In Tokyo they met the Imperial Family, visited a 16th-century shrine, toured car and computer factories, visited the Imperial stock farm and watched a performance of the Royal Ballet. Four days in Hong Kong saw the Princess visiting everything from housing estates to military headquarters, and enjoying both the sight of luxury stables at a local racecourse, and a dinner in the officers' mess of the Queen's Gurkha Signals. In Pakistan she ate hot curries – a great favourite with President Zia, toured a refugee camp near the Afghan border, and visited the Khyber Pass under heavy security against bandits and kidnappers.

These eventful foreign trips apart, Princess Anne's official year followed a familiar pattern. As Chancellor of London University she was able to announce in January that £125,000 had been raised by students to off-set the effects of Government cuts in further education, and she presented grants totalling £70,000 for library books, correspondence courses and sports facilities. A visit the following month to Queen Mary College was called off, however, for fear of disruption by students demonstrating during a National Day of Action against those same Government cuts. The Princess was criticised for not braving the threat of trouble, particularly after she had put up such a good fight for the Chancellorship over two years earlier. Nevertheless, that decision found a parallel in the cancelled visit to Lucas Aerospace in Birmingham in May, because men on a six-week-old strike were thought to pose a threat. Among a few novel experiences for the Princess were a game of bingo, played with great poise, at the Inter-Continental Hotel during the Poppy Appeal in October, and a visit to the Moulin Rouge in Paris where she and Captain Phillips attended a performance of "Girls, Girls, Girls" – many of them topless, and one of them finding it difficult to curtsey and keep her ostrich feathers in place. The Princess' reactions varied from enjoyment to embarrassment and mild distaste.

Princess Anne's successful public life during the year was not matched in the equestrian arena. In September, she sold her one-time favourite eventing horse, Stevie B, after an attempt to sell for a reported £30,000 foundered on the strength of an unfavourable veterinary test. On the other hand, the Princess registered six novices during the year, two of which, at six years old, she is desperately trying to bring on for three-day eventing. She competed on one of them, Charlie Brown, at the British Horse Society Trials at Hagley, Worcestershire in April, and was very pleased with his performance. The other, Mission Lake, has yet to be blooded. It was for that reason that Princess Anne – who hunted with the Beaufort Hunt in November and attended lorinery classes in London in December – was for the second year running unable to compete at Badminton in 1983.

Captain Phillips, in a year heavy with equestrian engagements, did compete, though his hopes of being the first person to win five Badmintons were dashed when his horse, the nine-year-old Classic Lines, threw him during the cross-country. Lincoln, on whom he won in 1981 and who may have been preferred to Classic Lines, had strained a tendon in a one-day event earlier and had to be withdrawn.

Indeed the year was peppered with misfortunes. The whole complement of the stables at

Gatcombe was struck down with influenza in July, and it was not until September that Captain Phillips competed – only to be eliminated in the cross-country at Tetbury. He was injured twice – once at Melbourne in October, when his horse failed to clear a fence and fell on his leg, and again in May when he was unseated and fell heavily on his shoulder at Gatcombe. There were two, more sinister, happenings. In April, 17-year-old Rebecca Weston was killed when her horse fell on top of her at Hagley, where Captain Phillips was competing. He competed three weeks later at the Amberley Horse Trials at Cirencester, when a young girl was murdered near the course.

But there was a moderate degree of success for Princess Anne's husband. He won the two-day event at Fontainbleau in September – a tournament to which the Princess and her mother-in-law went – and spent a successful month in Australia, competing and teaching three-day event techniques at Melbourne, Canberra and Perth. In January he won the individual competition in the Martell Championships at Upminster, and led a team of three-day event riders to an unexpected and conclusive victory: "It must have been beginner's luck", he said. Two months later he won a novice competition at Weston Park in Shropshire on Pacemaker, and finished sixth on Lincoln in an advanced section.

"Princess Anne and I have had a lot out of the sport, and we would like to put something back into it", said Captain Phillips in September 1982. As a result, August 1983 has seen the beginning of an annual one-day event – the Gatcombe Horse Trials – which has entered the National Equestrian diary. Captain Phillips organised and laid out a course round the 1,000 acre estate, so as to allow for competition for two classes, and a total of eighty competitors. Croft Original sponsored the 1983 event, and the BBC bought television rights. Captain Phillips hoped for a gate of 30,000, and at £7 a car – with a maximum of six passengers – it seemed a realistic objective. As he organised it, he cannot compete, though Princess Anne can. And before long, Master Peter Phillips, seen several times during the year confidently astride quick, sizeable ponies, may well be in the running too.

At the other end of the seniority scale, Peter Phillips' great-grandmother, Queen Elizabeth the Queen Mother, enjoyed a moderately successful season with her horses in 1982/83, for despite her years her enthusiasm for steeplechasing, fired at a reception over thirty years ago, has never waned. She is still bringing on new horses, although two of them, Lunedale and the five-year-old Highland Piper, still have a long way to go. Lunedale was unplaced in three races, while Highland Piper's fourth place at Sandown in March was the best he could manage all season. Another five-year-old, Sun Rising, whose sire Sunyboy ran for the Queen Mother in the mid-1970's, winning five races, finished the season with a win, two second places and two thirds, while the six-year-old Highland Line repeated a dismal 1981/82 season with only two places before unseating his rider at Kempton over Christmas. The Queen Mother's two best horses continued in good form. Cranbourne Tower, who came second in four races in his previous season, won by twenty-five lengths at Worcester in September 1982, while Master Andrew, the eight-year-old gelding, an eightieth birthday gift to the Queen Mother from the Jockey Club, came close to his previous season's brace of victories by winning once at Warwick in December, and coming second at Ascot in April. He blotted his copy-book only once when he fell at Kempton in February.

The Queen Mother, no mere armchair enthusiast, continued her practice of attending racemeetings, and Kempton, Sandown Park, and Cheltenham all played host to her in a private capacity. During her visit to the Cheltenham three-day festival in March she stayed, as she usually does, with her great friend and contemporary the Duke of Beaufort, her enjoyment of the racing marred only by the security scare when an unidentified man entered the unsaddling enclosure and actually shook hands with her! Off the course she lent her express support, along with the Queen and the Prince of Wales, to the recurring appeal to maintain the Aintree Grand National, and there was a delightful incident in January when, while staying at Sandringham, she called almost unexpectedly, at his modest home in Wolferton, upon Len Bradley – former keeper of the royal horses at the Queen's Norfolk retreat. She came away, felt-hatted and mackintoshed, carrying a plastic bag of plants which Mrs Bradley had given her in appreciation for this kind gesture, which shows that she does not easily forget old friends.

The Queen Mother's consuming private interest in horses further leavened a year which had already begun felicitously for her. On 4th August, her 82nd birthday, she lived through a triple celebration. The first was at Clarence House, where the well-established custom of her public appearance on the balcony and at the gates was perpetuated yet again. A crowd of five hundred or more cheered her as, to the tune of "Happy Birthday to You" from the 1st Battalion Grenadier Guards, two children slipped through the police cordon to give her a marigold and a box of Smarties. These two gifts were added to the sackfuls which, according to her staff, had arrived from well-wishers all over the country.

The second celebration followed almost immediately, as she left Clarence House for the short drive to Buckingham Palace, where great-grandson William was to be christened. By the time the private service was over and the official photographs were being taken, the infant Prince had grown vociferously hungry. He cried in his mother's arms, bawled in the Queen's, but reserved his longest and loudest protest for the Queen Mother. She was vastly amused: helpless to stop him, she praised him for the soundness and power of his lungs! But the pictorial record of the linked generations was made, comparable with historical photographs of Dowager Queens with great-grandchildren, and in one of many birthday eulogies of the Queen Mother she was described most aptly as "a great grandma fit for a Prince".

The third celebration took place in London's theatreland that night when she attended a performance of *The Pirates of Penzance*. The visit backstage proved no ordinary one: a huge cake encased in white, pink and green icing awaited the Queen Mother's knife. Eighty-two candles had to be blown out first, however, and the royal visitor received some gallant assistance from a member of the cast. As it happened it was a little late for the Queen Mother to taste any of the cake, though after her departure the story ran that the cake was demolished in no time and the commemorative candles soon found their way onto the black market. Meanwhile the Queen Mother was on her way for a holiday at the Castle of Mey, Britain's most northerly fortress, and its owner's place of annual pilgrimage. This time of the year is chosen as the most favourable climatically, when the copious crops of flower and fruit reach maturity. Here too, the Queen Mother's thirty-strong herd of Aberdeen Angus pedigree cattle are being selected for fattening – in 1982 to good purpose, since she won third prize at the Smithfield Show in December with her entry Eodima, a heifer weighing almost half a ton. And the Queen Mother broke new ground in September when she allowed television cameras into the grounds and gardens of the Castle of Mey for a film report shown the following January on the BBC programme *Nationwide*.

Remarkable though it may seem the Queen Mother did not lessen the number of her official engagements during the year. Some four score of them were accomplished in the public eye, quite apart from the smattering of private audiences she gives from time to time, and this despite her initially alarming *contretemps* with a salmon bone in November. The bone lodged in her throat late one evening during a supper she was giving at Royal Lodge Windsor for a party of fourteen, including Princess Margaret. She was rushed to King Edward VII Hospital for Officers in London for an operation, said to be "relatively straightforward", under a general anaesthetic. But to everyone's surprise, she emerged 36 hours later, bright, breezy, declining the shelter of an umbrella in the persistent drizzle, and showing no sign of the bruising which the operation was said to cause to the neck. During her short stay the Hospital was deluged with cards and gifts. "We have always known that she is close to the nation's heart", said one member of the staff, "but no-one had expected this kind of response". The Queen Mother, who is said to have joked, "At last the salmon has got its own back", spent the next week recuperating at Clarence House, and Princess Michael of Kent undertook her public engagements on her behalf. Within a week she had resumed her schedule, though on her first engagement afterwards she reported that she was "still suffering from jet lag".

Understandably, perhaps, for a lady of her years, many of her other public engagements carried a touch of nostalgia about them. In November she attended the Royal Variety Performance, accompanied by Princess Alexandra, Angus Ogilvy and Lady Sarah Armstrong-Jones. She admitted that seeing a performance of *Underneath the Arches* – reminiscent of the days of Flanagan and Allen, much loved by the Royal Family in the 1940's and 1950's – made her cry. In February she struck a celebratory champagne bottle – specially weakened, we are told – against the hull of a new bulk carrier, the *Pacific Patriot*, during her first visit to the Govan shipyard in Glasgow for 41 years. Then, she had accompanied King George VI to the launching of the aircraft carrier *HMS Implacable*. Later that month she visited Sadler's Wells Theatre for the first time since 1960 to see a performance of *The Count of Luxembourg*. In March she attended a reception of the Indian Army Association – an occasion which reminded one of the oft-forgotten fact that the Queen Mother was not only the last Queen-Empress of India, but must also be one of the few people alive now who enjoys strong official association with the days of the Raj. Two days later she was at St Mary's Hospital, Paddington, where Prince William was born nine months earlier, to lay the foundation stone of the new £21 million development to replace the present buildings, of which she herself opened the Lindo Wing in 1938. In April she remembered another parallel when unveiling the foundation plaque of the new Clore Gallery for the Turner Museum. "I vividly remember coming here with the King in 1937", she said, "to open a new sculpture gallery". And in July she loaned the set of twenty-six paintings of Windsor Castle by John Piper, which she had commissioned in 1941 and which normally hang in Clarence House, to the King's Lynn Festival.

That festival has long been a great favourite of the Queen Mother's and was specifically mentioned by Prince Charles in an interview he gave in July 1982. It cropped up as a childhood memory, and one in which the Queen Mother herself featured strongly. The Prince recalled how his grandmother had taken him to concerts at the festival and recalled "being excruciatingly bored by some of it, but my grandmother was one of the chief influences in the sense that she always made everything such fun, so exciting and enjoyable that I think I owe her a lot..." That tribute spoke volumes for the Queen Mother's ability to relate to the young in the 1950's, and she is still doing it today. In December she delighted fourteen Children of Courage by posing for photographs with them at Westminster Abbey after presenting awards to them for the bravery and determination which brought each successfully through some major personal crisis. In April the children of Brixton, both West Indian and white, crowded Railton Road to see her arrive to open an elderly folks' day centre, and were equally bucked by her easy-going informality in an area which only two years ago had been tense with anger and fierce with racial violence. "She is the best person we could wish to see", said one of the borough's councillors, commenting on the Council's unanimous first choice. But perhaps the most profound appreciation came from one unemployed youth whom she met during her visit to St Katherine's Dock in London to tour Operation Drake projects. Having hopped on and off barges, and clambered down narrow hatch-steps with the agility of – as Queen Victoria was once likened to – a she-goat upon the mountain tops, she left the young, tattooed rocker, whose belt and armband was bristling with studs, confessing admiration. "I'd been told she was a bit of a Fascist, and all that", he said. "But I think she's alright. A nice lady."

A great lady, according to the title of a video produced that year. The late David Niven narrated the film documentary of her life *Portrait of a Great Lady* which won the Video Business Magazine's best documentary prize of 1982. A courageous lady too, braving the dangers of renewed violence in Northern Ireland in June to visit the Territorial Army on their 75th anniversary, and to offer "my heartfelt thanks for your dedication and loyalty which have won you an honoured place in the service of the Crown". And, as one who has been doing her bit for over 60 years, she should know.

The Queen Mother's younger daughter, Princess Margaret, enjoyed a year almost entirely free from the scandal and public curiosity that seems to have dogged her for so many years. Any such attention could reasonably be called self-induced, for the new biography of her which appeared in April under the straightforward title *Princess Margaret* was, by all accounts, her own creation. She either initiated, or readily agreed to its being written by one of her life-long admirers, Christopher Warwick. To him she afforded full co-operation, numerous interviews and, according to the author, "a patience which proved limitless".

The co-operation included the facility of making alterations where necessary and the combined work of subject and champion made it inevitable that the result would be regarded as less than impartial. The inevitability was strengthened by the undoubted truth that the book appeared in this way as a reaction against two earlier publications: a biography of Lord Snowdon, which its subject condemned as "a scissors and paste job", and Nigel Dempster's best-selling biography *HRH Princess Margaret; A Life Unfulfilled*", for which, despite its author's claims to the contrary, Kensington Palace denied that the Princess had ever given her approval. In that light it was good to have a book clearly bearing the stamp of royal co-operation, even its objectivity must and will be tested under the unavoidable and unforgiving microscope of information, both official and personal, which must at present remain forbidden fruit to the historian.

Though the Princess is no longer the controversial figure she used to be, memories of less happy days seemed to colour the book's reception by the reviewers. Of its critics, the most kindly said it was solemn, or "slightly cloying" while others labelled it "a crochet job" which put the blame for the breakdown of the Princess' marriage squarely upon Lord Snowdon. Another critic asked whether "this was really the way for a Princess to behave". More tolerant spirits praised the author for a gallant attempt at the difficult job of rehabilitating the Princess in the eyes of the press and public who up to now have had a field-day in prurience at the Princess' expense. Yet another applauded the absence of scandal, and gobbled down those snatches of personal reminiscences which, for some, increased her charisma.

The charisma has not disappeared, despite the fact that she is no longer third in line of succession to the throne – as she was, for instance, at the time of the Townsend affair – but, following the birth of Prince William, eighth. Indeed, so influential is her hold on some of her closest friends that Earl and Countess Alexander of Tunis named their daughter Rose Margaret in her honour, and asked her to be godmother at the christening in July 1982. She agreed, but a fairly severe bout of gastric 'flu prevented her from attending the ceremony, as well as an official visit to the Royal Opera House, the Berkeley Square Ball, a visit to an international Guide camp in Scotland, and the Falklands commemoration service in St Paul's Cathedral. She recovered in time to spend a long weekend in Italy, combining a holiday in Tuscany with some public engagements in Venice, helping with fund-raising events for the Royal Ballet and the Royal Opera House, visiting a Canaletto Exhibition, and attending a performance of *Romeo and Juliet*. During her stay in Venice, petrol was poured on the doors of the British Consulate where she was being accommodated, though only slight damage was sustained when it was ignited.

The holiday had been prepared for some time before, and it was impossible to change her plans when the Prince and Princess of Wales announced the date of Prince William's christening. Consequently Princess Margaret was one of the few family members not to attend the celebrations. But she was at Balmoral two weeks later to celebrate her 52nd birthday with the Queen and her family, enjoying, with the Queen Mother, picnics and outings based at one of the many log cottages on the estate. And on the subject of picnics, the Princess contributed a short essay to a book published the following May called *The Picnic Papers*. It described her most memorable picnic. An indoor one at Hampton Court Palace, it consisted of smoked salmon mousse, cold meats and "beautiful and delicious salads" – with a butler on hand to see that everything was all right. That, as they say, is class.

In a year of ninety or so official engagements, Princess Margaret's duties varied from the sublime to the ordinary. The commemoration of her thirty-year service as Patron of the National Society for the Prevention of Cruelty to Children by the presentation to her of a silver goblet in April was perhaps the most timely reminder that behind the adverse publicity, the Princess's public life goes on, often unnoticed. In May she became Patron of the Halle Orchestra – its first royal patron since the death of the Princess Royal in 1965 – thus adding another branch of the musical arts to her long list of protégés. At the other end of the scale she was seen among local shoppers, inspecting the well-filled shelves of a Sainsbury's supermarket in Bath, and emerging with a bag of shopping which, disappointingly, had not been her own purchases, but had been given to her by the management. The same month, December, she took part in an uproarious Christmas party for the Friends of Covent Garden, and went on stage at the Royal Opera House to be hoisted up serenely into a heaven of mock clouds, and later to lead the singing of *Hark, the Herald Angels Sing*.

A few of her engagements had distinct family connections. In October she went to the Kodak library in Holborn to view the Earl of Lichfield's photographs of royalty, recently published in his book *A Royal Album*. It is said she admired the large group photograph of the Prince and Princess of Wales' wedding, complimenting Lord Lichfield – as we all should – on being clever enough to snap the entire assembly of over fifty with their eyes open at the same time. Three months later she visited the National Film Archives to see part of the film *Victoria the Great* starring Anna Neagle, and a contemporary documentary film made by the Office of Works about the coronation of King George VI and Queen Elizabeth – an event of which the Princess, then almost seven, will no doubt have vivid memories.

But it was a year in which her own family must have preoccupied her more than ever before. Both her son David, Viscount Linley, and her daughter Sarah ventured into pastures new, and this under the watchful eye of the press. In September Princess Margaret went to the former New Zealand High Commission residence in Regent's Park to look at an exhibition of woodwork, amongst which were two of Viscount Linley's creations. These included a chest made of sycamore and grey leather, designed and fashioned entirely by him at his Dorking workshop, and sold the following month for a reported £2,500. He also had orders for a folding screen he had made earlier, and by January his order book was full. Another exhibition at the Park Lane Hotel in February included a sycamore screen and a collapsible desk, and the Theatre Royal at Bath commissioned a set of fourteen cafeteria tables from him. In the same month he sent two more of his pieces over to Miami, Florida – his first venture into a foreign market, but one which he desperately wanted to make. The previous September he had remarked that the traditional "sheep-like" demands of the British market did not give him the same scope as more go-ahead American design-consciousness.

Outside his chosen career, David – "titles inhibit people and set me apart", he said in May – was frequently seen enjoying the social life expected by and of all young viscounts: the wedding of Cosmo, the son of Lord Snowdon's original choice of best man, Jeremy Fry, in October; a disco dance in Camden in December; and visits to parties, nightclubs and shows. He spent his 21st birthday in November watching the State Opening of Parliament from a side gallery in the House of Lords, and with his father attended the funeral in Sussex of Lord Rupert Nevill, Prince Philip's Private Secretary and a great friend of the Royal Family, who died in July 1982. The following May he was proudly sporting his restored MGB Roadster, bought for £600 in 1981, stripped down and rebuilt by him over two years, now in full working order and said to be worth over £3,000. Another early achievement for a creative spirit.

His sister's creativity has yet to find an outlet. Lady Sarah Armstrong-Jones obtained a single A-level in Practical Art at the end of her last term at Bedales School, and was accepted for a foundation course at the Camberwell School of Arts. Sleeves rolled up, bag slung over her shoulder, she jauntily arrived for her first day there in September. She has been unfettered by press interest since then and has enjoyed glowing reports of her appearance and behaviour at the few public functions she has attended, such as the Cartier Dinner-Dance in October, the Royal Variety performance in November, and the visit with her father to Sadler's Wells on his 53rd birthday in March.

That month her mother was busy denying another press rumour – to the effect that she was contemplating the sale of her holiday home in Mustique, and the purchase of a plot of land on a coconut plantation in neighbouring St Lucia. That particular hare was started after she had just spent her usual February holiday on Mustique – travelling economy class from London to Barbados with a party of friends. For once, the company she kept was almost uncommented upon. The reported presence of Norman Lonsdale, a much-noticed companion in 1982, warranted no more than a mention. The most promising prospect did not go to Mustique. He was Derek Deane, a 29-year-old principal dancer with the Royal Ballet, who had been seen dancing with the Princess in Venice the previous August and accompanying her to the Strand Theatre in January to see a play. He had the tact to admit that the Princess and he were friends, and to leave it at that. The press did not bay for more, and Princess Margaret was thus left in relative peace.

Another royal lady can, perhaps with much greater confidence, hope for a quiet future. "I must retire, with regrets but also with relief, from the many commitments of the past years": thus

Princess Alice, Duchess of Gloucester, at the end of her charming autobiography, published in March. The book represented over two years of planning and research, initiated at the suggestion, it is said, of Rosemary Collins, her great-niece and the wife of the head of a department of Collins Publishers. Its appearance was hailed as something of a breakthrough, Princess Alice being the first member of the Royal Family to pen an autobiography since her namesake, Princess Alice of Athlone in the mid-1960's. Furthermore it was all her own work. The historian and biographer Philip Ziegler collaborated with her and dispensed advice, "but she's such a determined and talented lady that there's been no question of a ghost", he confirmed. Two serialisation contracts preceded publication of the first printing of 10,000 copies. They were sold out in less than three months and a reprint was ordered in June. For the first six weeks the book featured in successive best-seller lists, hovering around fourth and fifth until it reached second in two charts at the beginning of May. By that time the Princess had recorded a delightful and informative interview at Kensington Palace with the interviewer Russell Harty, recounting her memories with honesty, clarity, more than a degree of relish, and an abundance of rather wry but nevertheless emphatic humour.

Literary critics often take their titles too literally and criticise rather than judge, but there was not a single reviewer who had anything but praise for this work. Some applauded Princess Alice's "wonderful eye for detail", others the book's discreet confidentiality, yet others her endearing asperity when she spoke of people or circumstances which failed to meet her full approval. Her tolerant, yet at times vaguely irreverent treatment of her husband – "there was no formal declaration", she said of his proposal of marriage: "I think he just muttered it as an aside during one of our walks" – provided a tactful yet revealing insight into a relationship which has been very much private property for almost fifty years, and her uncomplaining acceptances and rationalisation of the tragedies which beset her in the early-1970's explain her continuing, admirable serenity today.

Her intention to retire is proving no empty threat. Her engagements were dramatically reduced – to around thirty – during the year. What were once holidays in Barnwell and in Scotland are gradually turning into a pattern of retirement retreats, with just a few journeys to London for official duties. In her quiet yet decisive way she has told us she has had enough, yet despite this, despite her assertion that she is "failing in sight and limbs", it is difficult to believe it as she carries out her schedule with purpose and poise. But much as we may marvel at those persistent octogenarians of recent royal history, enough is clearly enough. In her biography she said that, at 34, she had had a good innings as a spinster: she now feels, understandably, that at almost 82 her second innings should be declared. May her years in the pavilion be restful and rewarding.

To fill the space she is gradually vacating are her surviving son, Richard Duke of Gloucester, and his wife. Little did they think at the time of their marriage in 1972, that the burden then being borne almost entirely by Princess Alice would fall on them. Resentful though they may have been not only by the personal anguish of successive cruel twists of fate but also by the wholesale alteration of their plans which they occasioned, they have adapted to the pressures of an unwanted public life with good grace. Princess Alice confided that their circumstances were not and are not all that conducive. "They work as hard as ever we did, and incomparably harder than we did before the war. But they cannot afford a chauffeur, a lady's maid or a valet. We have to share such help as best we can and for much of his day's business, the Duke dodges about London on his motor-bike."

Of course, like most members of the Royal Family, the Gloucesters are able to arrange a suitable combination of business with pleasure. As farming enthusiasts, visits to the Royal Show or the East of England Show benefit both them and their hosts. As a keen architectural conservationist, the Duke supports heritage bodies, and his engagements invariably reflect that support. He attended, for instance, a reception for the Heritage of London Trust at Marlborough House in January, and another in Kensington in March to celebrate the 25th anniversary of the Victorian Society – despite the fact that the old Victorian Town Hall at Kensington had only recently been demolished! And as patron of the Richard III Society he proposed the toast at a dinner to mark the 500th anniversary of that controversial monarch's accession. "Celebrating his 500th anniversary may seem eccentric", he said. "But it marks the beginning of what might have been a long and glorious reign. This was not to be: it wasn't only his crown and life he lost, but also his reputation." It is the reputation of that former Richard, Duke of Gloucester which the present Richard, Duke of Gloucester is determined to clarify and, if possible, redeem.

The Duchess of Gloucester has become increasingly busy in recent years and in March she assumed three new patronages, those of the London Suzuki Group, the Helen Arkell Dyslexia Centre, and the Women's Caring Trust. She also carried out a solo visit to the USA in May, attending the *Britain Salutes New York* celebration, a function in connection with the Victorian Society, and the launch of an exhibition of Churchill's paintings on Fifth Avenue. Threats from NORAID, the American organisation supporting the IRA, were ignored. "Security will not worry the Duchess", said a member of her staff.

The Duke and Duchess were abroad quite frequently during the year. In October the Duke paid a week-long visit to India as President of the British Consultants Bureau. On the way back he called in at Cyprus to visit his regiment, the 1st Battalion Gloucesters, and to join his wife who was visiting the Royal Army Education Corps, of which she is Colonel-in-Chief. Later the same month the Duke went to Brussels to visit the European Commission, and in March he and his wife were in Paris for three days, where the Duke toured an agricultural show. Shortly after the Duchess' return from New York in May, the Duke paid a five-day visit to South Korea to attend celebrations marking the centenary of diplomatic relations between South Korea and Britain. While there he laid wreaths at Commonwealth cemeteries for the casualties of the Korean War, and attended a performance of *Sleeping Beauty* at the Royal Ballet.

Generally regarded as one of the more private members of the Royal Family the Duke consented to appear on television for a brief interview in connection with the series *The Royal Family*. The first episode illustrated the history of royal palaces, and the Duke's architectural expertise was put to good use as he explained the design of London palaces, his ideas for a purpose-built modern-day palace, and his life as a child brought up in St James's Palace in the 1940's and 1950's. That apart, perhaps the only other insight we were given into the Gloucester's well-protected private lives is that the Duke prefers milk to coffee, orange juice to wine, and oysters not at all. So when in October he opened the Colchester Oyster Ceremony to inaugurate the new season on the Essex coast, the traditional fare of oysters and wine was tactfully refused.

For the Duke and Duchess of Kent, much of the year's events followed a familiar pattern. As Colonel of the Scots Guards, however, the Duke of Kent was obliged to make adjustments to his schedule in July to allow him to welcome back soldiers of his regiment from the Falklands Islands, to visit some of the casualties in hospital, to inspect the battalions at Chelsea Barracks, and eventually to help in the long ceremony to distribute South Atlantic Medals at Buckingham Palace in November. His long association with the Scots Guards, and his equally long service as a senior aide-de-camp to the Queen led Her Majesty to promote him, on the morning of her official birthday in June, from Lieutenant-Colonel to the rank of Major-General – effectively bypassing intervening ranks.

By early the previous September, the Duke and Duchess were well into the swing of their public engagements, the Duke's concentrating on the export drive and British technology and industry, the Duchess' on nursing and the arts. She has for long been regarded as genuinely sympathetic towards those suffering from handicap and disease, and supportive of those who work to fund and operate the means of overcoming them. Thus a typical random selection from her engagements list showed her opening a scanning unit at Ipswich, a cancer clinic at Brighton, a burns unit in Essex, a rheumatology department in Stoke-on-Trent and a care unit at Wolverhampton. In addition she attended meetings and receptions for the National Society for Cancer Relief and the Spastics Society.

Her concern in this field derives much of its intensity from her personal experience. In the last six years she has suffered persistent medical and psychiatric problems herself, and the jinx fell again in April when she was admitted to the King Edward VII Hospital for Officers for an operation to remove an ovarian cyst. The treatment – similar to that which Princess Anne received over a decade before – was safe, relatively straightforward and uneventful, and was performed by Sir Hugh Lockhart-Mummery, with the Queen's surgeon-gynaecologist Dr John Batten and Mr George Pinker in attendance. The Duchess' condition was pronounced "excellent" afterwards, and she left to recuperate at York House at the beginning of May. Her engagements for the next week or two were, of course, cancelled but there was growing concern as the list of cancellations increased and the Duchess showed no sign of emerging from her convalescence. On receipt of official denials of a relapse, anxiety pre-supposed the return of the nervous stress of three years earlier. Her office at York House denied this just as emphatically, stating that the Duchess merely needed much longer to recover from her operation than was originally thought necessary. Eventually, late in July she was seen, a picture of health again, singing in the Bach Choir at a King's Lynn Festival concert attended by the Princess of Wales, and at the end of the month she left for a two-week private holiday in Canada with her younger son Lord Nicholas Windsor. Meanwhile she had missed two particularly favourite sporting engagements – the F.A. Cup Final in May, and Wimbledon in June and July.

The Duke and Duchess made several trips abroad in the course of the year, visiting a total of seven countries. In October the Duke left for a visit to Australia and New Zealand in his private capacity as a Director of BICC Ltd before joining his wife who had left London meanwhile to attend a series of official engagements in Hong Kong. They were back in time for the State Opening of Parliament early in November, and it was not until January that the two-part arrangement was repeated. This time the Duke spent five days in Northern Italy to attend the Kandahar/Martini SkiingChampionships and to present prizes, then flew to Germany where he met the Duchess for two days of touring British manufacturing fairs and exhibitions. Finally, in mid-March, the couple paid a ten-day official visit to Saudi-Arabia and Jordan.

Another member of the family who spent rather longer abroad was the Duke and Duchess' elder son George, Earl of St Andrews. He spent his 20th birthday, in June 1982, halfway through a four-month trip to India where he worked on a poor relief project with the Save the Children Fund in Calcutta, Madras and Kashmir. He returned in mid-August, according to a colleague, Adrian

Evans, "very fit and well. He found it a very interesting experience. He went entirely on his own and I know that he feels he got a lot out of it." He began his undergraduate career that autumn, studying Law and History at Downing College, Cambridge, and working hard, by all accounts, to redeem the disappointment of the two low-grade A-levels which obliged him to attend a cramming school in Cambridge from November 1981. As yet his future plans are vague, but one ambition is to preserve his comparative anonymity. "Fortunately", he was reported as saying in May, "I am never going to have to carry out official engagements like my parents. I have managed to remain anonymous so far in life, and I want to remain that way."

That may be more possible for him than his sister, Lady Helen Windsor, whose stunning portraits by Lord Snowdon to celebrate her 18th birthday marked her out as a potential beauty worthy of the attentions of the most eligible of Europe's princelings. Her school career at Gordonstoun finished with a "C"-grade A-level in Art and, like her brother, she went to "crammers" to prepare for examinations which she re-took in June. Said to be a serious girl who does not make friends easily, her most publicised friendship was with old Etonian John Benson, a student at Edinburgh University. They met in June 1982, have been seen together several times in London since, and went off on a fortnight's skiing holiday at a rented villa in the Val d'Isère in March, with seven other companions.

Princess Alexandra, the most junior ranking member of the Royal Family in receipt of a Civil List payment, and her husband Mr Angus Ogilvy celebrated their twentieth wedding anniversary in April, as quietly and modestly as the wedding itself had been grand and spectacular. The weekend anniversary fell conveniently between two very ordinary public engagements for the Princess – a thanksgiving service at Westminster Abbey on the 23rd and a visit on the 27th to the new Queen's Road housing development which borders Richmond Park, the setting for the Ogilvys' private residence, Thatched House Lodge.

The Princess has gained a reputation for guarding her personal privacy while fulfilling her public obligations with enthusiasm and thoroughness, so there was no public celebration of a twenty-year union generally accepted as serene and happy despite the wretched consequences for Mr Ogilvy of the Lonrho affair, and his own recurrent indispositions. By design or coincidence, however, a new biography of Princess Alexandra appeared in October, written by Geoffrey Elborn, and containing some interesting, original, mainly anecdotal material which threw a measure of new insight onto the Princess and each member of her family. It was a pity that in some areas it also betrayed a dearth of really authoritative information, arising presumably from the small degree of effective assistance available from the Princess' household – another inevitable consequence, alas, of the perfectly understandable struggle to remain as private as royal status will allow.

The success of the Princess' marriage is perhaps best publicly demonstrated by the number of occasions on which she and her husband are seen together on official engagements. Mr Ogilvy has been able to steer an uncontroversial course between going everywhere with his wife and being branded a parasite, and never being seen with her and risking talk of mutual antipathy. He thus accompanies the Princess to most evening engagements – gala performances, concerts, plays and the like – and usually goes with her on visits abroad. In October for instance, they went together for a twelve-day visit to Thailand to celebrate the 200th anniversary of the Chakri Dynasty now represented by the present King Bhumibhol, and in April they visited Washington with her for the official handing-over of the Ditchley Bells – the replicas, cast at the Whitechapel foundry in London, of the Westminster Abbey bells, and which now hang in the old Post Office Tower in Washington's Pennsylvania Avenue. Mr Ogilvy also accompanied his wife on semi-official occasions such as the memorial services for Princess Grace of Monaco in November and for ex-King Umberto of Italy in April. Indeed, he represented her at numerous memorial services in London which her own schedule, and the rule of protocol under which members of the Royal Family are generally present at the memorial services of personal and close friends only, did not permit her to attend.

Both the Princess and her husband will be relieved that her official programme – and indeed private life – have progressed without controversy, a seemingly rare achievement for any member of the Royal Family in an age when publicity seems to intrude ever more aggressively. The nearest they ever came to it was in August when, shortly before they were due to attend the première of *Who Dares Wins*, a film based loosely on the Iranian Embassy siege of 1980, the Princess received an open letter from the chairman of the Campaign for Nuclear Disarmament, protesting that "the film associates our campaign with Eastern European-inspired terrorism," and threatening that her arrival at the cinema would be met with a silent protest by sympathetic actors and actresses. In April, there was some long drawn-out speculation about Mr Ogilvy's position as a director of Sotheby's, when that company became the object of the attentions of two American industrialists angling for a take-over, but otherwise probably the worst thing that happened was the hasty removal in October of the Princess and her staff from their three-roomed offices at Friary Court, St James's Palace, after severe damp caused plaster to fall from the walls. An estimated £15,000 was spent putting in a damp-course, before occupation was resumed in January.

Of the Princess' two children the younger, Marina, celebrated her 17th birthday at the end of July 1983, and the end of her penultimate year at St Mary's School, Wantage where she has shown promise as a pianist and aptitude on the stage. She has appeared in two school productions – *Salad Days* and, saving her aunt's presence, *Kiss Me Kate*. Nineteen-year old James spent his year, since leaving Eton with thirteen O-levels and three A-levels, in a variety of ways. Following a spell at a study school in an attempt to improve his A-levels, he took a short-term factory job, said to have been acquired through his local Jobcentre. Meanwhile, he co-edited the magazine *Freeway*, a "freebie" magazine distributed to executives in London: he had launched the publication in 1982, jointly with Alex Hambro and Rupert Goodman, and the third issue came out in May 1983 with a run of 5,000 copies. His passion for photography has not abated, and he took the family photograph which officially marked his parents' departure for Thailand, using an automatic shutter release to ensure that he could be part of the picture as well.

Strictly speaking, of course, Prince and Princess Michael of Kent do not carry out official engagements. As the second son of the late Duke of Kent, Prince Michael does not receive funds from the Civil List, has no obligations to carry out royal engagements, and his activities are not recorded in the Court Circular. But being royal he and his wife are in great demand, and between them attended just over a hundred functions during the year. They ranged as wide in nature as the engagements of any member of the Family – everything from visits to youth clubs to ceremonial attendances – but significantly over a third of their tally of outings concerned the motor trade and sport.

Prince Michael undertook twenty-one engagements in connection with the motor trade in his capacity as President of the Institute of the Motor Industry, itself a reflection of the keen interest in cars he has shown for many years. Thus, in between visiting the 1982 Motor Show and various motor car factories in the Midlands and East Anglia, the Prince was spotted taking his 1964 Mark II Cobra two-seater for a farewell spin, before selling it to an American for a reported £25,000. His particular enthusiasm for vintage and veteran cars led him to two meetings of the National Motor Museum at Beaulieu and in London, and prompted him once again to take part in the annual London to Brighton rally in November. Unfortunately the 1899 Wolseley he drove broke down at Croydon.

In the slightly less rarified realm of sport, Prince and Princess Michael were present at some of the most important of the year's fixtures, though perhaps their most enduring connection was with the America's Cup. At the beginning of March they flew to the Bahamas to visit some of the team training for the Cup, and Princess Michael went to Hamble at the end of March to name the British challenger *Victory 83*, Peter de Savary's modified version of the 1982 entry which she had also inspected. In May she and Prince Michael attended a dinner for sixty guests given by de Savary in Manhattan, while *Victory 83* was undergoing trials off the American east coast. And the following month Princess Michael opened the America's Cup exhibition in London.

The couple also attended the Cup Final replay in May, and the final days of Wimbledon, the Princess substituting for her sister-in-law the Duchess of Kent during the award ceremony after the finals of the ladies' championships. Bobsleighing, skiing, motor racing and acrobatics also won their attention during the year, though perhaps equestrianism remained their forte.

As in previous years, the Prince and Princess attended Royal Ascot, Epsom and Badminton, but they own horses themselves and are keen riders and competitors. They go for early morning rides in Hyde Park from time to time, and join various hunts in the area around their country house at Nether Lyppiatt in Gloucestershire. They rode with the Cotswold Hunt in November – the Princess was thought to have given up riding side-saddle – and the Prince followed his wife by car as she hunted with the Quorn in January. Even though she was riding astride, she came a cropper in a spill near Widmerpool in Nottinghamshire. Worse was to happen six weeks later: both of them fell from their horses during an outing with the Beaufort Hunt at the end of February, but the Princess at least redeemed her fortunes the following month when, competing in her first point-to-point at Didmarton, she finished twentieth out of a field of thirty-five in a three-and-a-half-mile novices race. Her horse, Benny's Gold, was "perfect, and did everything he was asked", she said. And a little more – he fell at the last fence.

One sport that has failed to derive much royal patronage is that of ballooning, but here again Prince and Princess Michael are expected to blaze a trail. The Princess was reported to have gone ballooning in September, and both she and her husband were taken up in the Famous Grouse Whisky craft owned by Giles Bellew in February. Bellew said that "they enjoyed themselves very much and said they would like to do a course with me so that they could eventually fly solo". His opinion that the Princess seemed the keener of the two coincided with preparations for the Ideal Home Exhibition – which the Princess was to open in March – which included the building of a replica of Montgolfier's balloon as its main decorative attraction.

The exhibition – "They're cross with me because I'm running late", she said on her inspection, "but that's because it's so good", – began with a burglar alarm fanfare for the royal visitor, and later produced another rather more serious alarm. A young man from Oxford, dressed up as a wolf with enormous teeth, suddenly leapt out at the Princess – apparently as a publicity stunt for an exhibiting furniture firm. He did not actually touch her, but she was temporarily stunned though "very composed and took it all in her stride", according to her lady-in-waiting afterwards. The Princess herself said the following day that "there was a bit of excitement, but I think it's been somewhat exaggerated". The police, who lost no time collaring the offender, did not press charges.

The Princess, it seems, is no stranger to excitement. While presenting the Dettol Midwifery Care Award in Birmingham in March, she revealed that "my husband felt he was really a little more qualified than I to make this award because our son Freddie was making a very determined bid to arrive in the car on the way to hospital". On 6th April 1983, Lord Frederick Windsor's fourth birthday was marked by charming portraits of him in the nursery at Kensington Palace. A further portrait of his sister Gabriella commemorated her second birthday three weeks later. Already, according to Princess Michael, her children are showing signs of developing their characters and interests. Lord Frederick, presently attending a nursery school in West London, is thought to be destined for Sunningdale Preparatory School before going on to Eton. He has a collection of Dinky toys, which he loves, and spends hours playing garage games with them. He likes to be taken on the estate tractor by Prince Michael, while back at the house he is showing a pronounced interest in painting and advanced jigsaws. Lady Gabriella seems to prefer the feminine stereotype which has become decidedly unfashionable among Women's Libbers: she is "already feminine and quite maternal", said Princess Michael. "She seized her first doll with shrieks of delight."

The Princess admits that she sees less of her children that she would like. First thing in the morning and bedtimes are musts: lunch and tea too, but only if work allows. And work, quite apart from her public engagements, includes her biography of Elizabeth of Bohemia, now nearing the end of its second year of preparation. The book – "I've written the happy chapters and now I'm on the sad ones" – is being researched in The Hague, where the Winter Queen lived in exile, in Heidelberg and in Czechoslovakia, and Professor J.H. Plumb of Cambridge University is giving the Princess advice. One of her preoccupations has been to see if Elizabeth ever had a lover, "but I've decided she remained faithful to the end".

Of her own marriage, Princess Michael says, "Being a Catholic is a problem I didn't envisage". She had hoped her children might be brought up as Catholics as some sort of compromise, so that her marriage to Prince Michael in 1978 might be recognised by the Vatican. On the other hand, the Church of England synod refused in February to countenance a change in the 1701 Act of Settlement – under which Prince Michael, though not his children, is debarred from the succession to the Throne – when the Rev Richard Brindley of Reading raised the "bizarre and haphazard" effects of the statute. Well, to some extent, the Princess' problems have been eased. Late in July 1983, over five years after her wedding, the Vatican recognised it officially. On 29th July – the Prince and Princess of Wales' own second wedding anniversary – their union was blessed at Westminster Cathedral.

That should give Princess Michael a feeling of achievement, though even before the Vatican's change of heart, she and Prince Michael rarely showed any discouragement as they blazed through their increasing number of duties. The Prince has a quiet, unhurried confidence, the Princess a sense of obligation. "I don't go along thinking I'm going to enjoy it, but 'Let's do our very best to ensure everyone enjoys it, so they get their money's-worth.'" If one of the organisers of the British Foundation for Age Research is to be believed, it works. "Quite simply", he said, "she's an enormous crowd puller."

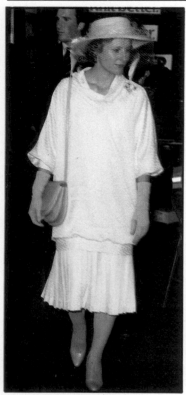

William.
The Duchess' visit to Stoneleigh came two days before she and the Duke celebrated their tenth wedding anniversary. They still share the modest, retiring sort of nature which craves obscurity and the peace of the countryside, and which – by some accounts – prompted them to plan setting up home on the Isle of Dogs before Prince William's early and tragic death at the age of 30 left them with the prospect, which soon materialised, of public duty for life. Princess Alice recently paid tribute to their dedication. "They work incomparably harder than we did before the war," she wrote. "But," she added, as an example of relative financial strictures, "for much of his day's business, the Duke dodges about London on a motorbike."

The Duchess of Gloucester was among the visitors to the Royal Show on 6th July, touring part of the massive site which for many years has found a permanent home at Stoneleigh in Warwickshire. No branch of the Royal Family is more readily associated with farming than the Gloucesters. The late Duke ran farms at the country home, Barnwell Manor in Northamptonshire, in partnership with his wife, Princess Alice, and their elder son Prince

(these pages) she was in the Home Counties, visiting Croham Hurst Place, a home for the Blind at Sanderstead in Surrey. This was one of her last public

As patron of the London Association of the Blind, Princess Alexandra attended its 125th Anniversary celebrations early in July. On 27th July

duties before a two-month summer break. A new schedule of appointments beginning in October included a ten-day visit to Thailand as the guest of King Bhumibhol and Queen Sirikit, for the 200th anniversary celebrations of the Chakri

dynasty. Princess Alexandra's son James took a family photograph marking his parents' departure for Bangkok: a keen photographer, he used an automatic release so that he could be included in the picture along with his parents and sister Marina.

Parliament, press and people – even the Queen was reported to have been amazed – and triggered a review of the complicated and perverse law of criminal trespass.

At Scotland Yard, whose royalty protection squad is responsible for the Queen's safety, London's

In spirits as bright as her cherry-red outfit, the Queen visited the Royal Military Police Training Centre at Chichester on 28th July, fascinated by demonstrations of karate and impressed by the smart discipline of the mounted guard of honour (right). Auspicious though the day was for the Military Police, however, the civil police endured a more harrowing ordeal in a month of fundamental breaches in Palace security. Central among a succession of scandals were Michael Fagan's two intrusions into Buckingham Palace in June and July, entering the Queen's bedroom on the second occasion to hold an unscheduled early morning conversation before she could summon help. At his trial in September, his acquittal of a charge of trespass stupefied

and guard dogs and a new burglar alarm system at Sandringham. In February a police sergeant on duty on the morning of Fagan's second entry was required to resign on admitting neglect of duty, after 27 years' service. The Fagan case ran parallel with that of Commander Trestrail, the Queen's personal detective. Threatened by exposure of his relationship with a male prostitute, he resigned in July 1982. Under intense Parliamentary pressure, the Home Secretary initiated an inquiry under the chairmanship of Lord Bridges. His report in November cleared Trestrail of breaching security, and recommended only minor changes in the vetting procedures which had failed to detect his homosexuality.

Police Commissioner Sir David McNee penned a personal letter of apology – "perhaps the most difficult I've ever had to write" – to the Queen, while his assistant, John Dellow, prepared a full report. In November, McNee's successor, Sir Kenneth Newman, ordered an investigation into the "gaping hole" in Palace security. This resulted in an increase in the police guard on London Palaces from 76 to 138, a three-tier electronic eye security alarm system at Buckingham Palace in January,

regatta. Taking the helm in the Yeoman class yacht which has served him for many years, and casting only an occasional, furtively suspicious eye at the photographers (below) he crossed the line in second place, only 90 seconds behind the winning craft, Highland Fling. After attending a Royal London Yacht Club reception and a Royal Yacht Squadron Ball at Cowes Castle the following day, he boarded the Royal Yacht *Britannia* on 3rd August for Balmoral, and another Highland fling, before visiting Holland to compete in the World Driving Championships.

The Queen has occasionally been there, Prince Charles has often raced and windsurfed there, Princess Anne and Prince Edward used to sail there and Princess Alexandra and her husband Mr Angus Ogilvy were frequent spectators there. But Prince Philip is the one member of the Royal Family for whom attendance at part of Cowes Week at least is an annual event. He was there again on 1st August, competing for the Queen's Cup – the major award in the Royal Southampton Yacht Club's opening

to go the way of many of his other outdoor interests, it was a day when he wore two teams' shirts – one for the Maple Leaf team, and one for Les Diables Bleus – and had no inhibitions about changing them in public. Nor did he think twice about

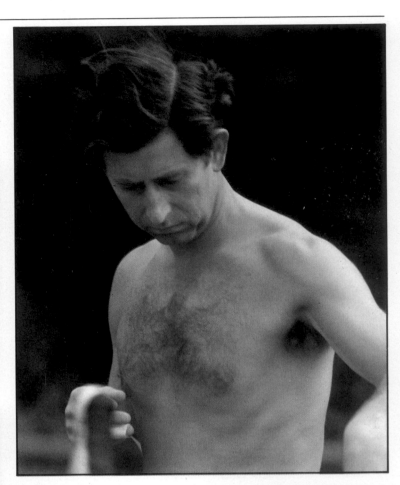

The Princess of Wales, keeping a low profile save for one official appearance at the Falklands service in London a few days before, was absent from Cowdray Park in Sussex on 2nd August. For her husband, whose enthusiasm for polo has refused

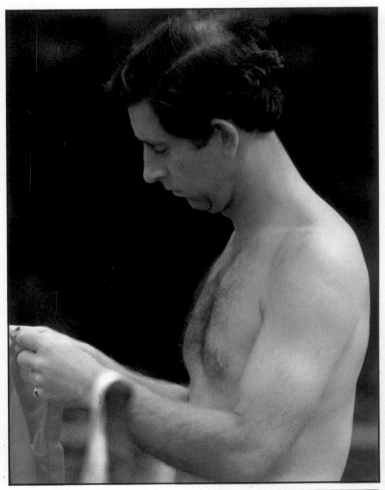

dodging behind the most convenient hedge to answer the inevitable call of nature as inconspicuously as possible (far right), nor again about nailing the old myth that royalty is not to be seen with glass in hand, let alone drinking from it (opposite page, top left). This was one of his last

adventures on the polo field. By the middle of August he and the Princess had made for Balmoral to join the Queen on her annual Highland holiday, leaving the English polo season to play out its last couple of weeks. Normally that would have meant no more polo for almost ten months, but in the event his tour of Australia in March 1983 gave him the opportunity to

limber up again for a couple of matches at Warwick Farm near Sydney. Understandably he found himself a little rusty after seven months off the field, but nevertheless contrived to be on the winning side on both occasions, justifying his commendable handicap of four with some well-praised shots, yet unable to avoid one of those legendary falls from the saddle.

It did not wholly comprise British royalty, because King Constantine of the Hellenes was in it, a representative of Greek royalty in exile and/or the Queen's vast and increasing cousinhood, royal or otherwise. With him was his wife, Queen Anne-Marie – the younger sister of the Queen of Denmark. In the King's team was his more immediate cousin the Duke of Kent (below left), the Duke's brother-in-law the Hon. Angus Ogilvy (opposite page, top right) and Captain Mark Phillips (opposite page centre), rejoicing in overall victory. The Team's victory was not much

On 8th August, the North Wales Shooting School on Deeside was the scene of an assembly of no fewer than eight royalties. They took part in a celebrity challenge shooting match organised by the champion racing driver Jackie Stewart, between eight not-too-loosely formed groups of guns. Most competitors were from the worlds of sport and entertainment, but the competition was graced by the inclusion of two rather upmarket teams. One, headed by the Earl of Lichfield, represented Britain's aristocrats and was named The Lords. The other represented Britain's royalty and, avoiding any charge of vulgarity by calling themselves The Royals, opted for a much more classy put-down in the title The Team.

present and load new cartridges while the competitors held the guns open. In this way Princess Alexandra, her daughter Marina Ogilvy, Princess Anne and the Queen of Greece took an active and, as the stewards overruled objections by the runners-up, successful part in securing victory for royalty – a lesson, perhaps, in how to survive in a world of republics. Lord Lichfield (bottom left) was not amused.

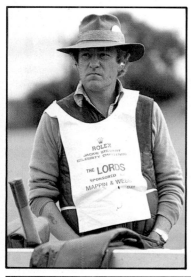

appreciated by the other contestants. The last and crucial round – in contrast to the more sedate standard clay-pigeon shoot or the picking off of dummy hares between straw bales – involved a marathon shoot of clay-pigeons propelled into the air at random. Time was of the essence and the reloading of guns had to be done quickly. Contestants in all other teams took up and put in their own cartridges but, shooting last, The Team engaged their respective ladies to

The increasing modern-day demand for the dramatic made it almost obligatory that, on her return journey from the Falklands conflict, *HMS Invincible* should not arrive home unless she loomed out of the fog in the process. Circumstances obliged on 17th September. Through the murk, almost six months after she had left amid a frenzy of patriotism and good wishes, *Invincible* slipped noiselessly towards her home harbour, her flight decks puddled with precipitation and patterned with Harrier jets and Sea King helicopters. Beside one of them stood the latest member of the British Royal Family to go to war, Sub-Lieutenant HRH Prince Andrew. Looking confident after his ordeal, feeling ineffably pleased and relaxed after a return journey taken up more with parties and sunbathing than with military exercises, he now awaited the culmination of his experience – to be reconciled with his family and to be part of one of the most patriotically effusive public welcomes any part of the British Isles had seen in almost forty years.

The Queen, now well over half way through her summer holiday at Balmoral, and Prince Philip, shortly to leave for Brisbane to open the Commonwealth Games, arrived with Princess Anne at Portsmouth Dockyard and were taken by barge to Spithead, two miles out to sea. From the bobbing barge they climbed up narrow wooden steps onto *Invincible* and were led to the Admiral's cabin for a private twenty-minute reunion with Prince Andrew. For all the royal party's outward calm, the Queen's decorous appearance, the Duke's Admiral of the Fleet uniform, the meeting must have been intensely emotional, but

the public facade was quickly regained for the photocall on one of the ship's decks (above) and the slow progress, as the last of the morning mists cleared, into harbour. Prince Andrew took the Press toward his helicopter (right) and was soon chatting freely about his adventures. He admitted feeling "different" after experiencing war at first hand. "I think my life has gone round the corner since I left five and a half months ago," he said. He had got on well with his companions – they proved it

by some good natured heckling as he spoke. "I couldn't forget this lot," he smiled. "They're an absolutely fantastic bunch. I would gladly keep going – particularly with this ship's company and the men I have served with in the Falklands." With just an inkling of the noises and the sights which lay immediately ahead of him and his ship, the war and its aftermath may have seemed a long way off, but there was time for a spot of self-analysis. "I felt lonely more than anything else," he confessed. "When you are down on the deck, when there are missiles flying around, then at that precise moment you are on your own and that's all there is. On the odd occasion I was terrified. To overcome fear I tried to adopt a positive mental attitude. I can't actually remember what I thought of – what I put in my mind – but I just remember telling myself 'I am going to survive this.'"

Survive he did, as did a crew of almost a thousand souls. Ahead of them lay Portsmouth harbour, busy with the unceasing movement of 55,000 relatives and friends anxious for the first sight of their loved ones. Half an hour after mid-day, the ship's

giving a rose to every returning crew member on the *Canberra,* the *Queen Elizabeth 2* and the *Hermes* in the previous three months. Perversely, it might seem, the public concentration on Prince Andrew, understandable though it was, was not particularly welcomed by the Prince himself. While he and the Queen were responding to calls from the crowds of "Well done, Mum, we're glad Andy's home," the appearance of a couple of private detectives, and of a Palace footman who came to pick up his baggage with its blue pointed labels from the single-berth cabin that had been his for almost six months, reminded him that royal rank would re-form the barrier which life

among his shipmates had effectively broken down. Well might he have thought – to paraphrase Queen Mary in 1945 – "Here I've been anybody to everybody, and back in London I shall have to begin being Prince Andrew all over again!" What he did say, more simply, was, "I'm not looking forward to going back to being a Prince. I'm a pilot."

"Being a Prince" started immediately. He was back in the world of public relations and walkabouts. The Queen and Prince Philip had agreed to see some of the thousands of other relatives crowding the quayside, and for a hundred yards they chatted casually with many of them. Prince Andrew was, of

Swordfish bi-planes performed the Royal Navy's own fly-past in honour of its heroes, and crews of ships from other NATO countries – Belgium, the Netherlands and Western Germany – joined in the celebrations. The dockside was itself a sea of faces – some cheering, some weeping, all searching – and of a multiplicity of banners identifying by name those who would be as welcome in their own parishes as Prince Andrew on a day when all *Invincible's* sailors were equal. But, of course, attention still focused on the royal crew member, and the public delight when he was presented with a long-stemmed red rose by 10-year-old Mandy Blythe was exceeded only when he voluntarily stuck it between his teeth for all to see (above). Then he removed the rose from his mouth with one hand, snatched off his white-topped cap with the other, and waved it high as he leapt into the air in a gesture of unrestrained joy and relief. The Queen, though more circumspect about her reactions, was equally delighted and certainly amused by the presentation to her of a single rose and a basket of red roses by the patriotically-dressed David Connolly (opposite page, bottom right), a florist from Croydon who was responsible for

engines were shut off and in bright sunshine a host of small boats of all descriptions bustled towards *Invincible's* path. On the quayside official bands struck up with tunes as resounding as *Rule Britannia* and *Land of Hope and Glory,* and as folksy as *Congratulations.* The crowds weighed in, and the sailors lining the rails of *Invincible* couldn't resist joining in as well. At a signal 4,000 red, white and blue balloons were sent soaring into the air, quickly gaining height and floating off as little dark dots. Coloured smoke was simultaneously released from canisters, sirens shrieked, tugs spouted fountains of water, a formation of historical

course, constrained to join in and with his ready reputation as a lady's man – he had been rumoured to have written letters to several girl friends during his absence – there was no shortage of requests from young ladies for a quick embrace. He refused, though tactfully, on the ground that "If I kissed you, I would have to kiss all the girls." The Queen was comparing notes with another mother, who confessed herself constantly worried for her son's safety. "I know how you felt," replied the Queen. "It's wonderful to have Andrew home." Home was not very far away. The Queen, Prince Philip and Princess Anne, having met their own family member and shared in the greetings for a thousand others, left the bustling, noisy harbour and its occupants to the joys of their own reunions.

Prince Andrew left with them, but made his way to London for the evening before returning to Portsmouth to fly his helicopter back to its base at RNAF Culdrose in Cornwall. There, a champagne celebration awaited him and other members of 820 Squadron – in spite of the Prince's own admission, at Portsmouth, that what he really looked forward to was a pint. "Of what?" he was asked. "Of milk. We haven't had any real milk for months." From Culdrose on the evening of 18th September, he flew to Balmoral to rejoin his parents, his

18th October, it was the end of what he described as "one hell of an experience." Not surprisingly, the Queen chose a photograph of him with his helicopter for her personal Christmas cards that December.

brother the Prince of Wales, and the Princess of Wales who was just back from Monte Carlo where she had been attending Princess Grace's funeral.

Politically, economically and socially the effects of the comparatively short Falklands skirmish were, and are, continuing, wide-ranging, and the subject of furious debate and enquiry. Even the celebrations were not over – a massive military parade was held in London the following October – and the sadness and waste had still not fully sunk in: that would happen when the container-loads of coffins sent from Teeside early in September brought back the human cost of battle. But *Invincible's* return was the last of the great triumphant homecomings, and for Prince Andrew and his colleagues, happily anticipating a month's shore leave before reporting back to Culdrose on

On 20th September, Prince Philip left London Airport for Los Angeles, as President of the *Federation Internationale Equestre,* to attend meetings in connection with the 1984 Olympic Games which are to be held there. From there he flew to Brisbane, the capital of Queensland, Australia to open the 12th Commonwealth Games (previous page) on 30th September. Forty-three countries competed and all were represented in the immense ceremonial at which the Duke presided. Unfortunately the weather proved unseasonal, an icy wind ripping across the vast, filled stadium. Raelene Boyle, the Australian sprinter for whom these Games proved a successful swan-song, delivered the baton carrying the Queen's message on the last stage of its journey across the globe. In

the week between the opening of the Games and the arrival of the Queen for a short visit to Australia, Prince Philip paid several calls to the various Games stadia to watch events as diverse as bowls and weight-lifting. On 6th October (far left), for instance, he witnessed a high-scoring friendly match between the 1982 Victoria League football finalists, Carlton and Richmond. But perhaps the most colourful interlude was his trip to Queensland's Gold Coast, then in the full swing of an interstate surf carnival. Soft, bleached sand and brilliant sunshine

outside help. But there was also time for demonstrations of sea rescue (below), the almost inevitable parade of life savers in their distinctive strip (above), a chat to some of the competitors (bottom left) and the presentation of gifts – probably the only circumstances in which Prince Philip would risk his reputation by letting a scantily-clad girl near him (top left). An attempt by 17-year-old Sonya Fawdry to present a toy koala bear to the Prince, and to give him a kiss, was quickly foiled. Conscious of a security alert, which had coincided with his arrival on 29th September, and of the delicate state of race relations in Queensland, security men grabbed the koala, and the girl disappeared, emerging later to explain that "there was no bomb in it."

provided the perfect setting for the surfing competitions – after one of which the Duke had to console a winner who was disqualified for receiving

It seemed appropriate that the Queen should arrive in Brisbane in an aircraft called "Windsor Town". It was the end of a hot afternoon, and with a strong breeze sweeping the airbase, the ceremonies were short and low key, highlighted by the presence of Queensland's popular Premier, Joh Bjelke-Petersen, the army's regimental mascot, a two year old ram called Private Don – and enthusiastic groups of young Scouts, Guides and Red Cross students who persisted with their bouquets and home-made gifts. At least one didn't succeed. "No, you have it," said Prince Philip to a little girl who offered him her stick of streamers.

"Welcome Your Majesty – and thanks for the loan of the theatre." Thus compere Rolf Harris – almost as famous in Britain as in Australia – at a Commonwealth variety performance at Her Majesty's Theatre, Brisbane on 7th October. A spectacular guard of honour was formed by teams of dancers, acrobats and Aborigine and Polynesian groups (centre), a cast of 250 represented the 47 countries of the Commonwealth, and an example of the extremes in cultural art forms was displayed by the distinctive, yet quite different, talents of the Aborigine David Gumpalil and the French singer Sacha Distel (far right). An appreciative audience, matching the enthusiasm of the crowd of

nearly 2,000 outside the theatre, paid $100 a ticket for the privilege of attending, and the Queen and Prince Philip came down from the dress circle to speak to the whole cast on stage after the show.

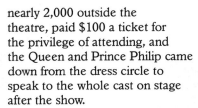

Few cities anywhere can rival Brisbane in their enthusiasm for the Royal Family, and few citizens of Brisbane fall hook, line and sinker for them as readily as Mrs Jess Anderson of nearby Bardon. "I'm the royalest royalist that ever lived," she announced. "I saw the Queen's mother here when she was Duchess of York in 1927." No sooner had the Queen begun her walk than hundreds of spectators dodged beneath

barriers to follow her, causing alarm among the police and concern among the Queen's own retinue. But the Queen, escorted by Lord Mayor Roy Harvey (opposite page, far right), smiled through it all, collecting so many bunches of flowers that members of her household and even the journalists following close on their heels were delegated with the responsibility of carrying them to the City Hall.
Prince Philip was faintly amused by the growing chaos, but even he was nearly swamped by

swirling crowds as soon as he stopped to chat. Nevertheless, he feasted his attention on the children and their sporting interests. Had they been to any of the Commonwealth Games? Which ones? Which did they like best? What sport would they like to take up? Were there any potential weight-lifters here? If so, they'd better eat plenty

of spinach. So it went on, until he finally commented, "Look at all these children. You must be great breeders around here."

Meanwhile, the Queen, ignoring

the flock of people pushing forward behind her, had a special word for Mrs Dorothy Kennish (opposite page, below), a 99-year-old Englishwoman who has lived in Australia for over half a century. Her niece had sneaked a chair to the front of the crowd for her so that she could present a white English rose to the Queen. "I'm so excited I can't think," she said afterwards.

Up a grand flight of steps to King George Square, past a splendid equestrian statue of

her grandfather, the Queen was eventually led to City Hall for a civic reception. This fairly innocuous engagement was not without its little history of trouble – Alderman Campbell, regarded, said one newspaper "as being a member of the socialist left of the Australian Labor Party" refused to attend. In his place – for better or worse, it seemed – were a dozen koalas, brought from a local zoo and set in five potted eucalyptus trees, waiting for an admiring glance from the Queen as she passed. A glance was all they initially got, so their owners brought them off the trees to give the Queen a closer look (top right).

National Bank

On the evening of her arrival in Brisbane, 6th October, the Queen made her first acquaintance with the Commonwealth Games with a visit to the Chandler Aquatic Centre for the final session of swimming and diving. Her

ceremonial entry was accomplished with some difficulty and only at the second attempt, since the excitement of previous events had already left the spectators noisy and vociferous, shouting to a background of constant whistles and blowing of horns. But the march in formation of two dozen yellow-coated officials hushed the noise, and the Queen appeared again, to a frenzy of applause and the artificial sound of the Royal Anthem on a Hammond organ (top left). Though she hardly ever

applauded, she relaxed a lot, sitting with legs crossed and conversing with the Prime Minister, Malcolm Fraser, against the sporadic chanting of supporters as they banged on the metal barriers.

The Queen moved from the Royal Box to present one set of medals – after the Australian Tracey Wickham had won the ladies' 400 metres. Jackie Wilmott (far left) won the silver and June Croft the bronze, both for England. After an informal walk along the side of the pool, during which she chatted to

Canada were disqualified. It was ironic that, for the only time that evening, the Queen joined in the applause – just as a disgruntled Canadian swimmer kicked over a chair in disgust! A tunnel-full of graffiti was the only problem the next day when, following their visit to City Hall, the Queen and Prince Philip toured the Commonwealth Games Village at Griffith University. The tunnel (opposite page, top right) links two sections of the campus, and for the past fortnight had been a playground for the literary wits of the sporting world. Whether she saw the adage, "Keep Australia beautiful, plant a Pom" is not certain, but she didn't seem to mind what she did spot. Nor did the Duke, who actually stopped to read one or

officials and competitors and collected a large number of pin-badges commemorating the Games, the Queen watched two more events, including the controversial men's medley relay, won by Australia after

two thoughts – and may have added a few of his own if he'd had the chance.

The royal tour of the Village took them to areas as diverse as the physiotherapy room and the refectory (opposite page, bottom right) where groups of waitresses and orderlies stood around in neat groups as the royal couple interrupted snack meals for a minute or two at a time to chat to competitors. The Duke clearly bowled over one Scottish girl: "It made my day," she gasped, wide eyed," – a bit of a shock." Another lady mused over the fact that when she was a nurse at Westminster in the 1930s, she used to watch the Queen and Princess Margaret when they were taken around London as little girls.

The Queen and Duke were taken past a display of Canadian cowboy whip-cracking, and a didgeridoo performance, and within the throbbing sound of a colourful tribal dance by Aboriginals in suberb white head-dresses and bright yellow skirts. Eventually, they were taken to a studio where they watched video recordings of some

events the Queen had missed. The Duke seemed to have seen them all, because he provided a running commentary for his wife: "Look at this – she just ran out of steam....Look! Here she goes...Now, this was tremendous..."

The Queen saw for herself an hour later, during her visit to the Queen Elizabeth II Jubilee Centre, for two hours of athletics. Two days later she would be there again for the closing ceremony.

Photography of royal investitures is usually heavily restricted and the ceremony at Brisbane on 8th October was no exception. But that tended to lend an exclusivity to the event, as all the recipients of honours on that warm fine day will testify. The lofty, balconied chamber within the city's Parliament building was lit by natural daylight and by two massive chandeliers, each bearing eighty-eight lamps. A table covered with medals awaited the Queen's pleasure, and gleamed as she entered to a fanfare of RAAF trumpeters. After the Royal Anthem, an officer announced: "Your Majesty has graciously consented to award the following," and the list of those about to be honoured was read out at intervals of approximately a minute. The Queen took each medal from a deep blue, gold-braided and tasselled cushion proffered to her, while an equerry whispered to her the nature of each beneficiary's services. For each, there were twenty seconds or so of royal conversation, unheard by the assembly because of the music coming from the orchestra outside. Only one dubbing took place – that of Sir Jack Leggo (above) for services to motorists, charities and the community.

Sea-green and aquamarine were the Queen's favourite evening dress colours for each of two

visits to art galleries: sea-green at Brisbane on 8th October; aquamarine at Canberra four days later. The Brisbane event was special from the start. The Queen arrived at the Queensland Cultural Centre by river, her barge gliding past multiple fountains and under bridges magnificently bathed in white and coloured lights. The festive feeling among the thousand-strong crowd was nurtured by Premier Bjelke-Petersen whose arrival gave his many admirers the chance to practise their cheering. An enormous explosion of fireworks as the royal craft came to a halt excited them even more. Sprays of red, white and blue, changing to falling gold and silver, were followed by great radial bursts of flame and spark, and five minutes of continuous noise and illumination. Eventually, as a Commonwealth Games symbol

floated in fire down the river, a fanfare sounded for the Queen's disembarkation, and her much applauded progress into the Centre.

A gallery walkway acted as a balcony from which the official

speeches were to be made, and as the Queen and Prince Philip reached it a resounding drum roll introduced the Royal Anthem, played with such vigour and at such a decibel level that it set the security alarms off. The Premier had to compete with the continuous hoot of a klaxon as he spoke his brief words of

welcome; the Queen kept a straight face while the Duke looked quizically around him, furrowing his brow deeper as scuttling officials attempted, unsuccessfully, to switch off the alarm. Both the Premier's speech and the Queen's reply were unremarkable, the Queen dwelling, as she must on these occasions, on the worth of the Commonwealth and the contribution being made by Queensland to it. And no sooner was her back turned on the picture she had unveiled to commemorate her visit to this part of the centre than it was whisked away to be stored until its rightful place among the other exhibits could be found the following day.

"Nothing could demonstrate better," said the Queen, when declaring open the Australian National Gallery in Canberra on 12th October (opposite page, top right), "the enhanced standing of Australia than this fine National Art Gallery." Few could possibly have disagreed with her. Conceived by the Menzies Government in 1965, an art collection was begun in 1969, and Gough Whitlam's government paid over $1,000,000 for a single painting in 1974.

Now Prime Minister Malcom Fraser, in his welcoming speech, announced his own government's contribution of $27,000,000 to the gallery to finance additions in time for the Australian bi-centenary celebrations in 1988. In all, it was a fascinating, and rather educational evening. And, as the Gallery's chairman said, "The Gallery is born tonight."

The Queen closed the Commonwealth Games on 9th October and the competitions seemed almost incidental by then. In a thrilling afternoon's finals England, thanks partly to a wonderful 1,500 metre run by Steve Cram (above), nudged Australia off the top of the overall medals table. Keith Connor's triple jump was the second longest in history. Raelene Boyle retired amid unending praise and applause. The day's weather, performance and spirit were perfect. The Queen had time to enjoy it – and record it (right) – before pronouncing the closing words (above left). Matilda, winking coquettishly at all and sundry, was the most popular feature, even when swathed in coloured smoke from the Chinese dragon (left). The Queen even told her driver to slow down for her own final lap of honour.

playing of the Royal Anthem, and Prince Philip's reading of the Lesson.

After the service the Queen and Duke drove back to Canberra (these pages) to visit the War Memorial – a large courtyard inset with a rectangular pool, overlooked by a copper-domed Hall of Memory. Around the sides of the courtyard, high walls record the endless roll of honour, classified by battle or war zone – South Africa, Indian Ocean, Gallipoli, Flanders, Java, and so on. In a short,

quiet ceremony, the Queen placed a wreath of daisy, chrysanthemum and hibiscus on a commemorative stone before being invited into the adjacent museum and shown, among other things, one of eight scarves which Queen Victoria crocheted for Empire soldiers during the Boer War as a reward for bravery. Outside, the crowd awaited a chance to see the royal visitors.

The royal tour moved that evening to the Federal capital, Canberra. The following morning the Queen and Prince Philip attended morning service at Ainslie, a suburb of Canberra, in a church which had once been a railway halt for a Sydney municipal cemetery. That trains – pulling six or eight carriages full of relatives grieving over coffins of their dead – once ran through what is effectively the aisle of the present church is unthinkable, so pleasant and welcoming it now all is. The only overt reference to the presence of royalty was the

On the evening of 10th October, the Governor-General of Australia, Sir Ninian Stephen and his wife, seen (opposite page, below) standing between Prince Philip and the Queen, gave a dinner at Government House, attended also by Mr and Mrs Malcom Fraser. On 11th October the royal visitors flew to Mount Druitt to open a new hospital which serves a large dormitory area for Sydney. It took its first patients during

I think she ought to bottle it." From Mount Druitt the Queen and Duke flew to Bathurst, a visit arranged at the Queen's request: she had not been there since 1954 and wanted to meet its people again. They turned out in their thousands to line the long, wide streets as she drove and walked to the City Hall for a State reception (remaining pictures).

the previous month and the Queen and Duke were able to tour the wards, talking with working staff and with patients (below). The Duke had a few jovially crisp comments about hospital food, compulsory prayers and the legibility of doctors' handwriting, but the Queen perked up one patient, Mrs Dorothy Hilmer, handsomely: "She looked so young, she has a warmth about her, so friendly. The best medicine I've ever had.

drummers and bag-pipers in blue shirts and dark blue wraps bearing a bright orange bird of paradise design, played them into the inspection of the guard of honour (bottom right). Gun salutes drew whoops of surprise from the vast crowd sweltering in the heat, patiently awaiting

something on the lines of a walkabout – but there was none. Within a short time the royal party was on the long, winding road to Port Moresby's Hubert Murray Stadium, passing endless lines of people standing

The Queen and Prince Philip arrived in the land of almost a thousand languages when a Royal Australian Air Force plane brought them from Canberra to Port Moresby, capital of Papua New Guinea, in the early afternoon of 13th October. Over 750 languages and 400 dialects are spoken in this heavily tribal country, though on occasions like this they all seem to fall silent. The Queen and Duke were welcomed by a white-uniformed Governor-General (below) as a band of pipers,

hair, along with the odd hibiscus bloom or circlet of frangipani. With the memory of the excitable children of Canberra still fresh, the comparative silence was eerie. Yet the sentiment was clear, epitomised by one banner sporting the first example of pidgin-English the Queen may have seen that day: "Welcum Misis Kwin Anytime."
That evening the Queen and Prince Philip were guests at a State dinner given by the Prime Minister Mr Somare (below) at

which 160 guests were present. The hotel selected for this occasion – the Papua Hotel – was an unpretentious one as, in an attempt not to overstrain National resources, a balance had to be achieved between luxury and cost. Almost in keeping with that concept, the guests were not all decked out in dinner jacket and black tie. Some of the men wore the skirt

common to the South Pacific Islands, others wore lounge suits and ties, others wore open-necked shirts and slacks, and the variety of footwear was equally comprehensive. But it was a gratifyingly informal sort of State dinner for which the Queen, who had seemed to flag earlier in the day, may well have been grateful. A modest menu comprised chilled avocado

shoulder to shoulder and often four or five deep. Most held flags of independent Papua New Guinea in brilliant red, yellow and black; many waved them and a few had acquired Union Jacks as well. For some it was enough to stick them upright in their

and tomato soup, noisette of lamb with local vegetables and salad, orange and passion fruit mousse and Highlands coffee. Papua Highlands, that is, not Scottish. And the wines were Australian.

On their first afternoon in Papua New Guinea, the Queen and Prince Philip were entertained at the Hubert Murray Stadium by a tribal carnival drawn from all over the country's lowlands.

Thirty thousand people had packed the stadium to see the royal party arrive to the rhythmic beating of welcoming drums.
Magnificent head-dresses stood four and five feet high, bristling with feathers of every conceivable indigenous bird but, proudest of all, with the much prized plumes of the dozens of species of bird of paradise. Protected by law, they may be captured only for the use of their feathers in head-dresses, which become priceless tribal heirlooms. Grass skirts, beautifully fashioned, abounded, as did festoons of horn necklaces and hosts of baubles symbolic of wealth or rank. The dancing seemed to go on for ever, several groups in various parts of the huge field performing simultaneously, none stopping without another taking up. The continuous throb of tom-toms quickened and slowed the pace of ritual movements, stout poles hung with shells were banged on the ground to induce changes of tempo, and all the while the small armies of dancers charged, bobbed, swung and gyrated until, almost perversely, a band from the Royal Yacht *Britannia,* pith-helmeted and red-sashed, were marched on to herald the Queen's departure. For once their polished excellence was swamped by the burnished, primitive splendour around them.
The following day the Queen and

Prince Philip flew to Mount Hagen in the Papuan Highlands to watch a sing-sing – a festival of song and dance, very similar to that given at Port Moresby, but pertaining to tribal life in the highlands. Communities had been on the march for days to be here, and the day had been declared an "amnesty day" when, in this tribally hostile region, bows and arrows may not be

carried except for cultural purposes. Here again was a vast assembly of scores of tribes, painted and dressed a hundred different ways (overleaf) and all limbering up to give their best performance for Misis Kwin and for Man Bilong Kwin. But it all went horribly wrong. As the Queen arrived, a storm was already gathering. As she and Prince Philip drove around the enclosure many dancers, fearing for their precious head-

gear, were fleeing, and droves of spectators followed them as the elegant royal thrones on the thatch-covered podium were filled. The rain started as the Queen began her reply to the Premier's speech of welcome; a clap of thunder marked its conclusion, and when the Queen looked up only a handful of people met her gaze. The full fury of an icy cold storm followed and the royal party beat a hasty retreat back to Mount Hagen airport and thence to the scorching heat of the capital.

The Royal Yacht *Britannia* took the Queen and Prince Philip from Port Moresby to the Solomon Islands, giving them the agreeable bonus of three days' relaxation as they neared the Equator. Early in the morning of 18th October, the Yacht anchored off-shore and the royal barge brought the travellers (opposite page, bottom left) to

fish casually swimming in the harbour's clear pool.

The guard was duly inspected (opposite page, top left), the local dignitaries duly introduced (left) and the royal party taken to Lawson Tama, a large recreation stadium in Honiara where the sound of the conch shell and a fierce but traditional warrior challenge heralded their arrival. Here they watched a succession of

Honiara harbour. The far quayside was thick with spectators who covered four wide jetties, climbed every tree and waded as far as necessary into the water to see the proceedings. Umbrellas were put to good use (left) as a brilliant sun shot the temperature into the thirties – even at 9.30 in the morning – and illuminated the bright colours of the numerous parrot

dances by groups from the various Solomon Islands, and inspected displays of local culture and handicrafts – copperware, the making of shell money, canoe manufacture and household interests. The Queen stood under a white parasol, held for her by a local official (opposite page, bottom right) as she replied, thanking the islanders for their gifts of wood carvings and for the star of the Solomon Islands she had just received as the first recipient of the highest of the Islands' honours. It was a short drive to the Central

Hospital, whose open-air corridors were beautifully decked out with flowers and bunting (opposite page, top right) and smelled of frangipani and hibiscus. The Queen was in her element as she visited the maternity wards, but the Duke came away less pleased. He had been told that the Islands' population growth rate was almost 5% – the highest in the South Pacific. He warned that "in twenty years' time there will be an economic crisis and you'll be blaming it on everyone else." "Five per cent!" he muttered to himself. "They must

be out of their minds!" Pointedly he did not rejoin the Queen for the remainder of her tour of the maternity unit. Babies appearing at that rate had clearly lost their appeal.

The Queen had changed into a
cool, blue outfit with a
flamboyant feather-trimmed hat
for the visit to the National
Museum late that afternoon.
Here she and Prince Philip saw
an exhibition of the history of
the Islands before they became a
British protectorate – a period
going back into the unknown and

pleased to see activities
connected with his Award Scheme.
At the National Archives the
Queen and Prince Philip toured
an exhibition of wartime
photographs and met five
veterans (left) of the fierce
fighting to defend the Solomons.

winningly referred to as
"Solomon Time Before." From
there they passed through a
bamboo grove into Coronation
Gardens, where the children's
rally awaited them. The Queen
received a bouquet from four-
year-old Indy Tapalia – Indy
being short for Independence,
since she was born on Solomons'
Independence Day in 1978 – and
spoke to several groups of
Scouts, Guides and primary and
secondary school children (far
right). The Duke was a great
favourite (above) and was

The mid-point of a tour of exciting and sometimes refreshingly primitive island communities, the royal visit to Nauru was certainly the most thought-provoking. Nauru is only eight square miles in area and produces nothing save phosphate. Mined continuously since the 1890s, the phosphate supply is now close to exhaustion.

The Queen's welcome on her arrival from *Britannia* by barge

(below and opposite page) was as genuine as any, yet there was a strangeness in the surroundings. The red carpet she set foot on was imported from New Zealand; the 30-strong school band which struck up the National Anthems on her arrival and serenaded her through the day, had been flown in from Melbourne; the management and supervisory staff of the phosphate mines, which the royal couple toured, were English and Australian; the dancers who entertained them at

a garden party that afternoon were from Western Samoa, Kiribati, Tuvala – anywhere, it seemed, but from Nauru. Even the handsomely-decorated coffee table, inlaid with the Star of Nauru in phosphate rock, and standing on carved lion's foot legs – presented to the Queen during the official farewells (far left) – was tactfully described as "Made under the supervision of Nauruans."

sunshine.
The day was punctuated by ceremonies in maneabas, or meeting houses, where honours in the form of plaited cords (far left) and dried-leaf garlands (below) were bestowed, and where

Iosiabata was the name of the man brought from Maina Island to Kiribati's capital Tarawa, to ensure good weather for the Queen's visit on 23rd October. He justified the cost of his passage and food. As the Queen arrived, the early morning rains stopped, leaving the remainder of the day bathed in hot

the drinking of coconut water straight from the shell was as much a ritual as an opportunity for refreshment. Shortly before the Queen arrived, the tin roof of a house gave way under the weight of dozens of people using it as a vantage point. On the island of Betio that afternoon, the branch of a tree followed suit, when it became over-loaded with sightseers.

Prince Philip, accompanying the Queen to Tarawa's Tungaru Hospital (opposite page, top right) lapsed into chatty informality in no time. Told of the number of injuries caused by drunken drivers, he said, "I'm not surprised, judging by the quantity of empty beer cans around the island. You really ought to get someone to clear up the empties."

After a colourful parade of local schoolchildren at Tarawa's

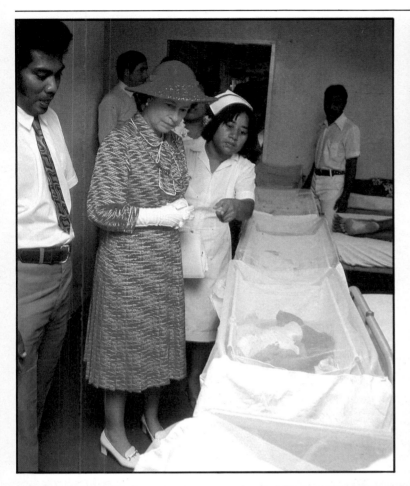

sports field (left) and a superb open-air lunch in the gardens of State House, close by one of Tarawa's long, wide beaches, the Queen and the Duke sailed for Betio where they separated – the Queen to see a display of village technology, the Duke to inspect a marine Training School and (facing page,top) find time for another quick drink. They met again in the Island's maneaba for a magnificent rendering of traditional songs and, to receive gifts before leaving for Tuvalu.

"If it's Tuesday, it must be Tuvalu," was certainly not one of the Queen's thoughts as she approached the island of Funafuti, capital of the former Ellice Islands. In a life where the well-prepared and even the spectacular may seem routine, there was nothing remotely mundane about the start – nor indeed the end – of her two-day visit, beginning on 26th October to Tuvalu. There is a harbour here, and the royal barge might have used it, but conditions were good enough for a more distinctive welcome. The barge was met by a flotilla of long canoes, whose paddlers were charged with the duty of conveying the Queen, Prince Philip and their party to the shore (opposite page, top). The canoes – built in a week, of light hardwood called puka, and costing no more than $270

(about £150) – were copies of those used locally for skipjack fishing, but the bright colours of protective paint marked their special purpose today.

Once ashore, the canoes and their occupants were – initially to the Queen's consternation – hoisted onto the shoulders of twenty six brawny men and carried along the sandy streets to be eventually set down on a tennis court beside the central maneapa. Like the maneapa itself, the tennis court was

strewn with matting (opposite page, bottom left) and before the Queen and Prince Philip went in, they were garlanded by necklaces made of shells. This was a gesture of great honour, traditionally afforded only to high chiefs of the islands and, as the Prime Minister said in his speech of welcome, never before bestowed upon anyone from overseas. It was, indeed, the first time the islands had welcomed their reigning sovereign, although Prince Philip, Prince Charles, Princess Margaret and Princess Anne had paid visits here in the previous

25 years. In her reply, the Queen was quick to assert that she had enjoyed her arrival and that she was glad that "my first visit to your charming country should be as Queen of Tuvalu." The tone for the entire visit was thus set, and affirmed by a performance of songs sung by 120 villagers, who found room to sway, clap and gesticulate as the narrative demanded, despite the density of the accommodation. The Queen and Prince Philip, applauding after each item, clearly enjoyed the experience immensely (opposite page, top right). At these

times the Queen seems not to give much away but she could not, and did not, fail to be warmed by this noisy, yet thoroughly polished performance. Prince Philip, his naval cap abandoned beneath his chair, gaily tapped his feet and patted his hands to the ever-changing but compulsive rhythms. The visit was only two hours old, yet its impact on the visitors was unmistakable as they gave a reception aboard the Royal Yacht that evening. They were among friends who knew how to balance respect with warmth and informality.

That night the celebrations continued. The Queen and Prince Philip were back in the maneapa for a traditional feast, served in an equally traditional manner. In a carefully rehearsed procession, bearers brought an amazing selection of food – legs of pork, quarters of chicken, crabs, lobsters and fish, even cooked blackbirds and bats, a whole succession of vegetables and fruit from the huge taros, or sweet potatoes, to the clusters of small bananas. The

Queen was visibly uncertain how to tackle this enormous spread, and seemed self-consciously to inspect and study its constituents, rather than to taste them. Prince Philip had no such reservations, and joked happily with his serving girl as he tucked into a variety of dishes. Afterwards, a ceremonial crowning, in which all the guests received decorative circlets of flowers, left the Queen with a cluster of densely arranged frangipani on her head, and the Duke with a more rakish version of straw and flame tree blooms on his – a result at which the Duke was openly amused (opposite page). This ceremony heralded the beginning of the evening's entertainment, and the Queen and Prince Philip moved from this table (far right) to watch a three-hour programme of non-stop singing. Every one of Tuvalu's

nine little islands was represented: singers from each community performing three or four songs – some of welcome, others of island legends, others versifying modern events like World War II battles, and the Apollo moon missions.

young children, while near the island's only hotel, the Queen laid a stone which will ultimately become part of Tuvalu's new Parliament building (bottom left). The visit of the Prince of Wales in 1970 was

The Queen and Prince Philip spent most of 27th October touring Funafuti, the island capital of Tuvalu. At the Princess Margaret Hospital, the Queen was delighted to find a set of twins in the tiny maternity unit (bottom right). Just outside, she and Prince Philip watched toddy (coconut water) being extracted from palms, and (above) sampled the result. At the primary school (right) they were serenaded with the Maori farewell, movingly harmonised by over a hundred

THIS STONE WAS LAID BY
H. M. QUEEN ELIZABETH II
27 OCTOBER 1982.

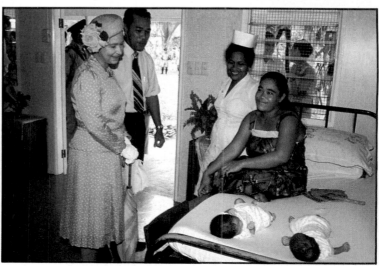

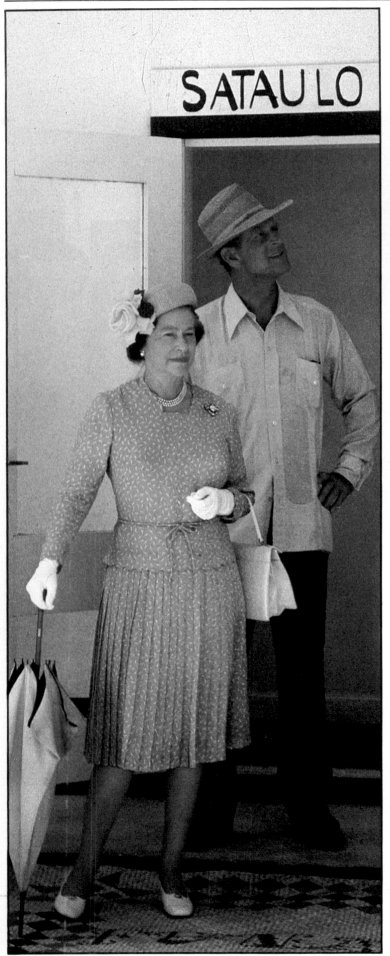

from – a quick refreshment before touring more mundane institutions such as the Police Headquarters, the Post Office and the National Bank, and watching the local game of ano being played on a recreation field.

recalled when they saw Prince Charles' coconut tree near the village centre. Here a villager shinned up a palm tree, hacked a couple of coconuts away, and threw them down, to be opened for the royal couple to drink

"Gifts," the Queen and Prince Philip were told that afternoon, "are the most important aspect of our culture." Whether, as in an open Land Rover, they arrived at the maneapa for the farewell ceremonies they realised how true that was is doubtful, but

the ensuing ritual – no less affirmative a term would suffice – was incredible, in its enormity, to novice eyes. Their arrival was proclaimed by the immediate singing of a chorus of 200 islanders, and no sooner had they sat down on steps outside the maneapa than a troupe of

traditional dancers performed a warrior-like routine, charging, retreating, gyrating and leaping in front of the royal dais. This – apparently a mere entertainment – was in fact the ceremonial prelude to the presentation of gifts, itself the subject of an intricate traditional procedure. Tuvalu custom makes it obligatory to bestow gifts, particularly on distinguished guests, yet

equally obligatory for the guest to demur. The Queen, it was felt, could not take part in a public charade of this nature so, on her behalf, one of the island's ministers did the refusing for her. This involved no mere shake of the hand, but rather a brisk chase which the minister was obliged to give to all those bringing their unending succession of presents. The result was a virtual free-

for-all as gift bearers, attempting to anticipate the minister's tactics, took running avoiding action, combining to outwit his energetic manoeuvres to prevent the gifts from reaching the Queen. She and the Duke found this enormous fun, the Queen fairly hooting with laughter, pointing with disbelief as the fray developed and all sorts of people began to fall over. She took the opportunity for a few private photographs. The presents began to heap up at her feet – a motley collection of mats,

feathered fans, grass skirts, necklaces, bead-covered pots, walking sticks and handbags. Then farewell speeches were made, the Queen's final word of thanks greeted with warm applause – and a downpour of rain. In the ensuing *sauve-qui-peut* for the shelter of the maneapa, the royal gifts were hastily packed into a carton and the Queen took a last drink of orange juice with the Governor-General and his wife amid totally unrehearsed and friendly informality, which seemed fittingly to epitomise the spirit of their entire visit.

The Queen and Duke left by the same route and in the same manner as they had come. Only the warm, saturating rain and the noticeable, underlying sadness of departure distinguished the two events. Anticipating the rain, the Queen had her transparent umbrella ready, but her hosts had provided a much more colourful substitute.

"Tuvalu," the Prime Minister had told the Queen, "has little in the way of land or natural resources, but we believe we have a happiness, culture and friendliness which are perhaps more important than pure material wealth." No-one who spent those two days on Funafuti could possibly doubt the truth of the assertion. Those qualities were evident everywhere and always, making Tuvalu one country at least that the Queen must have been genuinely sorry to leave.

A flotilla of craft from the Fiji Yacht Club escorted the Queen's barge for *Britannia* to Suva harbour on 30th October, three Second World War twenty-five pounders fired a twenty-one gun salute, and a sulu-clad contingent of the Royal Fiji Military Force (above) played resoundingly with trilling trumpet descants. But those were the only sounds of welcome for the Queen's fourth visit to Fiji during her thirty-year reign. Here they do things

quietly, with a courteous reverence unknown almost anywhere else in the world. So all official greetings on the quayside were performed in virtual whispers, every handshake followed by a half-kneel and the striking together of cupped hands – itself the most silent form of applause. Even the little girl who presented a bouquet of mauve, pink and white orchids (opposite page, bottom left) then sat crossed-legged on the matting, clapping her respect.

At Bau it was initially different. Although the inhabitants of this nearby island sat in complete silence awaiting the Queen and Prince Philip's arrival, the royal approach was noisy and active enough. Conch shells sounded out across the waters and a shrieking chorus of women's voices accompanied a mass waving of tapas, or straw mats, on

poles. A dozen young men, whose boat was escorting the Queen's punt, then dived into the water, swam ashore and began to chase the women-folk, as a hoarse shout from a village chief warned of the Queen's approach. Her procession from the shore to the village centre was much more dignified (above and top); as solemn as the subsequent ceremonies were time-honoured and long-drawn-out. After the presentation of whales' teeth kava was prepared and the Queen and Prince Philip accepted their measures, drinking them in a single draught as custom obliges.

Dressed in a splendid white evening gown, the Queen, with Prince Philip, attended a State

November. The Queen stayed for a further day, attending a Sunday morning inter-faith service at the National Stadium. That evening, the Queen gave a reception on board the Royal Yacht *Britannia,* before leaving the following morning for the town of Lautoka. Then it was on to Nadi Airport where a British Airways Tri-Star aircraft, named Princess Margaret Rose, waited to take the Queen back to Britain – just in time for the State Opening of Parliament on 3rd November. The final inspection (bottom right), the final farewells with the same dutiful courtesies from her hosts as marked her arrival, and the final cheery wave seemed to confirm that this long, colourful and above all friendly royal tour had been satisfactory and rewarding.

banquet in Suva, where again the speeches reflected the mutual rapport between Fiji and the British Crown since Fiji was ceded to Queen Victoria in 1874. The Prime Minister praised the Queen "whose life is based on Christian principles, and has a warm regard for the simple virtues of family life." He offered gifts of a painting, and a book about birds of the Pacific.

For the Duke of Edinburgh, this was the last function of the tour. After the dinner he left for Japan and Canada, before flying back to Britain on 11th

attempt to outshine her hosts, she chose a subdued yet elegant cerise evening dress with just a fraction of the sparkle sported by the Pearly folk and showed that, within sight of her 81st birthday and despite, as she herself admits, "failing in sight and limbs," she can still command respect as one of the most poised members of the Royal Family.

The Pearlies, quintessential representatives of the Cockneys whose affection for the Royal Family is well known, presented Princess Alice not only with a

Like her son and daughter-in-law, Princess Alice Duchess of Gloucester is a regular visitor to major farming exhibitions, and her presence on 6th July at the Royal Show at Stoneleigh (above and top) was the continuation of a practice which is perhaps almost taken for granted. After a two-month summer break, Princess Alice's official diary began in earnest with a visit to County Hall in London to attend the Pearly Kings' and Queens' annual charity ball on 1st October (opposite page). Eschewing flamboyance herself, and in any event wisely deciding not to

bouquet of freesias and asters (opposite page, centre) but also with a Pearly doll (opposite page, bottom right) which has no doubt found its way into the hands of one or both of her grand-daughters, Lady Davina and Lady Rose Windsor.

Her second engagement of the autumn, on 11th October, involved a short trip from her London home at Kensington Palace to the Royal Albert Hall, to watch a gala of Gilbert and Sullivan operas – where else to meet the Yeoman of the Guard? (right) – presented by Solid Rock Foundation in aid of the Mental Health Foundation and the

D'Oyly Carte Opera Trust. Princess Alice was at this time putting the finishing touches to her memoirs, but in the meantime one of her former butlers, Peter Russell, had published his own highly entertaining – if on the face of it a trifle far-fetched – anecdotal memoirs, *Butler Royal*. They confirmed the generally held view that the late Duke had a temper worthy of any military man, but that Princess Alice soon learned how to draw upon her reserves of resourcefulness and determination to circumvent it.

the Year Show at Wembley on the 4th (far left), and at the annual Poppy Ball at London's Intercontinental Hotel (below left and bottom left) on the 7th.

Her aunt, Princess Margaret, visited the Kodak Library in Holborn on 21st October (below) to view the Earl of Lichfield's royal photographs, including those featured in his book *A Royal Album,* published that month.

The Duchess of Kent's long held interest in music took her on 7th October to the factory, in Edgware, of Boosey and Hawkes, where she watched musical

instruments being made (left), while her sister-in-law Princess Alexandra opened the Elizabeth Fitzroy home for the mentally handicapped in Richmond, Surrey on 5th October (below) and inspected preparations for the International Fruits of the Earth festival at Westminster Abbey on the 29th (opposite).

Persistent critics of Princess Anne tended to turn a blind eye to the fact that, unlike many of her relatives, her summer holidays were frequently interrupted by official duties – twelve of them scattered through August and September. They preferred to concentrate on speculation about her marriage, on no more convincing information than that Captain Phillips was allegedly not

scheduled to accompany her on any engagements between July and December. Then, early in October, the rumours went the other way and predicted a third baby for the Princess in the spring.

Amongst those October engagements were her attendance at the Riding for the Disabled Championships at the Horse of

When you are a major fashion show's guest of honour among 600 connoisseurs of Western chic, your entrance has to be spectacular. So on 9th November, while the Prince of Wales was tramping his estates in Cornwall, his wife put on her latest and most fetching evening dress for her visit to the Guildhall in London, where the charity Birthright was able to raise £30,000 gross towards funds for their research into the problems of childbirth. Preceded by a dinner, the show, organized by the Princess'

fashion advisor Anna Harvey, consisted of over a hundred British, and a few additional French designs, from the ultimate in gold-embroidered silk ball gowns to the less subtle allurements of plastic-boned bodices. Many of the Princess' own favourite designers were among the exhibitors. Unfortunately, Diana's slim look rebounded on her. Within a week she was widely and persistently rumoured to have contracted anorexia nervosa, the slimmers' disease which can cause death. Aware that her sister, Lady Sarah McCorquodale was once a victim, and that the disease is hereditary, a public genuinely anxious about the extremes to which the Princess appeared to be going to regain her shape after Prince William's birth was fed graphic newspaper accounts of her supposed decline. Palace denials did not convince many – and still have not – that she was at that time enjoying normal health.

gave, as President of the Tufty Club, was published. In it she revealed that her son Frederick was showing an early interest in painting, while his sister Gabriella was "already very feminine, and quite maternal".

On 12th November, almost two months after her death, a requiem mass in memory of Princess Grace of Monaco was held in the Church of the Immaculate Conception in London's Mayfair. The Queen,

whom the Princess of Wales represented at the funeral in Monte Carlo, was not officially represented at this service, but both Prince and Princess Michael (left and right) and Princess Alexandra and the Hon. Angus Ogilvy (top right) were present in their personal capacities. That evening, Prince and Princess Michael attended a London Philharmonic Orchestra concert in Whitehall (all pictures above and opposite page). Two weeks earlier Princess Michael broke new ground when an interview she

reference to Argentina being noted for bully beef, "but it was British beef that sent the bullies home." Prince Andrew was at the next day's ceremony, laying a wreath (above centre) for the first time, along with his father, brother and Prince Michael (below).

Remembrance Week ceremonies, and the Royal Family's leading role of homage, change little each year. The Falklands campaign, with its 255 dead gave added point to the Festival of Remembrance, attended by – among others – the Queen (top), the Prince of Wales (above), the Gloucesters (above right) and Prince and Princess Michael (right) at the Albert Hall on 13th November. The Princess of Wales arrived late, but smiling (top right). Only Charlie Chester, the compere, soured the occasion with a tasteless

called Valentine, to add to her already impressive possessions at the royal stables (left). Prince Claus' illness forced him to miss some engagements, but it was a smiling farewell for all on 19th November (right).

Eight members of the Royal Family were at Westminster Pier on 16th November to welcome Queen Beatrix and Prince Claus of the Netherlands for a four-day State visit. The visitors' arrival followed a trip in the ceremonial barge *Royal Nore* from Greenwich, where they were met by the Prince of Wales. In the customary exchange of gifts, Queen Elizabeth received a horse

If, as one newspaper asserted, it was a case of "all eyes on Diana", she responded in kind when she joined other members of the family at Westminster Pier for the beginning of the Dutch State visit. Health rumours continued to fly however, developing the anorexia theme into post-natal depression. Even the more authoritative information about Prince Claus' continuing psychiatric treatment in Switzerland failed to steer public curiosity from the Princess, who nevertheless appeared studiously to ignore it. The pensive moment at the Dutch Queen's State banquet at Hampton Court on 18th November (below) was perhaps forgivable in the circumstances.

After the explosion of reportage on the subject of Prince Andrew's exploits with the actress Koo Stark, it was inevitable that he should be idolised by a crowd of young girls on one of his rare public engagements. On 18th November, he was invited to switch on the Christmas lights in Regent Street. The rush to see the Prince gave the police a difficult job, but female screams were hushed long enough for him to complete the ceremony and say a few words. He referred to the long-held belief that Christmas trees – the theme of the illuminations – were introduced into England by the Prince Consort, and as he threw the switch he said, "I'm told there are 55,000 bulbs in those Christmas trees. I just hope they all work." Give or take one or two, they did and the Prince then attended a reception (these pages) given by the Regent Street Association.

The Duchess of Kent's engagements in Britain were interrupted at the end of October by an eight-day official visit to Hong Kong with the Duke, who himself had left London on 15th October for a private trip to Australia and New Zealand. The Duchess' home engagements began again on 3rd November, and among them was her visit to St John's School, Leatherhead, Surrey on the 24th (above and right). The previous day the Queen Mother left the King Edward VII Hospital for

Officers in London (left) after an emergency operation to remove a fishbone from her throat. The bone had lodged in her throat during a late night dinner party on 21st November at Royal Lodge Windsor, and in the early hours of the following morning she was rushed to London for the operation. The alarm caused by the news made it a foregone conclusion that a large crowd

would be outside the hospital to see her leave again, for a short period of rest at Clarence House. Her engagements for the next few days were undertaken by Princess Michael of Kent, but a week later the Queen Mother – a great believer in the maxim that "the show must go on" – was back in action (above left) attending the inaugural meeting of the Court of Patrons at the Royal

College of Obstetricians in London on 30th November. Two days later the Queen Mother travelled to Southampton to tour the Cunard liner *Queen Elizabeth 2,* and to unveil a plaque marking the fifteen-year-old ship's service in the Falklands campaign (this page). The Chairman of Cunard, Lord Matthews (right), was her host and she clearly enjoyed this

occasion which must have reminded her of the day the previous June when, on her way into Portsmouth in *Britannia,* following her tour of the Cinque Ports, she passed the *Queen Elizabeth 2* in the Solent. These associations were marked by the addition to the Royal Standard at the head of the commemorative plaque, of the Queen Mother's personal coat of arms.

Among almost forty engagements between his return from Canada on 11th November and his departure for Geneva on 5th December to attend equestrian sports meetings, Prince Philip attended a ceremony to award certificates as President of the National Playing Fields Association, at Buckingham Palace on 1st December (left). Meanwhile, the Prince and Princess of Wales spent two days touring Wales in the last week of November. At Aberystwyth, the

Princess settled the dispute over the colour of Prince William's hair – it was blond, not red, as Princess Michael had recently said. The Princess accompanied Prince Charles to Dolgellau (top), and at Barmouth named a new lifeboat after her (top right). At Wrexham's Guildhall (above and right) Prince Charles attended a function with his wife, but (far right) toured the Whitegate factory complex alone.

The Princess of Wales seemed very much at home in her husband's principality, which she had already visited several times before, and would again, on her own account. This was a popular trend: like most of Britain and indeed Europe, Wales could never see enough of its new Princess.

Prince William, by now five months old, was beginning to creep into the news in his own right and in August a whooping cough epidemic led some doctors publicly to urge the Prince and Princess to have him vaccinated. Speculation began to increase about whether the young prince would accompany his parents to Australia and New Zealand, a visit already planned for March and April 1983. In October the rumours put the Queen, who favoured him staying, at

loggerheads with the Princess, who was adamant that he should go. Buckingham Palace spokesmen denied the Queen's "veto" and insisted that nothing had yet been finalised.

No official pictures of Prince William had been published since his christening, and many people were anxious for new photographs. Despite the occasional sighting – Prince Charles was photographed carrying him down the steps of

the aircraft which took the royal trio to Balmoral in August, and the young Prince was spotted in the arms of his nanny Barbara Barnes during a brief outing near Highgrove in mid-November – one leader writer put in a demand for "a picture at once, please. Or at least he could be featured in the Queen's Christmas television broadcast. To see little William gurgling on Granny's knee would be a national treat."

The distinctive uniforms of the King's Troop Royal Horse Artillery were even more spick and span than usual on 30th November, when Princess Anne visited their headquarters in St John's Wood, North London. The headquarters being the home of horses as well as riders, Princess Anne was naturally doubly interested, and her husband left farming commitments at Gatcombe to be there too.

Rarely do the Prince and
Princess of Wales miss an
opportunity to assist with fund-
raising for the Mountbatten
Memorial Trust, and the European
premiere of *Gandhi,* held amid
enormous publicity at the Odeon
Theatre in London's Leicester
Square, was a case in point.
Countess Mountbatten was there,
as was Barbara Cartland,
together with a galaxy of
international film celebrities,
and those directly connected
with the film – Sir Richard
Attenborough, Sir John Gielgud,
Sir John Mills and Ben Kingsley.
The Prince and Princess'
entrance was impressive, the
Princess re-calling one of the
most elegant gowns of her 1981
wardrobe. Prince Charles was

quietly satisfied with all he
saw and heard, as everyone
craned their necks for a glimpse
of his glittering wife. She
suffered from the intense heat
of the brilliant television
lights – "If you stand here long
enough, you nearly pass out,"
she said during another premiere
six months later. And this
occasion failed to pass without
a reference to Prince William.
"He never stops eating," the
Princess told Sir John Mills.

sunlit morning of 6th December he joined the Quorn hunt for a chase over the snow covered countryside near Melton Mowbray in Leicestershire. The outing – the Prince was unaccompanied by his wife – did nothing to stem yet another newspaper report that their sixteen-month-old marriage was in difficulties. The *Daily Mail's* gossip columnist, Nigel Dempster, added fuel to that particular fire when, in an interview on American television, he branded the Princess of Wales a "fiend" who "is very much ruling the roost" and making Prince Charles "desperately unhappy". In Britain, Dempster refused to withdraw, on the grounds that if the Princess was "making the Prince unhappy, we should know about it." Buckingham Palace condemned the comments as "totally stupid" and revealed that the Princess was "very upset" by them.

Like Princess Anne, the Prince of Wales has become a devotee of fox hunting, and has attracted his fair share of critics for doing so. They failed to dissuade him when, on the crisp,

On 5th December the Queen Mother visited Westminster Abbey to attend a service marking the Diamond Jubilee of the Bible Reading Fellowship. Two days later, another in a long line of public buildings was named after her when she opened The Queen Mother's Hall at Westfield College, part of the University of London (top picture and left). As always, she found many admirers among the Londoners who saw her arrive (centre right).

Perhaps her visit to the Smithfield Show at Earls Court on 8th December (far right) interested her most. As the owner of thirteen Aberdeen Angus cattle at the Castle of Mey, she had entered a pedigree heifer – Castle of Mey Eodima – for the Supreme Fatstock Championship. It won third prize, and the Queen Mother congratulated the owner of the winner, subsequently sold for £14,000.

Barbican Theatre. The choice of play was no coincidence. Almost fifty years before, its author J. M. Barrie bequeathed the rcyalties from his book to the Great Ormond Street Hospital. Now under severe financial strictures, the hospital was grateful for the capital asset and royal support.

The Great Ormond Street Hospital for Sick Children made the most of its royal patronage in December. On the 2nd, the Princess of Wales visited the hospital amid a great show of popularity from nursing and administration staff. On 15th December, the Queen, who is the hospital's patron, attended a performance (these pages) of the Royal Shakespeare Company's new production of *Peter Pan* at the

With the approach of Christmas, the inevitable party season got under way, and the Royal Family were not left out. On 16th December Princess Michael of Kent went to East London to attend a Christmas party at Wanstead Almshouses (bottom left). A week beforehand her brother-in-law the Duke of Kent attended a Variety Club lunch with a particularly Christmas flavour about it. Staged at the London Hilton Hotel, the lunch marked the end of the Club's Christmas toy campaign in which 20,000 toys were distributed to

sick and deprived children throughout the country. It also featured the Variety Club's famous "Miss Christmases", drawn from the casts of musicals *Song and Dance* and *Cats*: they are seen (top right) with the Duke

at the pre-lunch reception. After the lunch, the Duke received a cheque for the RNLI, of which he is President, and which saved no fewer that 1,281 lives at sea in 1982.

The Duchess of Kent, meanwhile, kept a regular annual Christmas appointment by attending the Not Forgotten Association's Christmas party, held at the Royal Riding Stables at Buckingham Palace (pictures above). Publicity tends to be concentrated on the Association's older members, particularly the Chelsea Pensioners, but recent campaigns continue to result in many younger men and women benefiting from its efforts. The MP Hugh Rossi told an audience of 350 at the party that there were now over a quarter of a million disabled war pensioners, with ages ranging from 25 to over 100.

One of the oldest, 101-year-old

courage it can inspire made her encounter with fourteen children a moving experience. She was there to present the annual Children of Courage Awards (above, below and left), and to make the acquaintance of children who had overcome cancer, bone disease, brain damage and blindness to live active, useful lives. Others had performed mountain rescues, chased burglars and saved friends from collapsing masonry. Their citations were read out during the presentation ceremony, and the Queen Mother gave each an award – in the shape of a bird set in perspex – and a citation scroll. Then, in front of a Christmas tree in the Deanery Courtyard, they all posed with her for a photograph to commemorate a pleasant finale to an exciting year.

Frederick Page, who served in Persia and lost an eye at the Dardenelles, shared the ceremonial knife with the Duchess of Kent as this year's cake was cut. Baked by the Army Catering Corps, the cake was iced with a replica of the Association's badge. Like that in the Duchess' left lapel, it showed the head of an elephant. As Patron of the Spastics Society, the Duchess was present two days later (left) at the International Show Jumping Championships at Olympia in aid of the Stars' Association for Spastics.

The catalogue of misfortune calling the Queen Mother to Westminster Abbey on 15th December is hardly the stuff of which Christmas is made, but the

Prince William (previous pages), was among four royal infants absent from Christmas Day mattins at St George's Chapel. But, excepting Prince Edward and the Queen Mother, everyone else attended. Less familiar faces included Captain Phillips with son Peter (right) and the Kent children Nicholas, Helen and George talking to Viscount Linley and his sister Sarah (bottom right).

RAF Benson has received many royal visitors; the Queen's Flight, established by King Edward VIII in 1936 at Hendon, has been based there continuously for 37 years, and Prince Edward gained his glider's wings there in 1980. On 12th January Princess Alexandra – equal first with the Duke of Gloucester for performing the first royal public engagement of 1983 – paid a four-hour visit to the base. Elegantly and well wrapped up against a bleak winter's day, her first job was to join the officers of the Queen's Flight for a group photograph (below). A forty-minute inspection of the Queen's Flight followed, before the Princess was taken to the sergeants' mess for a reception at which she signed the visitors' book. Luncheon at the officers' mess was taken to the

accompaniment of a selection of waltzes and film themes played by the Salon Orchestra of the Central Band of the RAF. During the afternoon, the Princess toured the station's twelve-roomed sports pavilion, and the education section where she met some of the families of RAF

personnel at an informal, hour-long tea party.
(Above and top) Princess Alexandra, who is patron of the English National Opera Company, visited its rehearsal and production centre at Lilian Baylis House in Hampstead on 25th January.

Royalty from Britain and Spain met on 13th January when a tercentenary exhibition of paintings by the Spanish artist Murillo opened at the Royal Academy of Arts in London. The Duke and Duchess of Gloucester (below) arrived first, five minutes before Queen Sophie of Spain.

The Royal Academy of Arts again entertained royalty when the Prince and Princess of Wales attended a reception (left) in connection with "Britain Salutes New York" – a festival marking the bicentenary of the end of the American War of Independence. This was the Prince and Princess' first official engagement since their short but eventful, far-from-private holiday in Liechtenstein as guests of that principality's heir apparent Prince Hans Adam. Prince Charles and his wife rarely had a chance to avoid the attentions of photographers, both British and continental, and the entire holiday of just less than a week was ruined by cat-and-mouse tactics. After

some pretty harsh words from the Prince's detective, the British press cried off, but the foreign contingent was not so easily deterred. In the event it was surprising that the royal couple were in a mood to smile at all when they got back to London. The Duke of Kent was luckier. He went off on 20th January to Sestriere in Northern Italy to attend the Kandahar/Martini International Ski-ing Championships, and was able to find time to keep up his ski-ing practice in between attending receptions and awarding prizes during the five-day event (remaining pictures). Unlike January 1982 at Meribel, in France, his family did not accompany him.

"*Heat and Dust* is a film about the relationship between East and West," said one magazine article, "and it is an affair in which the West seems the loser." There was perhaps an element of reconciliation when Princess Alexandra arrived for the premiere of James Ivory's film

at the Curzon Cinema in London on 3rd February. Her evening dress shimmered like the finest enbroidered Oriental silk, and her heavy pendant earrings could have been the envy of any Indian maharajah. With her husband, Angus Ogilvy – they were described in one newspaper at the time as "the least stuffy, happiest royal couple" – she was full of animation in conversation with the cast after the performance (opposite page).

The Duchess of Kent was at the Langham Gallery in London on 14th February to open a BBC exhibition commemorating 60 years of children's broadcasting. In a considerate gesture which suggests that the message of the 1981 Year of the Disabled had not been forgotten, the BBC invited pupils from North London schools for the mentally and physically handicapped to see the exhibition. The Duchess, well known for her open sympathy for the less fortunate, met some of the pupils, including six-year-old Hazel Chadwick (below). The Princess of Wales paid two visits in five days to the Royal Albert Hall. On 30th January (right) she attended with Prince Charles a Great Gala held in aid of the centenary appeal of the

Royal College of Music, of which Prince Charles is President. Then on 3rd February she went alone (top left) to hear the annual Mountbatten concert in aid of the Malcolm Sargent Cancer Fund for children, of which she is patron. The Princess' superb lilac evening dress was much admired, as indeed were most of the latest examples of her winter wardrobe, on which she was alleged to have spent some £50,000 during the previous September.
"William is fast taking

and contriving to have their photographs taken with her. The following week (this page and overleaf) she spent five minutes publicly looking through a selection of Valentine cards when she visited the International Spring Fair at the National Exhibition Centre in Birmingham.

everything over," the Princess had told one mother during her visit to a community centre in Thornton Heath the previous day (opposite page, bottom right), "but he's not crawling yet." Plenty of children there were not only crawling but also flocking to meet the Princess,

Though by no stretch of the imagination a conventional housewife, the Princess' image as particularly domestically orientated made this exhibition – Britain's largest consumer goods trade fair, and one of the biggest in Europe – of great interest to her. She may not have appreciated its significance in terms of marketing and commercial practices, but with 2,750 exhibitors showing the very latest designs in housewares, ornaments and gift-ware of every conceivable kind, there was no shortage of items to attract her attention.

And in the Princess herself, growing ever more confident and undertaking regular solo engagements with the competence of a professional, there was plenty to attract organisations seeking her support and presence at their great occasions. In early February, as if to emphasise her own sense of independence, she started up her own equivalent of the Prince's Trust, called the Princess of Wales' Charities Trust, with a nominal £100 fund. Further additions to the Trust were subsequently made from the proceeds of galas attended by the Princess, and continue to be made so that charities can apply for occasional grants.

Count of Luxemburg. The diamond and ruby jewellery provided a contrast with her more functional race-course outfit a few days later when she visited Kempton Park to see three of her horses in action. Success was moderate – one horse won, one fell, one was unplaced.

The Sadler's Wells Foundation was 300 years old in 1983, and the Queen Mother was at the theatre on 22nd February to help them celebrate, where she watched a performance of *The*

It was a little late for Valentine's Day, but as it was just over two years to the day since her engagement, the Princess of Wales might have thought the heart-shaped bouquet (above) appropriate as she began her visit to Brookfields School for Mentally Handicapped Children at Tilehurst on 25th February. "She's a natural," was the most often repeated compliment. "I'd have her on my staff any day," added the school's headmaster.

western hemisphere she has ever undertaken. The royal couple arrived at Kingston, Jamaica (top left) in scorching weather which made sub-zero Britain seem light years away. The welcoming procedures (far left) were as standard as the following day's cultural "Salute to the Queen" was typically Jamaican. Scores

Just over three months after landing in London from a month-long tour of Australia and the South Pacific, the Queen left Heathrow Airport with Prince Philip on 13th February for the most extensive tour of the

Alexander Bustamente, preceded a medley of traditional folk tunes in celebration of Jamaica's twenty first year of independence. The Queen, showed genuine pleasure (left) at this

of thousands of almost uncontrollable Jamaicans forgot their everyday problems and put on their finest show of sometimes almost delirious enthusiasm (top and far right). An imaginative parade of fifteen historical effigies, from Christopher Columbus to Jamaica's first president, Sir

colourful show. "Every time Prince Philip and I come here," she told the Governor-General at a State banquet that evening, "you seem to have some special event to greet us." Earlier that day she had been to Gordon House to address the Jamaican Parliament. She praised the country's

maintenance of democratic principles despite what she termed "pressures and strains that have stretched its social fabric" – a reference to a period of tumultuous and bloody unrest at the time of the 1980 elections, in which the former left-wing premier Michael Manley was defeated. His aspirations

to turn the country into a republic were thought to have been effectively put in their place by the Queen's reference to herself as "Queen of Jamaica," but in fact this is her common practice in all countries acknowledging her as sovereign. A walkabout afterwards (bottom right) showed she certainly enjoyed great popular support.

On 15th February the Queen and Duke visited Montego Bay, and saw twelve thousand people packed into Sam Sharpe Square as she attended a civic reception (below) and watched a march past (opposite page).

European settlers (right) – before boarding a yacht rejoicing in the name of *Marlin Darlin* for a trip to Cayman Kai. The ninety-minute trip gave them time for lunch on board, prepared by the Caribbean Club, a high quality restaurant on Seven Mile Beach, and another walkabout (opposite page, top right) followed their

A total of 75,000 stamps and 20,000 gold and silver coins were produced to mark the royal visit to the Cayman Islands – home of fewer than 20,000 people, and almost 500 international banks and myriad companies seeking shelter from the assaults of Western tax inspectors. The Queen and Prince Philip touched down at

Owen Roberts Airport shortly before noon (top) to a welcome so patriotic and alive with Union Jacks (above) that one wondered what happened to the islanders' patriotism for their own country. Fireworks substituted for guns to provide the official marks of respect, before the royal couple were taken to Morgans Harbour. Here they found time for a short walkabout to meet the local population – a motley blend of indigenous islanders and

disembarkation, when the Queen opened a new five-mile-long road linking two districts of Grand Cayman. After a tour of other towns on the island, Prince Philip peeled away from the Queen's party to visit a turtle farm, where he saw how turtles bred for meat and shell were kept in captivity for at least fifteen years – until reaching sexual maturity. He refused to be drawn on the issue of

cruelty, nor to answer the insidious question "Whose side are you on?" except by replying "I'm on the side of the turtle." A well-fielded response.

On 17th February the Queen and Duke visited The Pines, an old people's home, and attended the Cayman Legislative Assembly (below). That evening they were in Mexico, where the next day they toured the Sicarsta Steel Works (top right and above right) in Acapulco.

It is said that the invitation for the Queen and Prince Philip to visit California was made on horseback, while Her Majesty and President Ronald Reagan took their celebrated early-morning canter through Windsor Great Park in June 1982.

The Queen and Duke arrived in San Diego on 26th February, and another memorable chapter began. And it began in style, with official ceremony (below and opposite page, top), followed by a trip round San Diego harbour to review a small section of America's mighty Navy, and a visit to the aircraft-carrier USS *Ranger* to

inspect some of the fighter and anti-submarine planes on board (top left and opposite page, below). With an appreciative eye towards blending the old and the new, the Queen and Prince Philip heard a recital of Shakespeare at the Old Globe Theatre, and visited the huge Scripps Institute of Oceanography – 230 acres of insight into the geological and biological secrets of earth, ocean and atmosphere. The Duke admired the technology but perhaps, like most of us, the Queen was more readily attracted to the more understandable achievements of intelligent marine life (left).

– though nothing like it would be in the days to come. That evening saw probably the most publicised royal event since the Coronation. At the studios of Twentieth Century Fox at Long Beach a dinner, billed by some quirk of understatement as Hollywood's social event of the year, brought together the Queen, her husband and 500 guests comprising the royalty of the film world. Mrs Nancy Reagan hosted the event and escorted the Queen into the midst of that film world's distinguished company – Frank Sinatra, Perry Como, George

Sunday 27th February was more relaxed, with a single morning's engagement in the form of Mattins at St Paul's Episcopal Church (these pages). The weather gave ample notice of its intentions: for the second day it was dull and threatened rain

Burns, James Stewart, Michael
Caine, Elton John, Fred Astaire,
Rod Stewart and Dudley Moore to
name but a very small section.
For all the outward confidence,
there was confusion in the
ranks. The evening did not get
off to the best start; partly
because of the atrocious weather
outside, partly because a group
of fifty pro-IRA demonstrators
heckled the Queen and Prince
Philip as they arrived. Inside,
meanwhile, the invitations
specifying informal dress had
put everyone into a quandary
over balancing informality and
respect. Dudley Moore spilt
soup onto his trousers in the
Duke's presence. Even Mrs
Reagan confessed, rather
shakily, that this was the first
event she had ever hosted alone.
There was also a whiff of
offence. Many American stars
had been placed too far away

from the Queen and Prince Philip at the top table ever to have a chance to speak with them. They argued afterwards – and some of the British stars agreed with them – that the Queen could meet her own countrymen anytime: this was an occasion when Americans should have pride of place. But the Queen apparently had wished it otherwise and

Michael Caine was her nearest, and very British fellow guest. For all that the show went without any obvious hitch. George Burns put on his famous drawling act of desultory monologue. Frank Sinatra and Perry Como sang – rather too lengthily, and badly under-rehearsed thought Elton John – and Dionne Warwick raised the

roof with a medley of popular numbers. Some of the tributes to the Queen tended to ooze with Hollywood's traditional fulsomeness – a characteristic which the Queen herself found somewhat amusing. But she enjoyed the entertainment as a whole, clapping in time with many of the songs, while Prince Philip chuckled away at George Burns' jokes, both old and new. The cynics wondered who wouldn't, after a sumptuous meal of papaya with bay shrimp, chicken pot pie, fresh spinach with bacon, toasted coconut ice-cream snowballs and rivers of Californian wines!

The first royal engagement of 28th February carried with it the risk that Prince Philip would upstage the Queen. The venue was the Rockwell International Corporation – the home of the American space shuttle – where a simulator was ready for inspection in the mock-up chamber. The Queen

entered the module first (far left) and activated the automatic pilot to simulate a descent to earth at over 400 miles an hour from 10,000 feet. Prince Philip's turn came, and with an expert's eye "took" the craft down from an even higher altitude. The Royal couple also saw the Apollo XIV command module, before being taken from the Centre to Los Angeles City Hall for a reception. Yet another burst of rain delayed the Queen's motorcade by thirty minutes, and yet another band of Sinn Fein supporters jeered and chanted as she arrived.

Afterwards, the Queen and Prince Philip went to Los Angeles Music Center (these pages) for a lunch consisting of such exotic dishes as limestone lettuce salad, asparagus spears wrapped in red peppers, and lemon sorbet in whole fruit shell. The meal was preceded by a brief appearance on the balcony outside (opposite page, top right) and followed by the presentation of a hand-painted porcelain sculpture.

Plans for the Queen to sail in *Britannia* to Santa Barbara on 1st March were scuppered by storms which put the city's harbour out of action, and she and Prince Philip had to fly from Long Beach to rejoin the Reagans, who were by now beginning to feel personally apologetic for the continuing bad weather. Their arrival was attended by all the hastily-prepared ritual of State – there followed a hazardous twenty-mile journey by car through the flooded roads winding up to the Reagan's 700-acre ranch in the Santa Ynez mountains.

The plans at the Reagan ranch
fizzled out equally effectively.
There was lunch of course, but
the invitation to go riding – a
reciprocal gesture for the
amicable episode at Windsor nine
months before – had to be
called off in favour of a simple
photo-call (left and right) for
which neither hosts nor guests
seemed to have much enthusiasm.
There was no let up in the chaos
caused by worsening rain during
the following few days. Things
reached an all time low when the
Queen and Prince Philip were
forced to book into a hotel in
San Francisco on the night of
2nd March, instead of spending
that night on board *Britannia*.
But the following evening all
seemed forgiven at the State
dinner given by President Reagan
at the de Young Memorial Museum.
"I knew before we came," mused
the Queen (below), "that we had
exported many of our traditions
to the United States. I had not
realised that the weather was
one of them."

After lunch at President Reagan's ranch on 1st March, Mrs Reagan took the Queen and Prince Philip to the Santa Barbara Mission, a capacious Latin-American-style church in warm cream and pink masonry, founded on St Barbara's Day, 1786. It has the unique distinction of being the sole survivor of twenty-one Californian missions built before 1823 as permanent homes for Franciscan padres, and it was the present incumbents who welcomed the small royal party to the building today (above). After touring the mission (top right), the Queen planted a tree in the grounds to commemorate her visit (bottom centre). The rain held off for that brief moment and the ubiquitous royal umbrella was not needed.

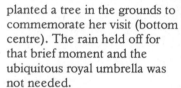

Of five engagements undertaken on 3rd March, a king-sized entertainment at the Symphony Hall, (opposite page, top) kept the Queen amused and delighted (above). Another involved a visit to Hewlett Packard's computer factory (top and far left). The following day the Queen and Prince Philip gave a dinner on board *Britannia* to celebrate the Reagans' 31st wedding anniversary (right and previous page). A more natural grandeur characterised their visit to the Yosemite National Park on 5th March (overleaf).

The Legislative Buildings (right) provided the background for the welcoming salutes as the Queen and Prince Philip arrived at Victoria, British Columbia, on 8th March. While *Britannia* tied up at Ship Point (far right) her barge (below) took the Queen to dry land. The inspection of the guard of honour (opposite page, top left) and the speeches were completed under the threat or reality of rain, but the warmth shown to the Queen during her walkabout afterwards (opposite page, centre right) demonstrated that her visit was long overdue.

The posy of spring flowers presented to the Queen (previous pages) by four-year-old Erin Johnson engaged a grateful royal smile at Victoria's City Hall. Here a civic welcome prefaced a royal walkabout from Centennial Square to the Gate of Harmonious Interest in the town's Chinese quarter, where the Queen and Prince Philip watched a lion

dance and chatted to some of the Chinese population (opposite page, bottom left). It was an enormously busy day. With two formal receptions behind them already, the Queen and Duke gave their own reception for members of the press on board *Britannia*, before lunching on chicken supreme at the Empress Hotel. The afternoon's engagements included a visit to Christ Church Cathedral, a tour of Craigflower School, recently restored, and tea at Royal Roads Military College, where 250 cadets provided the guard of honour (overleaf).

Britannia arrived in the impressive Vancouver Harbour on 9th March to a welcome by Prime Minister Trudeau and a mass of balloons proclaiming "Canada – With Love" (previous page). At the university of British Columbia a walkabout (these pages) linked a tour of the Museum, where Kwakiutl Indians danced for the Queen, and a visit to the Asian centre. Spring flowers (right) suggested

a fitting tribute to fine spring weather – at last – and the Queen had a word for even the youngest Brownie to present her with an unofficial bouquet (opposite page). That afternoon the Queen and Duke were at the site of Expo '86. The Queen set the ball rolling by extending an invitation "to all peoples of the world from the people of Canada" to visit the Exposition in 1986. No doubt she will be

there to open it and that, to the delight of British Columbians, will mean another royal visit in a quarter of the time it took the Queen to return for this one.

Bristol Hospital for Sick Children's intensive care unit (above, left and below) but only the young patients enjoyed her company as she sat on their beds, watched them at play, and told them not to suck thumbs. And after visiting wards where children were suffering from cancer and leukemia, she was told by one her hosts, "I have never seen anyone establish a rapport with patients in the way you have." A month later, on 2nd March, she opened a £7 million shopping precinct in Aylesbury (opposite page and pictures far left) and was highly amused to discover a cosmetic called Starkers. "I didn't know they made nude make-up," she said.

The combination of the Princess of Wales and children in hospital brings out the best in both. On 4th February, two thousand people saw her open the

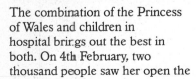

by visiting playgroups in Tavistock and Bovey Tracey. At the Tavistock playgroup (opposite page, bottom right) she joined in a birthday party, singing Happy Birthday to three-year-old Emma Parkin, and helping to blow out the candles on her cake. At Bovey Tracey, more bouquets of flowers were heaped upon her and all of the escort of six policewomen had to form a moving human chain to

The Princess of Wales was in Devon on 9th March – partly to accompany Prince Charles on an engagement to present the West Devon Borough Council with its Charter of Incorporation at the Town Hall, Tavistock (this page), and partly to launch an appeal for £400,000 for the county's under-fives facilities

off-load them all into car boots.

Apart from two engagements in London during the following week, this was the Princess' last public duty before her first tour abroad – a six-week visit to Australia and New Zealand beginning on 20th March.

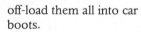

One of her last private engagements was as godmother at the Christening of the three-month-old daughter of Lord and Lady Romsey, named Alexandra Victoria Edwina Diana, at Romsey Abbey.

Exeter became the Queen's Maundy host on 31st March and 57 men and 57 women received her annual gift of specially minted money in the Cathedral. In good walkabout weather, the day (these pages and overleaf) was remembered for Prince Philip's gesture in lifting one little girl over a barrier and directing her, flowers in hand, towards the Queen.

There were no surprise royal visitors, and no surprise absentees, at the Badminton Horse Trials from 14th to 17th April. The Queen gave the event the prestige it habitually derives from her presence, much to the evident satisfaction of the Duke of Beaufort (below) who celebrated his 83rd birthday ten days beforehand. Prince and

Princess Michael (far left), active participants in hunting and point-to-points, attended again and the royal Phillipses were represented in full. Princess Anne, still trying desparately to bring on two young horses for eventing herself, watched the proceedings and carried her two-year-old daughter Zara around in between times, stopping for a quick look at a pair of draught horses (opposite page, top right). With them was five-year-old Peter, now in his second year at

Minchinhampton Blue Boys School. Lying sixth after the dressage – only 6.6 points behind the leader Mike Tucker of Dalwhinnie, Captain Phillips was forced to retire when his horse Classic Lines refused at the eleventh fence in the cross country, and threw its rider to the ground.

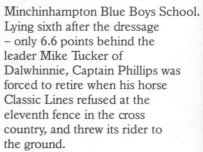

In a thrilling finish, it was Lucinda Green on Regal Realm who won for the fifth time. The Queen presented the Whitbread Trophy with the warm congratulations of a woman who appreciates good horsemanship. And, as usual (these pages), she was back on the Badminton estate on Sunday 17th April to attend the customary church service. She is seen (above) leaving Badminton House with the Duke of Beaufort, Prince Philip and Princess Anne that morning.

of York when she first visited the West Ham Mission in 1928, and on her fifth visit on 26th April 1983 – her sixtieth wedding anniversary – it was fitting that the hospice she opened should be named York House. The indefatigable royal visitor (right) seemed delighted with the coincidence.

Like the Queen Mother, the Queen, seen at Westminster Abbey

(Previous pages) A fly – past for Princess Margaret as she visited RAF Lyneham, Wiltshire on 13th April. A week later the Queen Mother paid a visit to Brixton, the scene of ferocious street fighting two years previously, to open a day centre for elderly West Indians. Despite persistent rain (above and below) she walked along Railton Road, where the worst riots had happened, and a large crowd including Rastafarian followers greeted her everywhere.

The Queen Mother was Duchess

for a service marking the centenary of the Co-operative Women's Guild on 9th May (below) did not enjoy much success on the Turf during 1983. But her visit to Newmarket to open the National Horse Racing Museum on 30th April (below left) must have provided some consolation. The museum is the first of its kind in tribute to the sport of kings, and will now become the repository of the folklore of some 300 years of racing

also on display.
The Queen was back in East Anglia on 5th May (these pages and overleaf), touring RAF

history. It is well supplied with the famous paintings of Stubbs and Munnings. The Queen herself lent a water-colour of Ascot race-course, dated 1756, while the Queen Mother loaned the well-known portrait of King George V by Sickert – a portrait chosen to grace the dust-jacket of the much-loved monarch's recent biography by Kenneth Rose. The Queen also lent the stuffed head of Persimmon, the first royal Derby winner – for the future King Edward VII in 1896 – and the King's own gift of a silk pyjama case to his jockey Jack Watts is

Coltishall, near Norwich – yet another royal visit enjoyed by the RAF during the year. Like most, it was a day full of displays, inspections and the inevitable walkabout.

The army had its share of royal favour during the year, too, and the Queen Mother was a frequent guest of honour. On 10th May she arrived at Colchester to visit the Royal Anglian Regiment. The weather proved less welcoming than her hosts: as she began her inspection of

the six guards of honour, a sudden downpour caught everyone unawares. She happily continued her inspection (top left) before watching a parade (left) and touring the Meeanee and Hyderabad Barracks (above and opposite page, bottom right). Security was tight on this occasion, but not nearly so stringent as for her visit to celebrate the 75th anniversary of the Territorial Army in Northern Ireland six weeks later. Then, the Queen Mother – who could well have justified staying at home – showed both personal courage and a confidence in the arrangements being made for her safety. A rash of bomb scares failed to deter her. Far from it: she fairly ambled through her schedule as if she were in the familiar surroundings of her own back garden. In so doing, she honoured her hosts, encouraged the local community and won for herself universal praise for putting duty first.

The Princess of Wales oozed confidence during her first public outing since returning from Australasia with Prince Charles. After her resounding success down-under, she was out doing her favourite thing, making friends with the young. It was 13th May, and the

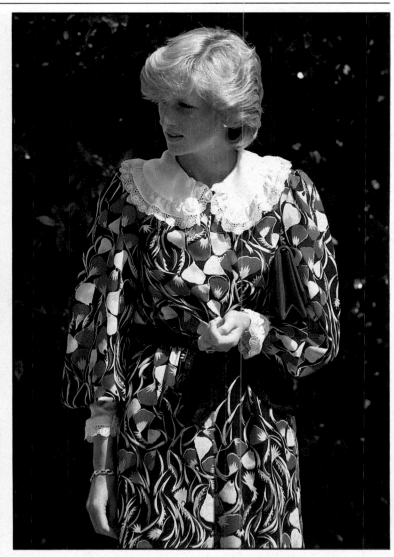

Princess visited two centres for handicapped children – the Gloucestershire Adventure Playground at Coberley – where she picked up and cuddled five-year-old Andrew Harrison, who ran towards her with great excitement – and Paradise House College at Painswick.

Prince Andrew piloted his own helicopter – a Queen's Flight Wessex – to Biggin Hill to open the International Air Show on 14th May. His brisk tour of the show included watching a Royal Navy rescue demonstration (below) and the familiar manoeuvres of the Harrier jump-jets (bottom right), an inspection of a Flying Fortress

aircraft and a look at the cockpit controls of a World War II fighter (right and above, far right). He also obliged those seeking evidence of his stereotype as a man with an eye for the girls, by meeting a line-up of Wrens.

In his final months at RNAF Culdrose, the Prince prepared for a transfer in September to 702 Squadron at Portland, to train as a Lynx helicopter pilot for six months.

It is only a short walk from Windsor Castle to the venue of the Royal Windsor Horse Show, and the inclusion of Prince Philip among the competitors was reason enough for the Queen, Princess Anne and her two children Peter and Zara (right), to be there – at least for the

weekend sessions. Prince Philip's event, the Carriage Driving Grand Prix, which he won in 1982, was sponsored for the first time by that royally patronised store Harrods, to whom the Queen lent some of her carriages for an exhibition there marking the show's 40th anniversary. Prince Philip competed on only three days of the five-day show. After the dressage section on 13th May, he led the field of seventeen competitors and looked well set

to retain the championship. But the following day his luck began to desert him. The Dutchman Tom Velstra streaked ahead in the marathon cross country into an almost unsurpassable lead, while the Prince had to be content with second place. In the final section on 15th May, he incurred ten penalty points when he knocked a cone over. That was enough to put him, and his team of Cleveland and Dutch bays, down into fourth place, 32 points behind Velstra who took the Grand Prix with over twenty points to spare. For him, sportingly, the Queen had a warm smile (above and right), as well as the coveted trophy.

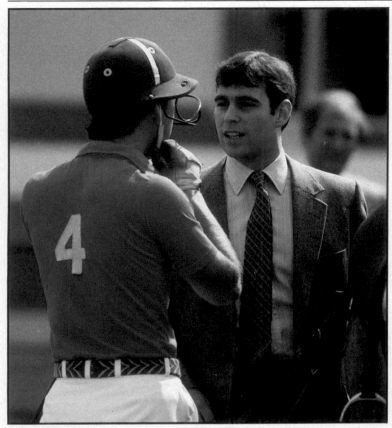

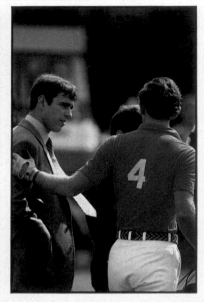

becomes almost newsworthy. Prince Andrew was at Smith's Lawn Windsor on 15th May to watch Prince Charles play in his first match since returning from Australasia, where he played three times and was on the winning side each time. Also present at Windsor were Lord and Lady Tryon, once fast friends of Prince Charles.

Prince Andrew, due to carry out solo engagements during his time in Britain that summer, was allotted a private secretary, Squadron Leader Adam Wise, formerly the Queen's equerry, from the beginning of October.

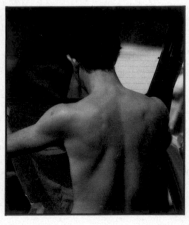

A spot of innocent horse-play never comes amiss, especially on the polo field, and when it develops between a couple of fun-loving brothers who happen to be first and third in succession to the Throne, it

One event Princess Margaret rarely misses each year is the Royal Caledonian Ball, held on 16th May at the Grosvenor House Hotel. A month previously, a new biography of the Princess – written by Christopher Warwick, who has admired her for many years – appeared very much as the Princess' own account of some of the controversies of her eventful and sometimes stormy life.

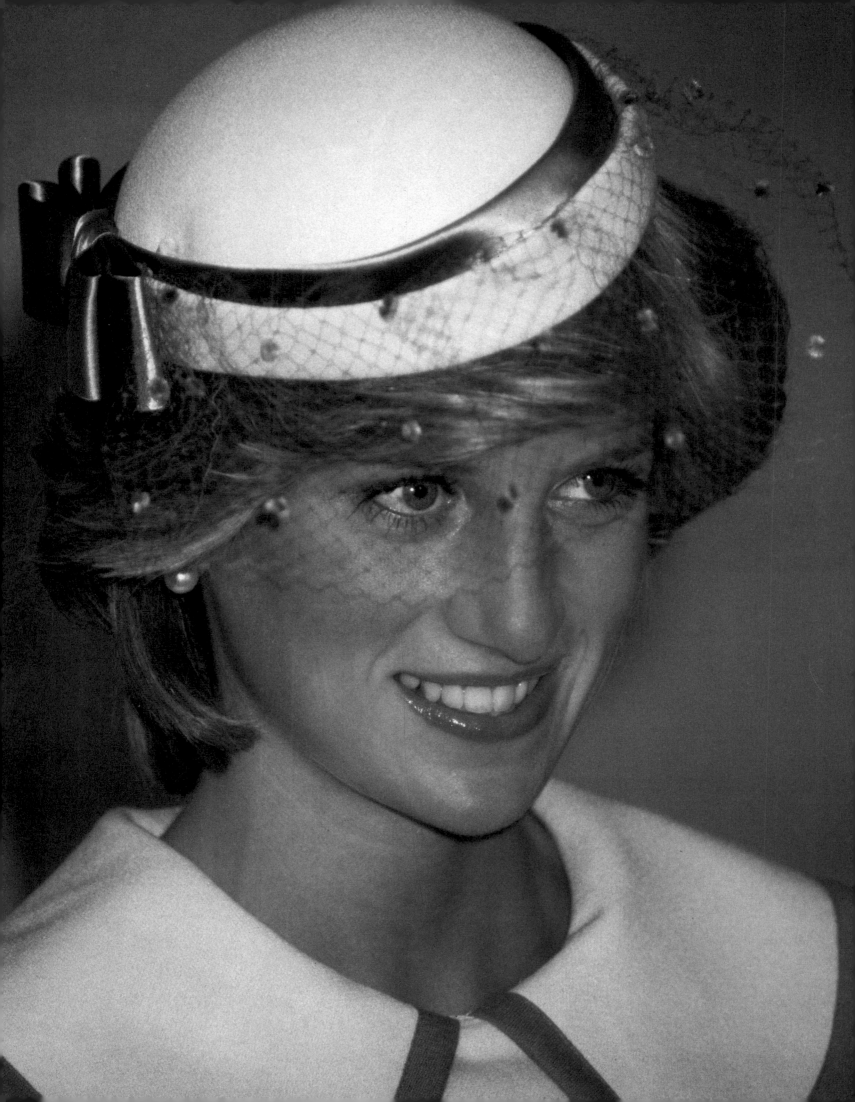

The Princess of Wales had not taken many steps from her car before she was drawn into an impromptu walkabout, and rewarded with a huge teddy bear for Prince William (below and top right). The place was Canterbury, the date 20th May, and the Princess was on her way to open Cranmer House, a housing

scheme for the elderly and infirm. Prince Charles has a soft spot for Canterbury Cathedral – he is president of its Appeal Trust Fund – and the Princess took the opportunity to visit it to declare open a new lift – the first of its kind – to assist disabled people from one level of the Cathedral to another. A sea of red, white and blue on a later walkabout (these pages) made it clear that she was a welcome visitor.

Prince Charles took his wife to the Dorchester Hotel on 24th May when he presented the Piper Champagne Award. The Princess, who has seen Prince Charles unseated at Cheltenham, and watched the Grand National with him in 1982, sported one of her splashier dresses. After a round of solo engagements, she seemed content to listen and watch as the likes of John Francome and Jonjo O'Neill received their awards.

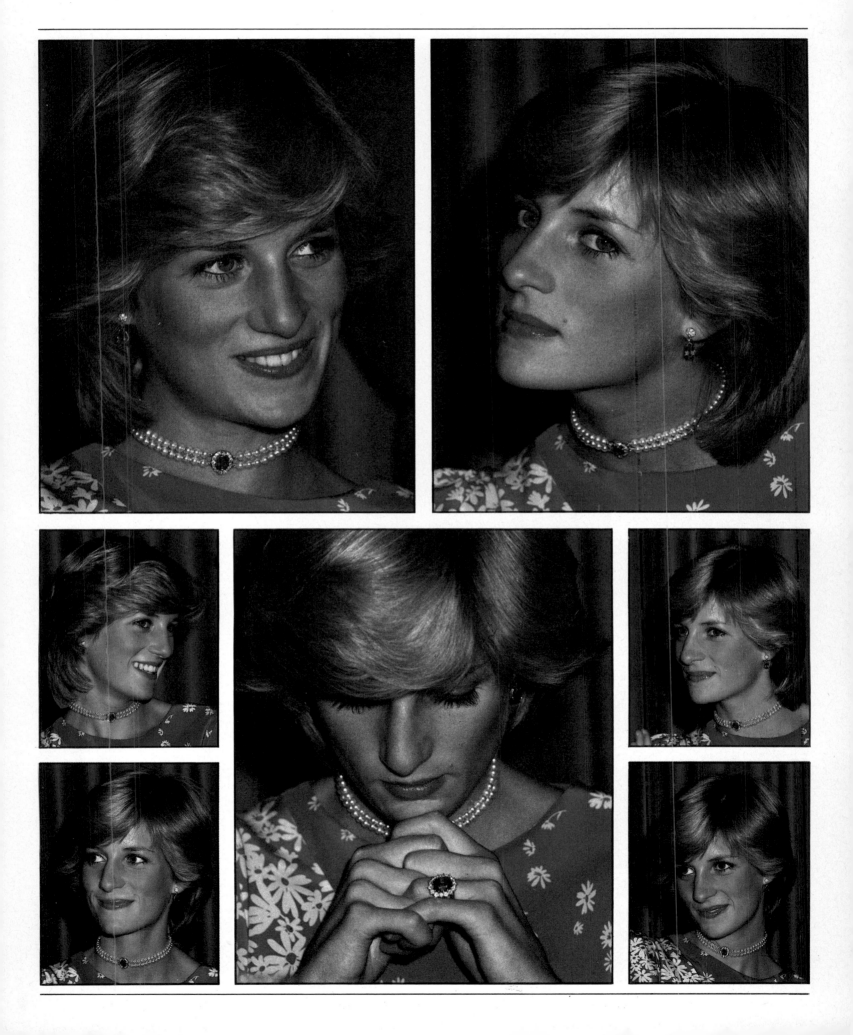

Prince Charles won a medal; his team Maple Leaf won a cup (below left); but the Princess of Wales won everybody's attention with her casual, stylish pedal-pushers, when she arrived at Smith's Lawn on 25th May. With sunglasses perched on her blow-away hair, she looked thoroughly relaxed, watching her husband's team beat Saracens.

A fine day enabled the Prince and Princess of Wales to be driven in an open car to celebrate the 650th anniversary of King Edward III's charter to St Columb, in Cornwall. While there Prince Charles received a book about British trees, published in 1906 and dedicated to King Edward VII.

Prince Charles spent another
Sunday afternoon on the polo
field, competing in the opening
tournament of the Queen's Cup at
Smith's Lawn on 29th May. The
Princess of Wales was again
present to watch him,
accompanied by Sinclair Hill
(overleaf, bottom left), the man
regarded as Prince Charles'
chief polo mentor. Earlier,
Prince Charles played in another
game, on the side of Galen
Weston's Canadian Maple Leaf
team, and looked pleased enough
with his performance (overleaf
bottom right).

The Queen had, perhaps, less to smile about at the Epsom Derby on 1st June (following pages). Her colt Special Leave had been withdrawn after an indifferent trials performance, and victory passed to the hands of others. But the presence of Prince Philip, Princess Anne, the Queen Mother and the Duke and Duchess of Gloucester made it a relaxing family event.

The Princess of Wales must have lost count of the number of times she has written "Diana" in visitors' books, but she did it again (above) when she officially opened the Royal Preston Hospital in Lancashire on 1st June. The Princess met many patients undergoing treatment in the wards (below), as well as in physiotherapy. No tour by the Princess would be complete without a visit to the children's ward, and that happened here too.

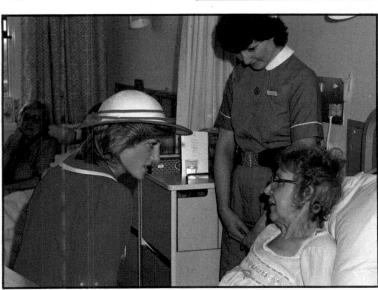

The 1st Battalion Grenadier Guards had the honour this year of trooping their Colour before the Queen at her Birthday Parade on 11th June. The Colour was guarded by soldiers towering up to 6'8" high, as everyone awaited the Queen's arrival. Her mother came first, of course, carriage-driven and floating her genteel wave to the applauding thousands as she rode with the Princess of Wales and the Duke of Beaufort. The eleven chimes of the Horse Guards' clock coincided with the approach of the Queen, followed by the Duke of Edinburgh, Prince of Wales and Duke of Kent. The latter had that morning been promoted to Major General – a promotion last accorded to a royal prince, the late Duke of Gloucester, in the reign of King George VI.

The Queen inspected her troops with her usual eagle eye – any irregularity, we are told, and the royal Colonel-in-Chief will want to know why. Then the intricate procedure, meaningful only to those who have to or who want to know, began to build up – to an accompaniment of music of every tempo and rhythm – to the climax of the Trooping itself. The Colour, all twelve square feet of it, blazed crimson with the Imperial Crown and a seventeen-point fired grenade, and shone gold with 44 battle honours and distinctions. After the relentless march past of eight ranks of guards, in slow and quick time, and the annual appearance of those popular drum horses, Caractacus and Coriolanus, the Queen's permission was sought and given for the march off. She led her troops away, following slowly the path of the clip-clopping horses which took the Queen Mother's carriage in advance to Buckingham Palace, for a family reunion on the balcony. The adults waved and smiled as the RAF performed its fly past salute. The children squealed and jumped with delight. And today's special royal visitors, Prince Philippe and Prince Laurent of the Belgians, seemed just a little bemused by it all.

Towards the end of April it was announced that the Queen had appointed three more Knights of the Most Noble Order of the Garter. These were the Duke of Norfolk, hereditary Earl Marshal of England, Admiral of the Fleet Lord Lewin and Lord Richardson of Duntisbourne. On 13th June, the Throne Room at Windsor Castle was filled with almost the entire complement of Knights as the new boys were installed at the annual chapter. After the customary lunch, the service of the Order was held in St George's Chapel, the Queen, Prince Philip, the Prince of Wales and the Queen Mother bringing up the rear of the impressive, slow-moving procession (overleaf).

The Royal Family was out in force again for the four days of Royal Ascot (following pages) from 14th to 17th June, bringing a touch of level-headedness to a meeting frenzied with preoccupation about hairstyles and dress lengths. The big fad this year was the coiffing of hair into effective hats – one head of long hair was teased up and lacquered to form a top hat; another was ranged radially to form a Japanese parasol. Mrs Gertrude Shilling caught the Queen's eye – but necessarily only fleetingly – with a messy turmoil of Union Jacks bearing the motto "Buy British" while a German designer, Besant by name, sported a hat comprising nothing but mirrors, explaining that "when the sun comes out it sparkles."

The nearest any member of the Royal Family got to extravagant styles was the cartwheel-brimmed hat which the Duchess of Gloucester wore on the first day. For the rest, it was noticed that the absent Princess of Wales' predilection for boaters had taken the Queen's fancy, and that pill-boxes were as popular with Princess Anne as ever. Pleasant though it was, the occasion may not prove particularly memorable for the Queen. She had not a single runner in the entire four-day programme, and the BBC's live broadcasting blackout deprived her of a television commentary in the royal box. The Queen Mother asked the BBC's racing correspondent whether he couldn't do his commentary on Ascot's closed circuit TV instead. "That was nice of her," he beamed.

The Queen was received officially as Sovereign at Croydon on 21st June, and unofficially as grandmother. On her walkabout with the Mayor, Mrs Margaret Campbell (above), she was presented with toys, some of which found their way to Prince William's nursery to help him celebrate his first birthday

that day, as well as endless bunches of flowers. For lunch (opposite) at the Fairfield Halls, Croydon's civic chef, John Golding, prepared a dessert called Sorbet aux Fruits Prince Guillaume and the Queen received congratulations and good wishes almost as if the achievement was hers alone. For all that, as the Queen was there to mark the centenary of the granting of Croydon's first municipal charter, there was work to be done. She toured the Hospital of the Holy Trinity and Taberner House, heard an afternoon concert given by the Croydon Youth Philharmonic Orchestra and visited the National Theatre. And she re-named the Town Hall gardens (top left) The Queen's Gardens, to mark both the charter centenary and her visit.

It was Prince Andrew's turn to honour the late Lord Mountbatten on 24th June. He had been invited to open the new Mountbatten Centre sports complex at Portsmouth. Prince Andrew's cousins Lord and Lady Romsey were there (right) and the Prince might be there again himself one day; he was given a life membership card and an inscribed squash racquet.

The State Opening of Parliament on 22nd June (overleaf and following pages) – was not quite the family occasion it usually is. The Queen was there of course, as was Prince Philip, Princess Margaret and the Duke and Duchess of Gloucester. Others were otherwise engaged – the Prince and Princess of Wales in Canada, Princess Anne on other royal business, the Duchess of Kent still recovering from an operation. Despite that, the colourful and impressive ceremonial left one feeling grateful to King Edward VII, who imaginatively revived it over eighty years ago.

If 1981 was celebrated for a spectacular Royal Wedding, 1982 for the birth of a future King, then 1983 became renowned above all for a programme of Commonwealth tours for the Prince and Princess of Wales, whose popularity in Australia, New Zealand and Canada exceeded all expectations. The tours themselves were tailor-made to emphasise the importance of youth, as shown by the young, informal trends set by the Princess, and by the unceasing contact both she and Prince Charles had with children. Prince William's presence in Australasia was an added source of excitement. After the uncertainty as to whether he would accompany his parents, it was a delight to see him being brought downs the steps of the aircraft when it landed in Alice Springs at eight o'clock

on the hot Sunday morning of 20th March. An effusive welcome awaited the royal couple the next day at the School of the Air (opposite page). This education-by-wireless service gives daily schooling to children living in the remote parts of the Northern Territory, and the Prince and Princess broadcast to them, answering their questions about Prince William's favourite toys and the number of rooms in Buckingham Palace.

No visit to the Northern Territory would be complete without a trip to Ayers Rock, and the royal couple toured this massive feature dominating the flat, scrubby landscape on a blazing afternoon. They even climbed part of the Rock, not far from where a dozen people had been killed in past years. After some tactful noises from a large press contingent, they turned their backs on the rock for a brief moment (these pages), posing for photographs amid a wave of cheering.

The Princess of Wales wore a hat for the first time on the tour, when she arrived with Prince Charles in Canberra (opposite page) for a two-day visit. Originally planned over three days, it was curtailed to allow them to visit the Cockatoo area of Victoria (this page) and meet the families affected by the terrible bush fires of the previous month. "I hope we are not intruding," said the Princess.

Sydney gave the Prince and Princess a cosmopolitan welcome as 10,000 people packed the forecourt of the Opera House. The royal couple drove in an open car (far right) to watch a programme of dancing and singing, and the crowds were so enthusiastic that one bouquet thrown into the car struck the Princess in the face. Things were less hectic that evening at Sydney's Wentworth Hotel, though the Prince and Princess' first dance together in public had the cameras clicking. To the strains of "The More I See You" the couple were the first to take the floor.

Even the relatively small communities of Maitland and Newcastle produced problems for the police on 29th March, but the Prince and Princess loved their fantastic reception (opposite page). The Prince told over 40,000 children at Newcastle, "Our ears are

ringing with all the noise you made." The Princess' ears burned at Hobart the next day when, at a glittering evening reception (these pages), the Prince said how lucky he was to have married her.
This was at the end of the first of two days in Tasmania.

At the last port of call, Launceston, there was time to plant a tree (left) and enjoy a walkabout in the city centre (below). The Princess' Easter bonnet the following day was a modest one, as she arrived for an Easter Sunday church service at Albury (right).

The Princess of Wales' wardrobe during the next few days (previous pages) included a cream and brown outfit at Adelaide, a black and white ensemble for a disco the same evening, and bright red and white the next day at Renmark. At Perth (this page) she wore a fuchsia-coloured dress, and a softer silver-grey outfit at Bunbury (opposite page).

The tiny church of St Paul, Holbrook was the Prince and Princess' venue for Holy Communion on 10th April. Sidesmen on duty ticked off the names of arrivals, after which a bell ringer rang a bell for less than thirty seconds, to call to worship the faithful already in attendance! An electric organ, borrowed from a neighbouring church to replace one that had broken down, was carted hastily in shortly before the royal arrival. During their walkabout afterwards, the Princess received a boomerang made "expressly for Prince William."

As for the Queen the previous October, so for the Prince and Princess, Brisbane bubbled over with enthusiasm on 11th April. The crowds surged up Queen Street Mall behind the royal party. It was the biggest welcome of their tour, though Prince Charles became worried for the Princess' safety.

The Princess seemed to have gained enormous confidence by now, and on no occasion did she seem remotely out of her depth. Six hundred eyes were upon her at a State reception at Brisbane (left); over two thousand at a garden party at Government House, Perth (these pages).

At Melbourne, young men from a college royalist society kissed the Princess' hand. IRA protestors heckled the couple as they arrived at Melbourne's Concert Hall (opposite page). The next day (overleaf) they rode Wells-Fargo style during a visit to Ballarat.

Prince William appeared again towards the end of the Australian leg of the tour. His mother held him in public at Melbourne (previous page) during their last day there, when the Prince and Princess attended a dinner-dance (opposite page). The family was reunited for the farewells the next day (these pages), Prince William looking healthy and bronzed.

New Zealand's welcome was typical. Prince Charles, already an expert in Maori greetings, performed his response to the warrior challenge with aplomb.

Much practised at coping with foul weather, the Prince and Princess enjoyed themselves on a soaking wet day at Auckland's North Shore. Even when their car failed to start for the return journey, they happily talked with the crowd until they could leave. It was in stark contrast to the serenity of the previous evening's night out at St James' Theatre (opposite page).

Premier Robert Muldoon escorted the Princess of Wales into a splendid State banquet at Wellington on 21st April (opposite page). Prince Charles' speech sparkled with wit as he thanked his host for their wedding present of a "seemingly endless" pure wool carpet. The next day, the Princess was besieged during her walkabout at Upper Hutt and Masterton. No effort was spared by some to get their gifts into her hands. The gifts for Prince William were now being counted in thousands.

With Wanganui only a short plane trip from Wellington, a meeting with Prince Edward was inevitable. The young Prince wore a Maori cloak as he met his brother and sister-in-law – much to Prince Charles' amusement. Prince Edward took it off for a photo-call in the grounds of Wanganui Collegiate, where he was about to complete his second and final term as housemaster and junior tutor.

Prince William had not been seen in public since his arrival in New Zealand, but his parents compensated for that by bringing him out onto the lawn of Government House in Wellington for a session with the press. There was a sense of occasion about it – it was St George's Day – but Prince William was not interested. He crawled, turned up the carpet, showed his seven precious teeth, bit his bright wooden toy bee, and took a few steps almost unassisted. His parents looked proud of him and Prince Charles let slip his family nickname, Wills. Everyone seemed quite bowled over.

The Princess of Wales wore this striking white hat with its wide black ribbon for a garden party at Government House in Auckland (left). She chose white again for the royal visit to Tauranga, where Prince Charles opened a community centre (above and right), and for a civic reception back in Auckland that evening (far right). Whoever said she was "absolutely exhausted" was hard put to find a photograph to prove it.

Prince Charles, robed in academic gown, re-opened Otago Boys' High School near Dunedin on 17th April. His wife unveiled a plaque, and both toured the library and gymnasium. There was a walkabout in Otago after lunch.

At Christchurch on 28th April a city-centre walkabout allowed thousands of rain-soaked citizens to see the Prince and Princess, if only for a few moments. Prince Charles wore the uniform of RNZAF Air Commodore in Chief, ready for a flying display at Wigram base.

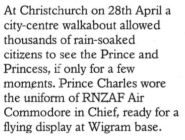

With tribal dances, the presentation of a jade fertility necklace, and a canoe trip across the Bay of Islands, April 29th was a day of high ceremony at Waitangi, where the Maoris conceded sovereignty to Queen Victoria in 1840.

Auckland's State banquet gave the royal couple a sumptuous official send-off. The Prince, in his speech, and the Princess, with her regal composure, rose to the occasion. They broke their journey back to London with a short holiday on Eleuthera, with no repetition of the previous year's harassment by photographers.

The Australasian triumph caused everyone to expect an anti-climax in Canada. But the Canadians gave the royal couple an unforgettable welcome at Halifax on 14th June. The Princess responded with her special brand of informality, and clothes matching the Maple Leaf flag. (Opposite) At a naval dockyard the next day.

Premier Pierre Trudeau seemed to fall in love with the Princess when he spoke at a banquet she and Prince Charles attended (previous pages) on 15th June. She was an instant success with the children too, shaking hands with hundreds of them at Rothesay two days later (this page). And those who kept an eye on her wardrobe admired her bold, flamenco-style clothes at Shelburne and Bridgewater on 16th June.

The Premier of New Brunswick followed Mr Trudeau in his admiration of the Prince and Princess of Wales, speaking fulsomely of the "triumph of love" at a State banquet on 17th June (left). Two days later, the population of St Andrews cheered them out of the mists as they arrived for Sunday morning service (this page and overleaf). The previous day they had been among the Micmac Indians, who had given the Princess (see page 307) a Red Indian outfit for Prince William.

Ottawa blazed in an 80° heat to give the Prince and Princess a formal welcome on Parliament Hill on 20th June (this page) and again at a banquet at Rideau Hall that evening.

The royal couple enjoyed a break from the Maritime Provinces' mists during a relaxing visit to the Ottawa Police Headquarters on 21st June. (Overleaf) The Princess in St John's, Newfoundland.

(Previous page) the Princess was a little embarrassed when she had to join in the singing of sea songs at St John's on 23rd June. But she and her husband enjoyed the endless festivities on St John's Day (opposite page) and a chat with the residents of Carbonear the day after (this page).

The Princess at Summerside (opposite page) and with Prince Charles (this page) on their first day in Edmonton, Alberta.

Klondike fashions dominated a barbecue at Edmonton, and the Prince and Princess (right) entered into the fun of the occasion. A more formal, but equally colourful farewell dinner the next day (this page) brought their second Commonwealth tour to a fitting end.

Royal Diary

The official engagements
of each member of the Royal Family
for a complete year
are listed on the following pages.
Generally the schedules are
confined to public engagements
and official duties
which are not public – audiences
in particular – have not been
included. The engagements for
Prince and Princess Michael of Kent
are not official, but have been
included where they were public
or undertaken on behalf of a
public organisation.

Engagements of **THE QUEEN**
August 1982-July 1983

August	**4**	Left Buckingham Palace for Aberdeen.
	5	Opened Aberdeen Harbour Fish Market.
September	**17**	Welcomed HMS Invincible home from the Falkland Islands, Spithead.
	30	Arrived at Buckingham Palace from Balmoral.
October	**4**	Left London for tour of Australia, Papua New Guinea, Solomon Islands, Nauru, Kiribati, Tuvalu and Fiji.
November	**1**	Arrived back in London from Australian and South Pacific tour.
	3	Opened new session of Parliament, Palace of Westminster.
	4	Held Investiture, Buckingham Palace.
	9	Held Investiture, Buckingham Palace.
	10	Visited London Central YMCA.
	11	Entertained the King of Malaysia to luncheon, Buckingham Palace.
		Left London for Northamptonshire.
	12	Toured exhibition and display of work, at Queen Elizabeth School, Corby.
		Toured the Derngate Centre and opened a Lift Tower, Corby.
	13	Attended Festival of Remembrance, Royal Albert Hall, London.
	14	Laid wreath at the Cenotaph for Remembrance Day, London.
	15	Attended the Memorial Service for Lord Rupert Nevill, St Margaret's Church, Westminster.
		Attended the Press Club's centenary reception, London.
	16	Welcomed Queen Beatrix and Prince Claus of the Netherlands to London, Westminster Pier.
		Gave a banquet for Queen Beatrix and Prince Claus, Buckingham Palace.
	17	Gave a reception for North Atlantic Assembly delegates, Buckingham Palace.
		Received and replied to addresses from the House of Commons and House of Lords, Buckingham Palace.
		Attended a reception to mark the Golden Jubilee of Book Tokens, Stationers' Hall, London.
	18	.Received and replied to an address from the House of Commons, Buckingham Palace.
		Entertained the President of Botswana, Buckingham Palace.
		Attended a State Banquet given by Queen Beatrix of the Netherlands, Hampton Court Palace.
	23	Held Investiture, Buckingham Palace.
		Received addresses from the Houses of Lords and Commons, Buckingham Palace.
	25	Held Investiture, Buckingham Palace.
		Left King's Cross Station for West Yorkshire.
	26	Visited the Police Academy, Wakefield.
		Visited Howson-Algraphy Factory, Seacroft, and Leeds.
	30	Held Reception for Diplomatic Corps, Buckingham Palace.
December	**1**	Visited Royal College of Defence Studies, Belgrave Square.
	1	Attended reception given by Board of Deputies of British Jews, St James's Palace.
	7	Held Investiture, Buckingham Palace.
	8	Entertained at dinner by the US Ambassador, Regent's Park.
	13	Attended a concert in aid of the Royal Society for the Protection of Birds, Royal Albert Hall.
	14	Held Investiture, Buckingham Palace.
		Received and replied to addresses from the House of Commons, Buckingham Palace.
	15	Visited Foreign and Commonwealth Office and the Overseas Development Administration, London.

January	23	Presented the Queen's Medal for general efficiency, King Edward VII School, King's Lynn, Norfolk.
February	3	Visited the Sue Ryder Home, Snettisham, Norfolk.
	7	Arrived at Buckingham Palace from Sandringham.
	8	Held an Investiture, Buckingham Palace.
	9	Opened the new wing of Arnold House, a Cheshire Home at Enfield, Middlesex.
	10	Held an Investiture, Buckingham Palace.
		Held reception for winners of the Queen's Award for Export and Technology, Buckingham Palace.
	13	Left Heathrow Airport to visit Jamaica, the Cayman Islands, Mexico, California and British Columbia.
March	11	Arrived back at Heathrow Airport from Canada.
	13	Attended Commonwealth Day Observance Service, Westminster Abbey.
		Attended Commonwealth Day reception at Marlborough House.
	15	Held an Investiture, Buckingham Palace.
	16	Opened new operating theatres at Westminster Hospital, and attended a reception in the Queen Mary Nursing Home.
	17	Held an Investiture, Buckingham Palace.
		Opened Henry Cole Wing at the Victoria and Albert Museum.
	18	Received members of the Arab League delegation, Buckingham Palace.
	22	Welcomed President Kaunda of Zambia, Victoria Station, London.
		Gave State banquet for the President of Zambia, Buckingham Palace.
	23	Visited Crown Agents to celebrate their sesquicentenary, Millbank, London.
	24	Attended State banquet given by the Prince of Zambia, Claridges Hotel, London.
	29	Held an Investiture, Buckingham Palace.
	31	Attended Maundy Service at Exeter Cathedral.
April	10	Attended Mattins for the Windsor Castle Chaplains, Windsor Parish Church, and a reception afterwards at Windsor Castle.
	13	Gave luncheon for Lieutenant Governor of Saskatchewan, Windsor Castle.
	14	Attended the service of the Royal Victorian Order, St George's Chapel Windsor, and a reception afterwards at Windsor Castle.
	19	Inspected the Queen's Company, 1st Battalion Grenadier Guards, Windsor Castle.
	30	Opened the National Horse Racing Museum, Newmarket.
May	4	Opened the Wall Walk, Tower of London.
	5	Visited RAF Coltishall, Norfolk.
	6	Visited St George's School, Windsor.
	8	Entertained the Governor-General of Canada to lunch at Windsor Castle.
	9	Attended a service of dedication for the centenary of the Co-operative Women's Guild, Westminster Abbey.
	11	Attended a reception given by the General Nursing Council, St James's Palace.
	16	Visited the 2nd Infantry Division, Imphal Barracks, York.
	17	Opened International Maritime Organisation Headquarters, Albert Embankment, London.
	19	Presented new standards to the Household Cavalry, Horse Guards Parade.
		Attended a garden party for the Household Cavalry, Burton Court, London.
	21	Boarded *Britannia* at Portsmouth for a four-day State visit to Sweden.
	25	Arrived in Sweden for State visit.

May 31   Dined with the Nulli Secundus Club, to celebrate their bi-centenary, Savoy Hotel, London.

June 1   Attended Epsom races.

7   Entertained the Prime Minister of Australia to lunch at Buckingham Palace.

8   Received the cricket teams taking part in the Prudential World Cup 1983, Buckingham Palace.

11   Took the salute at the Queen's Birthday Parade, Horse Guards Parade, London.

13   Held a Chapter of the Order of the Garter, Throne Room, Windsor Castle.
Attended the installation service for the Order, St George's Chapel, Windsor.

14   Attended Royal Ascot.

15   Attended Royal Ascot.

16   Attended Royal Ascot.

17   Attended Royal Ascot.

21   Carried out engagements in Croydon to mark the centenary of the granting of its first municipal charter.

22   Opened a new session of Parliament in State, Palace of Westminster.
Attended a reception given by the National Art Collections Fund, St James's Palace.

23   Entertained the Governor-General of New Zealand to luncheon, Buckingham Palace.
Received Prince Naruhito of Japan, Buckingham Palace.

24   Entertained the Rt Hon Malcolm and Mrs Fraser to lunch, Buckingham Palace.

27   Attended the Rhodes Scholars' reunion Garden Party, Rhodes House, Oxford.
Attended a reception at Oriel College, Oxford.

28   Arrived at the Palace of Holyroodhouse.
Visited Merchiston Castle School, Edinburgh.
Gave a reception to mark the 400th anniversary of Edinburgh University, Holyroodhouse.

29   Opened the renovated premises of the Royal Society of Edinburgh.
Gave a garden party, Holyroodhouse.

30   Reviewed the Royal Scots (The Royal Regiment) to mark its 350th anniversary, Holyroodhouse.
Attended a luncheon given by the Regiment, North British Hotel, Edinburgh.
Attended a reception given by the High Constables of Holyroodhouse, Abbey Court.
Gave dinner party, Holyroodhouse.

July 1   Visited the Royal College of Physicians and Surgeons of Glasgow.
Attended a Glasgow Chamber of Commerce reception, George Square.
Attended the Lord Lieutenant's luncheon, City Chambers, Glasgow.
Visited the Glasgow Herald, Albion Street, Glasgow.
Visited the Scottish Special Housing Association development, Calton, Glasgow.

2   Reviewed the Boys' Brigade, Holyrood Park.

3   Attended morning service, Canongate Kirk, Edinburgh.

4   Opened the Factory of Nippon Electric Company Semiconductors (UK) Ltd, Livingstone.
Received an address from the House of Lords, Holyroodhouse.
Attended a gala concert by the Scottish National Orchestra, Usher Hall, Edinburgh.

5   Left the Palace of Holyroodhouse for Birmingham.
Visited the Kingfisher Shopping Centre, Redditch.
Opened the restored Forge Mill and Museum, Redditch and visited Hymatic Engineering Co Ltd, Redditch.

12   Opened the new premises of the British Academy, Regent's Park.
Attended a Garden Party at the Holme, Bedford College.

Engagements of **THE QUEEN**
August 1982-July 1983 (*continued*)

July **15** Presented a new guidon to the Queen's Royal Lancers, Tidworth, Hampshire, and toured the barracks.

18 Took the salute at a performance of the Royal Tournament, Earl's Court.

19 Gave a garden party, Buckingham Palace.

20 Held an Investiture, Buckingham Palace.

21 Visited the Royal Welsh Show, Builth Wells.
Attended a service to celebrate the diamond jubilee of Swansea and Brecon Diocese, Brecon.

22 Visited *HMS Thunderer*, Manadon, Plymouth.

26 Held an Investiture, Buckingham Palace.

27 Gave a garden party, Buckingham Palace.

28 Gave a luncheon party for the President of the Ivory Coast.
Attended a Guild of Freemen of the City of London reception, Guildhall, London.

Engagements of **THE DUKE OF EDINBURGH**
August 1982-July 1983

August	**2**	Attended reception, Royal London Yacht Club, Cowes.
		Attended Royal Yacht Squadron Ball, Cowes Castle.
	3	Left Cowes on Royal Yacht Britannia.
	9	Visited Appleby Association Football Club, Cumbria.
		Left from Hull for Netherlands to compete in World Driving Championships, Apeldoorn.
	16	Returned to Britain, travelling to Balmoral via Dyce Airport.
September	**17**	Welcomed *HMS Invincible* home from the Falkland Islands, Spithead.
	20	Left London for Los Angeles as President of World Wildlife Fund International and of the Federation Equestre Internationale.
October	**6**	Joined the Queen for visit to Australia and the South Pacific.
	31	Left Fiji to visit Japan and Canada.
November	**11**	Arrived back in Britain from Canada.
	13	Attended Festival of Remembrance, Royal Albert Hall, London.
	14	Laid a wreath at the Cenotaph for Remembrance Day, London.
	15	Attended a Memorial Service for Lord Rupert Nevill, St Margarets Church, Westminster.
		Attended the Press Club's centenary reception, London.
		Attended Council of St George's House meeting, Windsor Castle.
	16	Welcomed Queen Beatrix and Prince Claus of the Netherlands to London, Westminster Pier.
		Gave banquet for Queen Beatrix and Prince Claus at Buckingham Palace.
		Chaired a panel of judges for Tiger Club "Dawn to Dusk" Competitions, Buckingham Palace.
		Attended a Burnbake Trust Symposium, London.
	17	Gave a reception for North Atlantic Assembly Delegates, Buckingham Palace.
		Presided at a meeting of the Trustees of the Duke of Edinburgh's Award, Buckingham Palace.
		Chaired a meeting of the Royal Mint Advisory Committee, Buckingham Palace.
		Attended a meeting of the Royal Academy Trustees, Buckingham Palace.
		Attended a performance of "Camelot" in aid of Boys Clubs, Apollo Victoria Theatre, London.
	18	Present at an audience by the Queen at which an address from the House of Commons was made, Buckingham Palace.
		Attended a State Banquet given by Queen Beatrix of the Netherlands, Hampton Court Palace.
		Attended a meeting of the Government Committee on the Education of Ethnic Minorities, Little St James's Street, London.
		Attended a meeting of the Lord Mayor's Appeal Committee, Buckingham Palace.
		Chaired a meeting of the Westminster Abbey Trustees, Buckingham Palace.
	19	Visited British Steel Corporation workshops, and other industrial sites, Corby, Northamptonshire.
		Toured Corby Civic Centre and an exhibition of work of the Corby Joint Industrial Development Committee.
		Laid the foundation stone of R.S. Components Ltd factory and toured the factory of Pakcraft Ltd, Corby.
	21	Left Luton for Switzerland to attend meetings of the World Wildlife Fund International.
	30	Returned to London from Switzerland and Germany.
		Attended reception for the Diplomatic Corps, Buckingham Palace.
December	**1**	Visited Royal College of Defence Studies, Belgrave Square.

Engagements of **THE DUKE OF EDINBURGH**
August 1982-July 1983 *(continued)*

December	1	Presented National Playing Fields Association certificates, Buckingham Palace.
		Presented South Atlantic Medals to Members of the Household Division, Buckingham Palace.
		Attended Central Council of Physical Recreation dinner, Hyde Park Hotel.
	2	Attended National Maritime Museum Trustees Meeting, Greenwich.
		Presented English Language Competition prizes for the English Speaking Union, Buckingham Palace.
		Gave a reception for Friends of the Duke of Edinburgh's Award Scheme, Buckingham Palace.
		Attended a dinner in aid of the Bowles Outdoor Pursuits Centre, Piccadilly.
	3	Toured factories in Chichester and Crawley, West Sussex.
	5	Left Lydd Airport to carry out engagements in Geneva.
	10	Returned to London from Switzerland.
	13	Attended concert in aid of the Royal Society for the Protection of Birds, Royal Albert Hall.
	14	Attended "Saints and Sinners" Club Christmas luncheon, Savoy Hotel.
		Presented the MacRobert Award Prize and Medal for 1982, Buckingham Palace.
		Received representatives of the Institute of Chemical Engineers, Buckingham Palace.
		Presented Albert Medal and Benjamin Franklin Medal, and attended a Royal Society of Arts Dinner, London.
	15	Chaired a Duke of Edinburgh's Award Scheme forum, Palace of Holyroodhouse.
	16	Chaired a General Council Meeting of the Duke of Edinburgh's Award Scheme, Assembly Rooms, Edinburgh.
January	17	Visited the training centre of the Construction Industry Training Board, Bircham Newton, Norfolk.
February	4	Carried out engagements in Mablethorpe, Lincolnshire.
	7	Arrived at Buckingham Palace from Sandringham.
	8	Attended reception for winners of the Duke of Edinburgh's Award, Gold Standard, at St James's Palace.
	9	Visited the new Billingsgate Market at West India Dock Road.
		Attended a luncheon of the Victory Syndicate, St James's Club, London.
		Dined with the Smeatonian Society of Civil Engineers, London.
	10	Chaired a meeting to select the Duke of Edinburgh's Designers Award and attended luncheon, Design Centre, London.
	10	Held a reception for winners of Queen's Award for Export and Technology, Buckingham Palace.
	13	Left Heathrow Airport with the Queen to visit Jamaica, the Cayman Islands, Mexico, California and British Columbia.
March	11	Arrived back at Heathrow Airport with the Queen from Canada.
	14	Attended Commonwealth Day Observance Service at Westminster Abbey.
		Attended Commonwealth Day reception at Marlborough House.
	15	Attended a Greater London Council luncheon, County Hall.
		Attended dinner for the Council of the Duke of Edinburgh's Award Scheme's 25th anniversary appeal, Lloyds of London.
	16	Attended reception for winners of the Duke of Edinburgh's Award Scheme Gold Standard, St James's Palace.
		Attended a masonic dinner, Freemasons Hall.
	17	Attended a meeting of the National Maritime Trustees, National Maritime Museum, London.

Engagements of THE DUKE OF EDINBURGH
August 1982-July 1983 *(continued)*

March 17 Attended 50th anniversary dinner of the British Fund for Jewish Relief, Guildhàll.
       18 Addressed Army Staff College, Camberley.
       22 Presented Schweppes County Championship Trophy, Buckingham Palace.
            Attended welcoming ceremonies for President Kaunda of Zambia, Victoria Station.
            Gave State banquet for President of Zambia, Buckingham Palace.
       23 Visited Crown Agents to celebrate their sesquicentenary, Millbank, London.
            Presented 1982 Prince Philip Awards and certificates for the Royal Association of British Dairy Farmers, Buckingham Palace.
            Chaired meeting of the Royal Mint Advisory Committee, Buckingham Palace.
            Left Heathrow Airport to attend meetings of World Wildlife Fund International, Gland, Switzerland.
       24 Returned to Heathrow Airport from Switzerland.
            Attended the State banquet given by the President of Zambia, Claridges Hotel.
       25 Visited 1st Battalion Ghurka Rifles, Church Crookham, Hampshire.
       29 Opened Billy Butlin Youth Recreation Centre, St John, Jersey.
            Attended Duke of Edinburgh Scheme Luncheon, St John, Jersey.
            Attended anniversary dinner of Crimea Club, Piccadilly Hotel, London.
            Chaired meeting of the trustees of the Westminster Abbey Trust, Buckingham Palace.
       30 Visited Ranfurly Library Service, Kensington Palace Barracks.
            Attended the viewing of film as President of the Aidis Trust, Buckingham Palace.
            Gave a reception as patron of the British Trust for the Conservation Volunteers, Buckingham Palace.
       31 Attended Maundy Service with the Queen, Exeter Cathedral.

April 8 Chaired the St George's House annual lecture, St George's Chapel, Windsor.
       10 Attended Mattins for Windsor Castle Chaplains, Windsor Parish Church, and a reception at Windsor Castle.
       11 Attended a council meeting of St George's House, Windsor Castle.
       13 Gave lunch for Lieutenant-Governor of Saskatchewan, Windsor Castle.
       14 Attended the service for the Royal Victorian Order, St George's Chapel Windsor, and a reception at Windsor Castle.
       18 Visited the exhibition of Driving Vehicles, Harrods, London.
       19 Inspected Queen's Company, 1st Battalion Grenadier Guards, Windsor Castle.
       21 Attended the start of the Sealink International cycle race, Barry Avenue, Windsor.
       23 Left Heathrow Airport to attend show jumping cup finals and meetings of World Wildlife Fund International, Vienna.
       24 Arrived back at Heathrow Airport from Austria.
       26 Attended the opening of Mantech Symposium, Fellowship of Institution of Civil Engineers, London.
            Attended the Outward Bound/Variety Club Luncheon, Grosvenor House.

May 3 Attended reception given by the English Speaking Union, Dartmouth House, London.
            Attended the premiere of *Educating Rita*, Leicester Square Theatre, London.
       4 Attended the opening of the Wall Walk by the Queen, Tower of London.
            Chaired Annual General Meeting of the Central Council for Physical Recreation, Fishmongers' Hall, London.
            Viewed a mobile education centre for the University of Salford, Buckingham Palace.
            Attended a New Fellows' dinner given by the Fellowship of Engineering, Apothecaries' Hall, London.

Engagements of **THE DUKE OF EDINBURGH**
August 1982-July 1983 *(continued)*

May 6   Visited St George's School, Windsor.
Attended a Duke of Edinburgh's Award Trustees meeting, Buckingham Palace.
Attended the Windsor and Eton Football Club reception, Harte and Garter Hotel, Windsor.

8   Entertained the Governor-General of Canada to lunch, Windsor Castle.
Attended the Grenadier Guards' Regimental Remembrance Day Service, Guards' Chapel, Wellington Barracks, London.

9   Opened the Maxibrite Smokeless Fuel Extension, Maxiheat Works, Mwyndy, South Wales.
Presented 1983 Design Council Awards, St David's Centre, Cardiff.

9   Attended Younger Brethren's dinner, Trinity House.

10   Presented 1983 Templeton Foundation prize for progress in Religion, Buckingham Palace.
Attended Annual Court, and luncheon, at Trinity House, and the Trinity House church service at St Olave's Church, London.
Chaired the British Commonwealth Ex-Services League Council meeting, Buckingham Palace.
Awarded the Air League flying scholarships, and attended a reception, at the Brewery, Chiswell Street.
Attended a Royal Society Club dinner, Carlton House Terrace, London.

16   Left Heathrow Airport for Zambia and Zimbabwe, joining the Royal Yacht Britannia afterwards to meet the Queen in Sweden.

28   Arrived at RAF Leuchars from Sweden.

31   Attended a dinner of the Nulli Secundus Club, Savoy Hotel, London.

June 1   Attended Epsom races.
Presented the 1983 Prince Philip medal, City and Guilds Institute, at Buckingham Palace.

2   Addressed the Royal United Services Institute, Whitehall, London.
Attended a reception for achievers of the Duke of Edinburgh's Award Gold Standard, Buckingham Palace.
Attended the annual dinner of the Incorporated Liverpool School of Tropical Medicine, Thornton Manor, Cheshire.

3   Opened the field studies centre, Deeside Naturalists Society, Connah's Quay, Clwyd.
Visited the British Association for Shooting and Conservation Headquarters, Rossett, Clwyd.

4   Took the salute at the second rehearsal of the Queen's Birthday Parade, Horse Guards Parade, London.

6   Attended the Anglo-Swedish Society's annual dinner, Hyde Park Hotel, London.

7   Entertained the Prime Minister of Australia to luncheon, Buckingham Palace.
Attended a Grenadier Guards Regimental garden party, Hounslow.
Attended a massed bands display of the Prince of Wales Division, Horse Guards Parade.

8   Received the cricket teams taking part in the Prudential World Cup 1983, Buckingham Palace.
Visited the University of Cambridge as Chancellor.

9   Continued visiting the University of Cambridge.

11   Attended the Queen's Birthday Parade, Horse Guards Parade.

13   Attended the Chapter and installation service of the Order of the Garter, Windsor Castle.

14   Attended Royal Ascot.

15   Attended Royal Ascot.

16   Attended Royal Ascot.

17   Attended Royal Ascot.
Attended the Grenadier Guards regimental ball, Syon House, Middlesex.

19   Left Heathrow Airport for Switzerland to attend meetings of the World Wildlife Fund.

Engagements of **THE DUKE OF EDINBURGH**
August 1982-July 1983 *(continued)*

June	22	Attended the State Opening of Parliament by the Queen, Palace of Westminster.
	27	Attended the Rhodes Scholars Reunion garden party, Rhodes House, Oxford.
		Attended a reception at Oriel College, Oxford.
	28	Gave a reception marking the 400th anniversary of Edinburgh University, Holyroodhouse.
		Opened the new headquarters of the 13th Commonwealth Games, Canning House, Edinburgh.
		Visited the Royal College of Surgeons, Edinburgh.
		Attended a reception for achievers of the Duke of Edinburgh's Award Gold Standard, Holyroodhouse.
	29	Left RAF Turnhouse for Canada.
July	7	Arrived back at RAF Turnhouse from Canada.
		Attended a dinner marking the 400th anniversary of Edinburgh University.
	8	Conferred Honorary Degrees at a Graduation Ceremony, Edinburgh University.
	9	Attended the University of Edinburgh General Council dinner, Students' Centre, Bristo Square, Edinburgh.
	12	Visited the new premises of the British Academy, Regent's Park.
		Attended a garden party, the Holme, Bedford College.
		Visited a Boys' Club centre, Woodrow High House, Amersham, Bucks.
		Gave a reception for the Shakespeare Globe Trust, Buckingham Palace.
	13	Gave a garden party, Buckingham Palace.
	14	Presided at a meeting of the Royal Mint Advisory Committee, Buckingham Palace.
		Attended a reception for achievers of the Duke of Edinburgh's Award Gold Standard, Buckingham Palace.
	15	Presided at Degree Congregations, University of Salford.
	18	Attended the Royal Tournament, Earl's Court.
	19	Gave a garden party, Buckingham Palace.
	19	Attended the Royal International Horse Show, White City Stadium, London.
	20	Attended a National Maritime Museum dinner, Arts Club, London.
	21	Visited the Royal Welsh Show, Builth Wells.
		Gave a reception in connection with the Duke of Edinburgh's Cup Golf Challenge event, Buckingham Palace.
	22	Visited *HMS Thunderer*, Manadon, Plymouth.
	23	Presented new colours to the 1st Battalion Queen's Own Highlanders, Tidworth, Wiltshire.
	26	Visited Birmingham Airport development site project office and terminal building.
		Opened the European six-a-side Football Championship for the mentally handicapped, Solihull.
		Visited Aston Science Park, and opened Birmingham Athletic Institute.
	27	Gave a garden party, Buckingham Palace.
	28	Gave a luncheon party for the President of the Ivory Coast, Buckingham Palace.
		Attended a Guild of Freemen of the City of London reception, Guildhall, London.
	29	Embarked in HM Yacht *Britannia*, Cowes, Isle of Wight.
	30	Attended the Elder Brethrens' reception on board *THV Patricia*, Cowes, Isle of Wight.
	31	Attended the Cowes Regatta church service, Holy Trinity Church, Cowes.
		Presented the Chichester Award at the Royal Yacht Squadron Club, Cowes.
		Attended the Cowes Combined Clubs reception, Cowes Castle.
		Attended a reception given by the Royal Thames Yacht Club, Royal London Yacht Club, Cowes.

Engagements of THE PRINCE OF WALES
August 1982-July 1983

August	5	Entertained Major General John Macdonald to luncheon, Kensington Palace.
	12	Attended National Youth Choir of New Zealand concert, Wembley Conference Centre.
	13	Visited Worshipful Company of Shipwrights Exhibition, Museum of London.
	17	Took salute at Trooping Parade of Gordon Highlanders, Aberdeen.
	19	Received round the world helicopter pilot Dick Smith, Balmoral.
	26	Opened Strathaird Fish Smoking Plant, Inverness.
	29	Present at return of the Transglobe Expedition, Greenwich.

September	1	Visited Graphic Information Systems Ltd, Blairgowrie, Perthshire.
	3	Visited Royal Star and Garter Home for disabled servicemen, Richmond, Surrey.
	8	Visited the Tummel Forest, Perthshire.
	17	Took salute at a Trooping Parade of Gordon Highlanders, Aberdeen.
		Reopened His Majesty's Theatre, Aberdeen and attended a Gala Charity Performance there.
	24	Visited Prince's Trust Youth Camp, Argyll Forest Park.
		Attended NATO dinner, Royal Naval College, Greenwich.

October	1	Attended Parachute Regiment Falklands Campaign Memorial Service, Aldershot.
	6	Opened Shell-Mex Gas Terminal, St Fergus, Aberdeenshire.
	9	Watched operations to recover the Mary Rose, Portsmouth.
	11	Present at the raising of the Mary Rose, Portsmouth.
	13	Visited Army Youth Adventure Training Unit, Fort George, Inverness.
	25	Attended meeting of the Cambridge Commonwealth Trust, Cambridge.
		Visited USAF Base, RAF Mildenhall, Suffolk.
	26	Attended Rostropovich concert, Barbican Centre, London.
	27	Left London for USA and Canada, on behalf of the United World Colleges.
	31	Arrived in London from Canada.

November	2	Visited Rolls Royce Diesels, Shrewsbury.
	3	Attended the State Opening of Parliament, Palace of Westminster.
	4	Presided at meeting of The Prince's Council, Duchy of Cornwall Office, Buckingham Gate, London, and entertained members to lunch at Kensington Palace.
		Attended Hunter Memorial Lecture, Institution of Electrical Engineers, London.
	8	Visited Scilly Isles, as Duke of Cornwall.
	10	Left Scilly Isles.
		Opened Victorian Heyday Exhibition, Portsmouth, Hampshire.
		Attended Banquet in aid of the Mary Rose Trust, *HMS Victory*, Portsmouth.
	11	Attended Friends of Covent Garden Luncheon, London.
		Visited Royal Institute of Oil Painters Exhibition, Mall Galleries, London.
		Attended a lecture, Society of Antiquaries of London, Burlington House, Piccadilly.
	12	Visited the Eastern District of the Duchy of Cornwall and attended a Tenants' luncheon at Radstock.
	13	Attended Festival of Remembrance, Royal Albert Hall, London.
	14	Laid wreath at the Cenotaph for Remembrance Day, London.
		Attended Remembrance Day Service, Guards Chapel and laid a wreath at the Guards Memorial.
	16	Welcomed Queen Beatrix and Prince Claus of the Netherlands to London, Greenwich.
		Attended the State Banquet for Queen Beatrix and Prince Claus, Buckingham Palace.
	18	Present at an audience by the Queen at which an address from the House of Commons was presented, Buckingham Palace.
		Attended a State Banquet given by Queen Beatrix of the Netherlands, Hampton Court Palace.

Engagements of **THE PRINCE OF WALES**
August 1982-July 1983 *(continued)*

November	19	Attended a performance of "Wild Oats" in aid of the Bristol and West Orthopaedic Trust, Theatre Royal, Bristol.
	23	Gave reception for the Wells Cathedral Preservation Trust, Kensington Palace.
		Entertained at dinner by the US Ambassador, Regent's Park.
	25	Visited Merioneth district of Gwynedd.
	26	Visited Wrexham area of Clwyd.
	30	Attended Conference on Forestry and Conservation, Royal Society of Arts, London.
		Visited City of London Archaeological Trust, and Billingsgate Museum, London.
		Attended Reception for the Diplomatic Corps, Buckingham Palace.
December	1	Presented South Atlantic Medals to members of the Household Division, Buckingham Palace.
	2	Attended Law Society's luncheon, Chancery Lane.
		Attended premiere of Gandhi, Odeon, Leicester Square.
	3	Visited Consett, Co Durham.
		Opened Northumberland County Hall, Morpeth.
	7	Chaired a meeting of the Royal College of Music Centenary Appeal, Buckingham Palace.
		Unveiled British Library Foundation Stone, Wardour Street, London.
		Attended Philharmonia Orchestra's gala concert, Royal Festival Hall.
	8	Presided at a Royal Jubilee Trusts meeting, Buckingham Street, London.
		Attended charity gala performance, Royal Opera House, Covent Garden.
	9	Visited RAF Brawdy, South Wales.
		Opened new coastguard Rescue Centre, Mumbles.
		Attended premiere of E.T., Empire Theatre, Leicester Square.
	10	Attended Chief of General Staff's Falklands briefing, Staff College, Camberley.
	14	Attended British Medical Association dinner, Tavistock Square, London.
	15	Attended the Cynefin Conference, St David's Hall, Cardiff.
	16	Attended Commonwealth Development Corporation meeting, Hill Street, London.
		Gave a reception, Kensington Palace, in connection with the Duchy of Cornwall.
	18	Attended Cheshire Regiment Memorial Service for those killed in the Ballykelly bomb explosion, Chester Cathedral.
	19	Attended the Friends of Covent Garden Christmas Party, Royal Opera House, Covent Garden.
	20	Visited Birkenhead Training Centre.
		Attended a Christmas celebration, Liverpool Cathedral.
	23	Visited members of the Cheshire Regiment injured in the Ballykelly bomb explosion, Queen Elizabeth's Military Hospital, Woolwich.
		Visited Duchy of Cornwall property, Manor of Kennington, London.
January	17	Attended a reception for the "Salute to New York" celebrations, Royal Academy of Arts, London.
	30	Attended a Great Gala at Royal Albert Hall, for the Royal College of Music Centenary Appeal.
February	2	Visited the Van Dyck Exhibition, National Portrait Gallery.
	3	Gave a reception for the Prince's Trust, Kensington Palace.
	7	Began a five-day farming visit to Duchy of Cornwall property in Cornwall.
	15	Held an Investiture on behalf of the Queen, Buckingham Palace.
		Attended the premiere of the film *To the Ends of the Earth*, Classic Cinema, Shaftesbury Avenue.
	16	Gave a reception for the Royal Jubilee Trusts, Kensington Palace.

Engagements of **THE PRINCE OF WALES**
August 1982-July 1983 *(continued)*

February	22	Held an Investiture on behalf of the Queen, Buckingham Palace.
		Visited the Duchy of Cornwall Office, Manor of Kennington, London.
	23	Attended the Operation Raleigh luncheon, Warwick House, St James's Palace.
	24	Visited 1st Battalion Welsh Guards, Pirbright, Surrey.
		Entertained at dinner by the Australian High Commissioner, Hyde Park Gate, London.
	25	Visited factories in Gwent and South Glamorgan.
		Attended the South Wales Constabulary dinner and ball, Cardiff.
	28	Attended the opening of Cestyll '83, Festival of Castles, Caerphilly Castle.

March	1	Visited Welsh Guards, Pirbright, Surrey.
	2	Opened new London offices of the British Technology group, Newington, London.
	2	Gave a dinner party in aid of the Prince of Wales Awards for Industrial Innovation, Kensington Palace.
	3	Presided at a meeting of the Prince's Council, Duchy of Cornwall Offices, London.
		Watched a video in connection with the Royal Jubilee Trusts, Independent Broadcasting Authority headquarters, London.
	4	Visited Prince of Wales Trust members in Glasgow and Edinburgh.
	9	Chaired a meeting of the Duchy of Cornwall Steering Committee for Dartmoor, Bovey Tracey.
		Presented a charter to the new borough of West Devon, Tavistock.
		Visited Duchy of Cornwall farms on Dartmoor.
	11	Chaired a meeting of the President's Committee, Royal Jubilee Trusts, at Kensington Palace.
	15	Opened an exhibition on telecommunications, Science Museum, London.
		Attended a committee meeting of National Hospital Junior Staff, BMA House, Tavistock Square, London.
	17	Attended 25th anniversary luncheon of the Royal Forestry Society, Grosvenor House, London.
	18	Left Heathrow Airport for royal visit to Australia and New Zealand.

May	11	Arrived home from tour of Australasia and holiday in the Bahamas.
		Attended a dinner given by the Company of Fishmongers, Fishmongers' Hall.
	12	Attended the dedication ceremony for the Maureen Production platform, Kishorn, Wester Ross.
	16	Attended a Royal College of Music concert, Exbury, Hampshire.
	17	Opened the exhibition *Renaissance at Sutton Place*, Guildford, Surrey.
	18	Received a degree of Civil Law during a visit to Oxford University.
	19	Attended the presentation of new standards to the Household Cavalry by the Queen, Horse Guards' Parade.
	20	Attended the Annual General Meeting of the Royal Naval Film Corporation, *HMS President*, King's Reach.
	23	Attended a concert given by the Royal College of Music, Royal Albert Hall.
	24	Attended a charity luncheon, Dorchester Hotel.
		Attended the *Live Music Now* dinner, Apsley House, London.
	26	Opened the new building at the London Business School, Regent's Park.
	27	Toured the Western Woodland in the Duchy of Cornwall.
		Visited St Columb Major, Cornwall.
	28	Attended the King Edward IV quincentenary concert, St George's Chapel, Windsor.
	31	Gave a reception for the British Medical Association, Kensington Palace.

Engagements of THE PRINCE OF WALES
August 1982-July 1983 *(continued)*

June 1   Entertained at dinner by the New Zealand High Commissioner, Chelsea Square, London.
     2   Presented the Prince of Wales Award for Industrial Innovation, BBC Television Centre, London.
     3   Presented new colours to the 10th Battalion, Parachute Regiment, Duke of York's Headquarters, London.
     4   Attended a ball in aid of the United World Colleges, Broadlands, Romsey, Hampshire.
     6   Received the Prime Minister of Australia, Kensington Palace.
        Attended the premiere of *Octopussy*, Odeon Theatre, Leicester Square.
     7   Took the salute at a massed bands display by the Prince of Wales' Division, Horse Guards' Parade.
     8   Attended the launch of the conservation and development programme for the UK, Logan Hall, University of London.
     9   Visited Duchy of Cornwall property in South Glamorgan.
    11   Attended the Queen's Birthday Parade, Horse Guards' Parade.
    13   Attended the Chapter of the Order of the Garter, Windsor Castle and the installation service at St George's Chapel.
    14   Left Heathrow Airport for an eighteen-day tour of Canada.

July 2   Returned to London from Canada.
     5   Gave a reception for those wounded in the South Atlantic and Northern Ireland, Kensington Palace.
     6   Attended a dinner in aid of the Help Poland Fund, Hatfield House, Hertfordshire.
     7   Visited the Prince's Trust Projects in Suffolk and Cambridgeshire.
        Attended a Cambridge Commonwealth Trust dinner, Trinity College, Cambridge.
     8   Visited Prince of Wales Committee projects in Gwynedd.
    12   Attended a meeting of the Duchy of Cornwall advisory group on archaeology, Cornwall.
        Visited Duchy of Cornwall property in the Eastern District.
    13   Attended a garden party, Buckingham Palace.
    14   Visited the India Office library, Blackfriars Road, London.
        Gave a reception for people involved in community relations, Kensington Palace.
    15   Visited the Cancer Help Centre, Bristol.
    18   Gave the inaugural Police Foundation lecture, Guildhall, London.
    19   Presided at a meeting of the Prince's Council, Duchy of Cornwall Office, London.
        Entertained members of the Prince's Council to luncheon, Kensington Palace.
        Gave a reception for the Royal College of Music Centenary Appeal, Kensington Palace.
    20   Attended a rock gala in aid of the Prince's Trust, Dominion Theatre, London.
    21   Attended a Variety Club luncheon, Guildhall, London.
        Chaired a meeting of the Prince of Wales' Advisory Group on Disability, Kensington Palace.
    22   Presided at a meeting of the Court of Governors of the University of Wales, Aberystwyth.
        Attended an official dinner at Pantycelyn, and switched on the illuminations in Aberystwyth.
    23   Presided at a degree congregation, University College of Wales, Aberystwyth.
        Visited the Ceredigion Museum, Coliseum, Aberystwyth.
    26   Visited the Welsh Guards Regimental Headquarters, Wellington Barracks.
        Attended a national service of thanksgiving for the life of William Wilberforce, Westminster Abbey.
        Dined with "A" Division, Staff College, Camberley.
    27   Attended a garden party, Buckingham Palace.
    30   Accepted the freedom of Merthyr Tydfil on behalf of the Welsh Guards.

Engagements of **THE PRINCESS OF WALES**
August 1982-July 1983

September	18	Represented the Queen at State Funeral for Princess Grace of Monaco.
October	26	Attended Rostropovich concert, Barbican Centre, London.
	29	Attended performance by Welsh National Opera, New Theatre, Cardiff.
November	2	Opened new extension to the Royal School for the Blind, Leatherhead, Surrey.
	3	Attended the State Opening of Parliament, Palace of Westminster.
		Visited Pre-School Playgroups Association meeting, Hyde Park Hotel, Knightsbridge, London.
	9	Attended a charity dinner and fashion show, Guildhall, London.
	10	Attended the opening of the Victorian Heyday Exhibition, Portsmouth.
		Attended a banquet in aid of the Mary Rose Trust, *HMS Victory*, Portsmouth.
	12	Attended a Tenants' luncheon, Radstock, Duchy of Cornwall.
	13	Attended Festival of Remembrance, Royal Albert Hall, London.
		Attended Remembrance Day Services, Cenotaph, London and Guards' Chapel.
	16	Attended welcoming ceremonies for Queen Beatrix and Prince Claus of the Netherlands, Westminster Pier.
	16	Attended State banquet for Queen Beatrix and Prince Claus, at Buckingham Palace.
	18	Present at an audience by the Queen, at which an address from the House of Commons was presented, Buckingham Palace.
		Attended a State Banquet given by Queen Beatrix of the Netherlands, Hampton Court Palace.
	22	Visited Cirencester Playgroup, Forum Youth Centre, Cirencester, Gloucestershire.
	23	Visited Capital Radio, Euston Road, London.
		Entertained to dinner by the US Ambassador, Regent's Park.
	25	Visited Merioneth District of Gwynedd.
	26	Visited Wrexham area of Clwyd.
	30	Visited Youth A.I.D. (Lewisham), Hearsay Community Centre, Catford.
		Attended Reception for Diplomatic Corps, Buckingham Palace.
December	2	Visited the Great Ormond Street Hospital for Sick Children, London.
		Attended premiere of Gandhi, Odeon Leicester Square.
	3	Visited DHSS office, Fleming House, London SE1.
	7	Visited Handsworth Cultural Centre, Birmingham and Belgrave Lodge, Coventry.
		Attended Philharmonia Orchestra's Gala Concert, Royal Festival Hall.
	8	Visited the Royal Marsden Hospital, Fulham Road.
	8	Attended a charity gala performance, Royal Opera House, Covent Garden.
	9	Visited Charlie Chaplin Playground for Handicapped Children, Kensington.
		Attended the premiere of E.T., Empire Theatre, Leicester Square.
	15	Opened the Neonatal Intensive Care Unit, University College Hospital, London.
	16	Gave a reception at Kensington Palace, in connection with the Duchy of Cornwall.
	20	Visited Birkenhead Training Centre.
		Attended a Christmas celebration, Liverpool Cathedral.
January	17	Attended a reception for the "Salute to New York" celebrations, Royal Academy of Arts.
	30	Attended a Great Gala at the Royal Albert Hall.
February	2	Visited the Van Dyck exhibition, National Portrait Gallery.
		Visited the Parchmore Methodist Church Youth and Community Centre, Thornton Heath, Surrey.

Engagements of **THE PRINCESS OF WALES**
August 1982-July 1983 *(continued)*

February	4	Opened new intensive care unit, Bristol Royal Hospital for Sick Children.
	7	Attended a reception for the launch of the Yorkshire Appeal for Cancer Relief, Garrowby, Yorkshire.
	8	Visited the International Spring Fair, National Exhibition Centre, Birmingham.
	9	Received the Freedom of the Grocers' Company, Grocers' Hall, London.
	16	Visited Nightingale House for the Elderly, Clapham, London.
	17	Visited the Royal Hospital for Sick Children, Glasgow and opened a Paediatric Renal Unit.
		Visited the Homesteading Scheme, Easterhouse, Glasgow.
	18	Attended the Ice Show at Wembley.
	22	Visited the factory of Glaxo Pharmaceuticals, Ware, Hertfordshire.
	24	Entertained at dinner by the Australian High Commissioner, Hyde Park Gate.
	25	Opened Brookfields School for the Mentally Handicapped, Tilehurst, Reading.
	28	Attended the opening of Cestyll '83, Festival of Castles, Caerphilly Castle.
March	2	Opened new shopping centre, Aylesbury, Buckinghamshire.
	4	Visited Prince of Wales Trust members in Glasgow and Edinburgh.
	8	Attended the Memorial Gala honouring Marie Rambert, Sadler's Wells Theatre.
	9	Attended the presentation of the Charter to the new borough of West Devon, Tavistock.
		Visited under-five playgroups at Bovey Tracey and Tavistock.
		Visited Duchy of Cornwall farms on Dartmoor.
	15	Accepted the Freedom and Livery of the Stationers' and Newspapers' Company, Stationers' Hall.
		Visited Baring Primary School. Lee, South East London.
	17	Attended the exhibition *Better Made in Britain*, Kensington Exhibition Centre, London.
	18	Left Heathrow Airport with the Prince of Wales for the royal tour of Australia and New Zealand.
May	11	Arrived back at Heathrow Airport after the tour of Australasia and a holiday in the Bahamas.
	13	Opened an adventure playground for the handicapped at Seven Springs, Cheltenham.
		Visited Paradise House training college for young people, Painswick, Gloucestershire.
	16	Attended the Royal College of Music concert at Exbury, Hampshire.
	17	Attended the opening of the exhibition *Renaissance at Sutton Place*, Guildford, Surrey.
	18	Opened the new bridge over the Tyne, and opened a new Findus Food factory near Newcastle-upon-Tyne.
	19	Attended the presentation by the Queen of new standards to the Household Cavalry, Horse Guards' Parade.
	20	Opened the Warden-assisted Housing scheme for the elderly, Cranmer House, Canterbury.
		Visited Canterbury Cathedral.
	27	Visited Duchy of Cornwall properties.
		Visited St Columb Major, Cornwall.
	28	Attended the King Edward IV quincentenary concert, St George's Chapel, Windsor.
June	1	Entertained at dinner by the New Zealand High Commissioner, Chelsea Square, London.
		Opened the Royal Preston Hospital, Lancashire.
		Opened the factory of Joseph Arnold and Company Ltd, Accrington.
	4	Accompanied the Prince of Wales to the Ball in aid of the United World Colleges, Broadlands, Romsey, Hampshire.
	6	Received the Prime Minister of Australia, Kensington Palace.

Engagements of **THE PRINCESS OF WALES**
August 1982–July 1983 (*continued*)

June	7	Attended the Taking the Salute at a massed bands display by the Prince of Wales' Division, Horse Guards' Parade.
	10	Took the salute at the Founder's Day Parade, Royal Hospital, Chelsea.
	11	Attended the Queen's Birthday Parade, Horse Guards' Parade, London.
	14	Left Heathrow Airport for an eighteen-day tour of Canada.
July	2	Arrived back in London from Canada.
	5	Attended a reception for those wounded in the South Atlantic and Northern Ireland, Kensington Palace.
	6	Attended a dinner in aid of the Help Poland Fund, Hatfield House, Hertfordshire. Visited the Elmhurst Ballet School, Camberley, Surrey.
	8	Opened the new Fisher-Price Toy Factory, Peterlee, County Durham.
	12	Opened Spencer House, St Andrew's Hospital, Northampton.
	13	Attended a garden party, Buckingham Palace.
	14	Gave a reception for people involved in community relations, Kensington Palace.
	15	Visited Kraft Producers in Dyfed.
	19	Entertained members of the Prince's Council to luncheon, Kensington Palace.
	20	Attended a rock gala in aid of the Prince's Trust, Dominion Theatre, Tottenham Court Road.
	21	Attended a Variety Club luncheon, Guildhall, London.
	22	Attended the opening of the 1983 King's Lynn Festival, Norfolk.
	26	Opened the new Grimsby General Hospital, Humberside.
	27	Attended a garden party, Buckingham Palace.

Engagements of **PRINCE ANDREW**
August 1982–July 1983

September	17	Returned in *HMS Invincible* from the Falkland Islands, Spithead.
November	13	Attended Festival of Remembrance, Royal Albert Hall, London.
	14	Laid wreath at the Cenotaph for Remembrance Day, London.
	18	Switched on the Christmas Lights and attended a reception, Regent Street, London.
December	10	Presented Royal Aero Club Annual Awards, RAF Museum, Hendon.
January	14	Attended the Aero Club's committee dinner, Piccadilly, London.
May	14	Visited Biggin Hill and opened the International Air Fair, Kent.
June	24	Opened the Mountbatten Centre, Alexandra Park, Portsmouth.
July	11	Opened the Falkland Islands exhibition, Fleet Air Museum, Yeovilton, Somerset.
	14	Left Heathrow Airport to attend the British America's Cup Ball, Newport, Rhode Island, USA.

Engagements of PRINCESS ANNE
August 1982-July 1983

August	4	Left London for Aberdeen, en route to Balmoral.
	5	Attended opening of Aberdeen Harbour Fish Market.
	22	Presented prizes at Junior European Three-Day Event Championships, Rotherfield, Hants.
	30	Attended Greater London Horse Show, Clapham Common.

September 8 Installed as Middle Warden of the Farriers Company, Innholders' Hall, London.
17 Welcomed *HMS Invincible* home from the Falkland Islands, Spithead.
22 Visited Dairy Farming Event and Agricultural Seminar, Stoneleigh.
23 Entertained President of Malawi, Buckingham Palace.
Present at NATO reception, Lancaster House, London.
28 Visited Wycliffe College, Stonehouse, Gloucestershire.
Attended prizegiving for Woman's Own Slimathlon '82, New Zealand House, London.
Attended Army Benevolent Fund Auction, Royal Hospital Chelsea.
29 Visited Royal Corps of Signals and attended a Falkland Islands reception, Blandford Camp, Dorset.

October 4 Attended Riding for the Disabled Championship, Horse of the Year Show, Wembley.
5 Admitted as Freeman and Honorary Liveryman of Carmen's Company, Guildhall, London.
6 Opened Integrated Care Wing of the Home Farm Trust, Frocester Manor, Stonehouse, Gloucestershire.
Attended reception for former members of the Royal Ulster Constabulary, London.
7 Opened runway extension, Manchester International Airport.
Visited Eastwood Heating Developments Ltd, Shirebrook, Derbyshire.
Attended Save the Children Fund rally, Worksop College, Nottinghamshire.
Attended Poppy Ball, Intercontinental Hotel, London.
8 Visited Pershore High School, Worcestershire.
Visited Army Medal Office, and West Mercia Police Headquarters, Droitwich.
Toured Royal British Legion flats, Redditch.
9 Attended the St John Cadet Spectacular, Royal Albert Hall, London.
11 Opened Spastics Society's riding school, Meldreth Manor School, Royston.
Visited Riding for the Disabled Group, Gaddesden Place, Hemel Hempstead.
12 Visited RNAS Culdrose.
19 Visited Westfield College, London.
19 Attended performance by Royal Winnipeg Ballet, Sadler's Wells Theatre, London.
20 Attended Annual National Service for Seafarers, St Paul's Cathedral, London.
Attended Horse of the Year Ball, London Hilton Hotel.
21 Attended Save the Children Fund Branches Meeting, Queen Elizabeth Hall, London.
Visited *HMS Raleigh*, Torpoint, Cornwall, and opened the Dauntless building.
Present at Trafalgar Night dinner, *HMS Raleigh*.
23 Left London for visits to Swaziland, Zimbabwe, Malawi, Kenya, Somalia, Djibouti, North Yemen and the Lebanon as President of Save the Children Fund.

November 12 Arrived back in London from the Lebanon.
16 Attended welcoming ceremonies for Queen Beatrix and Prince Claus of the Netherlands, Westminster Pier.
Attended a State banquet for Queen Beatrix and Prince Claus at Buckingham Palace.
20 Visited the 33rd Signal Regiment (Volunteers) at Liverpool.
Attended a regimental ball at the Alamein Territorial Army Centre, Liverpool.
26 Attended Royal Corps of Signals Dinner, Blandford Camp, Dorset.

Engagements of **PRINCESS ANNE**
August 1982-July 1983 *(continued)*

December	7	Attended a Save the Children Fund reception, St James's Palace.
	8	Visited the Save the Children Fund projects at Newcastle upon Tyne and Washington, Co Durham.
	9	Attended lecture organised by the Loriners' Company, Hackney.
	20	Attended "The Story of Christmas 1982" charity event, St George's Church, Hanover Square, London.
	23	Attended a Carol Concert for the Save the Children Fund, Royal Albert Hall.
January	19	Attended the presentation ceremony of London University degrees, Royal Albert Hall.
		Attended London University ecumenical service, Westminster Abbey.
		Visited the Linguists Group, Women's Transport Service, Duke of York's Headquarters, London.
	27	Presented British Forces Sporting Personality of the Year Award, Tower of London.
		Visited Headquarters of Save the Children Fund, Camberwell, London.
February	2	Attended the Court Ladies Dinner of the Farriers' Company, Innholders' Hall, London.
	16	Attended Central Council meeting of the National Union of Townswomen's Guilds, Baden-Powell House, London.
		Visited the YMCA Indian student hostel, Fitzroy Square, London.
	21	Attended the Farmers' Company livery dinner, Mansion House.
	22	Visited Canterbury Hall, University of London.
March	1	Planted a tree at Highfield School, Liphook, Hampshire.
		Visited Royal School for Daughters of Officers, Haslemere, Surrey.
		Attended a dinner given by Land Rover Ltd, Metropole Hotel, Birmingham.
	2	Visited the Poppy Factory, Richmond, Surrey.
	3	Visited Bilthoven, Netherlands, to attend the launching by Princess Juliana of the Dutch Save the Children Fund.
		Attended the Horse and Hound Dinner Dance, Grosvenor House, London.
	5	Attended the Rugby Football Union Lunch and the match between England and Scotland, Twickenham, Middlesex.
	8	Visited Wye College, Ashford, Kent.
	9	Attended the presentation ceremony of London University degrees, Royal Albert Hall.
		Attended the London University ecumenical service, St Paul's Cathedral.
	10	Attended a luncheon with members of the Saddlers' Company Council, Saddlers' Hall, London.
		Attended a reception to present life memberships, Students' Union, University of London.
	13	Attended a performance of *Fall in the Stars*, Hippodrome, Bristol.
	14	Attended the 30th Anniversary Dinner of the Bath Townswomen's Guild, Assembly Rooms, Bath.
	15	Attended a gala performance of "Y", Piccadilly Theatre, London.
	16	Attended a gala performance in aid of children's charities, Moulin Rouge, Paris.
	17	Presented the Ritz Charity Trophy, Cheltenham Race Course.
	20	Attended an awards ceremony for the British Academy of Film and Television Arts, Grosvenor House Hotel.
	22	Opened the new Crown Courts, Southwark, London.
		Attended the welcoming ceremonies for President Kaunda of Zambia, Victoria Station.
		Attended the State banquet given by the Queen at Buckingham Palace for President Kaunda of Zambia.

Engagements of **PRINCESS ANNE**
August 1982-July 1983 *(continued)*

March   **24**   Attended the State banquet given by President Kaunda of Zambia, Claridges Hotel, London.
        26   Attended the rugby match between Scotland and the Barbarians, and opened the East Stand, Murrayfield Stadium, Edinburgh.

April   **7**   Took the Lord High Admiral's Division, Britannia Royal Naval College, Dartmouth.
        10   Attended the Royal Lymington Cup yacht racing championships, Hampshire.
        19   Opened Elizabeth Curtis Centre for Disabled Riders, Bromham Hospital, Bedfordshire.
                Opened new galleries at Percival David Foundation School of Oriental and African Studies, Malet Street, London.
                Attended a charity evening of greyhound racing, White City, London.
        22   Left Heathrow Airport to visit Japan, Hong Kong and Pakistan.

May   **6**   Arrived at Gatwick Airport on her return from Pakistan.
       9   Attended a service of thanksgiving for King Edward VI Schools, Birmingham.
               Visited the factory of Metropolitan Cammell, Birmingham.
               Attended a reception and dinner in aid of the Missions to *Seaman*, Albany Hotel, Birmingham.
       10   Attended a performance of *Edith et Marcel*, Queen Elizabeth Hall, London.
       11   Opened Oaklands Community School, Southampton.
               Opened Cranleigh Paddock, Lyndhurst, Hampshire.
               Opened new extensions at Lymington Infirmary, and visited Lymington Hospital, Hampshire.
       12   Attended a floral luncheon in aid of charities, Savoy Hotel.
       17   Opened the exhibition *Signature Collection of Artists in Make-up* at Christies, London.
               Visited the Marconi Space and Defence Systems, Stanmore, Middlesex.
       18   Attended the Townswomen's Guild national council meeting, Royal Albert Hall.
               Attended the Launderers' Company banquet, Launderers' Hall, London.
       19   Attended the presentation by the Queen of new standards to the Household Cavalry, Horse Guards' Parade, London.
       20   Toured the Factory of Critchley Brothers Ltd, Brimscombe, Glos.
               Visited Selwyn School, Gloucester.
               Attended the presentation ceremony of the Gloucester Youth Association Football League, Gloucester Leisure Centre.
       26   Attended the Annual General Meeting of the WRNS Benevolent Trust, Seymour Street, London.

June   **6**   Visited Carlton Junior School, Gloucester.
              Toured the High School for Girls, Denmark Road, Gloucester.
              Toured the Gloucestershire Fire and Rescue Service Training Complex, Gloucester fire station.
       7   Attended the Variety Club Ladies' Luncheon, Hilton Hotel, London.
       8   Attended the Fishmongers' Company Court Ladies' dinner, Fishmongers' Hall, London.
       10   Attended a Farriers' Company luncheon, City Livery Club, London.
       11   Attended the Queen's Birthday Parade, Horse Guards' Parade, London.
       14   Opened the new extension to the computer centre, Guildford Street, London.
              Opened the Chest Unit extension, Medical School, King's College Hospital, Denmark Hill, London.
       17   Attended the Grenadier Guards regimental ball, Syon House, Middlesex.
              Opened Baggeridge Country Park, Staffordshire.
              Toured the factory of T I Tower Housewares Ltd, Stafford.
              Toured the Wombourne Ounsdale High School, Staffordshire.

Engagements of **PRINCESS ANNE**
August 1982-July 1983 *(continued)*

June 21   Attended the Lawn Tennis Championships, Wimbledon.
Attended the Garden Ball, Kensington.
22   Visited St Mary's Hospital Medical School, Paddington.
Attended the Vincent's dinner, Savoy Hotel, London.
23   Opened the new Advanced Technology Hercules Simulator, RAF Lyneham.
24   Entertained Prince Naruhito of Japan to luncheon, Gatcombe Park.
25   Attended a summer fete, Upton Park, Poole, Dorset.
26   Attended the Royal Signals Association reunion, Catterick Camp, Yorks.
27   Opened a new arena at Berril Farm, for the Ackworth Group, Riding for the Disabled Association, Yorkshire.
Opened the Systime Computers Ltd factory, Leeds.
Visited St John's Ambulance and Nursing Cadets, Roundhay Park, Leeds.
28   Opened Arnwood House, Carlisle.
Visited Carlisle Civic Centre, and the leisure centre.
Opened Lonsdale House, St Bees School, Cumbria.
29   Attended a garden party, Palace of Holyroodhouse, Edinburgh.
Visited Lanark Grammar School, Strathclyde.
Visited the Border Group, Riding for the Disabled Association, Jedburgh.
30   Reviewed The Royal Scots (The Royal Regiment), Holyrood Park.
Appointed as Colonel-in-Chief of The Royal Scots.
Attended a regimental dinner, North British Hotel, Edinburgh.
Attended a garden party, Palace of Holyroodhouse.
Opened the Old Course Golf and Country Club, St Andrews, Fife.

July 1   Took the salute at a march past by The Royal Scots, Princes Street, Edinburgh.
Attended a luncheon marking the 350th anniversary of The Royal Scots, City Chambers, Edinburgh.
Visited the Marine Biological Station, Millport, Cumbrae.
Attended the Royal Scots Regimental Officers' Ball, Assembly Rooms, Edinburgh.
2   Presented awards and attended a fete for the Save the Children Fund, Castle Howard, Yorkshire.
3   Attended a Farriers Company reception, Luton Hoo, Bedfordshire.
7   Visited RAF Wildenrath, BAOR, Western Germany.
11   Opened new extension to the sixth form centre, Felixstowe College, Suffolk.
Visited Haverhill Meat Products Ltd, Suffolk.
12   Visited the Coventry and Warwickshire Awards Trust Centre, Coventry.
Attended luncheon at Massey Ferguson Training Centre, Stareton, Warwickshire.
Toured the factories of T I Matrix Ltd, and J & J Cash Ltd, Coventry.
Opened a congress of Obstetrics and Gynaecology, Birmingham Town Hall.
18   Toured Maingay House for the elderly, Aylsham, Norfolk.
Visited Norfolk groups of the Riding for the Disabled Association, Salhouse.
Visited the St John's Nursing Cadets, Ike Centre, Norfolk.
19   Attended a garden party, Buckingham Palace.
21   Opened the Nailsworth and Forest Green Scout group H.Q. Gloucestershire.
Opened the mid-Counties Autistic Society's building, Minchinhampton, Gloucestershire.
25   Attended a gala charity concert, the Hexagon, Reading.
26   Attended a performance of the Royal Tournament, Earl's Court.
28   Opened a scanner unit, Broomfield Hospital, Chelmsford.
Toured the factory of Britvic, Chelmsford.

Engagements of THE QUEEN MOTHER
August 1982-July 1983

August	5	Opened Kessock Bridge, Beauly Firth.
	18	Opened Royal British Legion's Caberfeidh Court, Wick.
October	20	Visited Central Library, Aberdeen.
		Named British Rail Locomotive *The Queen Mother*, Aberdeen Railway Station.
	25	Visited Aberdeen-Angus Cattle Society Show, Perth.
	27	Received the Prime Minister of Luxembourg.
		Duties as Counsellor of State, Clarence House.
	28	Attended the Press Club's Centenary Reception, International Press Centre, London.
	29	Duties as Counsellor of State, Buckingham Palace.
November	2	Attended reception marking Diamond Jubilee of Past and Present Nurses League of St Mary's Hospital, Paddington.
	3	Visited Queen Mary's London Needlework Guild, St James's Palace.
	4	Opened the Cracking Complex, Mobil Oil Refinery, Coryton, Essex.
	8	Attended the Royal Variety Performance, Theatre Royal, Drury Lane, London.
	9	Laid the foundation stone of St Catherine's Hospice, Crawley.
	11	Planted a Cross, Royal British Legion Field of Remembrance, St Margaret's Church, Westminster.
		Attended WRVS reception, St James's Palace.
	12	Launched Keep Britain Tidy Group's Beautiful Britain campaign, Hyde Park.
	13	Attended Festival of Remembrance, Royal Albert Hall, London.
	14	Attended Remembrance Day Service, Cenotaph, London.
	15	Attended the Memorial Service for Lord Rupert Nevill, St Margaret's Church, Westminster.
	16	Entertained Queen Beatrix and Prince Claus of the Netherlands to tea at Clarence House.
		Attended State banquet for Queen Beatrix and Prince Claus at Buckingham Palace.
	17	Presented certificates and awards at the Royal College of Music, London.
		Attended reception given by London University Contingent Officers' Training Corps, Senate House, London.
	18	Attended a State banquet given by Queen Beatrix of the Netherlands, Hampton Court Palace.
	30	Attended inaugural meeting of the Court of Patrons, Royal College of Obstetricians and Gynaecologists, London.
December	2	Visited the *Queen Elizabeth 2*, Southampton.
	3	Attended service to mark the Diamond Jubilee of the Bible Reading Fellowship.
	7	Visited Westfield College, University of London, to open the Queen Mother's Hall.
	8	Visited Royal Smithfield Show, Earl's Court.
		Dined with Benchers of the Middle Temple.
	15	Presented Children of Courage Awards, Westminster Abbey.
	21	Attended a "Christmas Evening" in aid of charity, St James's Palace.
February	3	Named the bulk carrier *Pacific Patriot*, Glasgow.
	15	Opened St David's Hall, Cardiff and attended a concert there.
	22	Attended a performance of *The Count of Luxembourg*, Sadler's Wells Theatre.
	23	Lunched with the Court of Assistants of the Merchant Taylors' Company, Merchant Taylors' Hall, London.
		Visited St Martin-in-the-Fields, London.
March	1	Held an Investiture on behalf of the Queen, Buckingham Palace.

Engagements of **THE QUEEN MOTHER**
August 1982-July 1983 *(continued)*

March 8   Visited Queen Alexandra Hospital Home, Gifford House, Worthing, Sussex.
9   Attended a reception given by the Indian Army Association, St James's Palace.
10   Laid the foundation stone for a new building at St Mary's Hospital, Paddington.
14   Opened the Duke of Beaufort Court, Royal British Legion Flats, Gloucester.
17   Presented shamrocks to the 1st Battalion Irish Guards at Oxford Barracks, Munster, to celebrate St Patrick's Day.
21   Attended the Royal Film Performance, Odeon Theatre, Leicester Square.
22   Entertained President Kaunda of Zambia to tea at Clarence House.
       Attended the State banquet for President Kaunda at Buckingham Palace.
24   Attended the Annual General Meeting of Queen Mary's London Needlework Guild, St James's Palace.
       Attended the State banquet given by President Kaunda of Zambia at Claridges, London.
25   Attended a luncheon of the Grand Committee of Benevolent Society of St Patrick, Bucks Club, London.
30   Attended a performance by the Windsor and Eton Operatic Society, Farrer Theatre, Eton College.

April 12   Opened the Bomber Command Museum, RAF Hendon.
14   Attended the service of the Royal Victorian Order, St George's Chapel, Windsor.
19   Unveiled the foundation plaque of the Clore Gallery for the Turner Museum, Tate Gallery, London.
20   Opened the luncheon club and day centre for West Indian elderly folk, Railton Road, Brixton.
       Attended a dinner at Admiralty House for former Captains of the Ark Royal.
24   Attended the Queen's Scouts' Parade, Windsor Castle.
26   Opened York House, a new home and hospice of the West Ham Central Mission, East London.
27   Opened the Irradiation Unit, Royal Marsden Hospital, Sutton.
       Attended a reception given by the London Division of the Royal Naval Reserve, Fishmongers' Hall, London.
28   Laid a wreath on the grave of David Livingstone, Westminster Abbey.

May 3   Attended a Gala performance of *Manon Lescaut*, Royal Opera House, Covent Garden.
10   Visited the Royal Anglian Regiment, Colchester.
11   Attended a gala performance of the Magic Flute in aid of the Museums' Association, Coliseum Theatre, London.
26   Attended a performance of *Bugsy Malone*, Her Majesty's Theatre, Haymarket.
       Opened the Tradescant Garden, St Mary at Lambeth, London.
27   Attended a ceremony marking the restoration of the Lutyens Memorial to King George V, Windsor.

June 3   Attended a luncheon at University College London, to mark its 150th anniversary.
7   Opened the Australian Studies Centre, and the premises of the Institute of Commonwealth Studies, Russell Square, London.
11   Attended the Queen's Birthday Parade, Horse Guards' Parade, London.
13   Attended the Chapter of the Order of the Garter, Windsor Castle.
       Attended the Installation Service for the Order of the Garter, St George's Chapel.
19   Attended dinner with the Secretary of State for Northern Ireland, Hillsborough Castle, Belfast.
20   Reviewed units of the Territorial Army, St Patrick's Barracks, Ballymena.

Engagements of **THE QUEEN MOTHER**
August 1982-July 1983 *(continued)*

June	**23**	Visited the Helicopter Squadron, RAF Shawbury.
	24	Attended a reception for Commonwealth, American and European exchange teachers, Lancaster House, London.
	28	Attended the dedication of the Household Cavalry Regiment's Memorial stone, Hyde Park.
		Attended the Festival Service for the Friends of St Paul's, St Paul's Cathedral, London.
July	**1**	Left London for Oslo to attend the 80th birthday celebrations of King Olav V of Norway.
	5	Visited the 3rd Battalion, Light Infantry, Tidworth.
	6	Visited gardens in Camden and Islington, for the London Gardens Society.
	7	Visited the United Biscuits Factory, Harlesden, London.
		Visited the exhibition of Tudor and Early Stuart miniatures, Victoria and Albert Museum, London.
	8	Visited the Royal Windsor Rose and Horticultural Society Show, Windsor.
	9	Opened the Queen Mother Theatre, Hitchin, Hertfordshire.
	13	Attended a garden party, Buckingham Palace.
	14	Visited Chailey Heritage Craft School.
	19	Attended a performance of the Royal Tournament, Earl's Court.
	20	Visited the East of England Agricultural Show, Peterborough.

Engagements of PRINCESS MARGARET
August 1982-July 1983

September	8	Opened 6th Congress of Anaesthesiology, Royal Festival Hall.
	9	Attended the American Medical International Staff Association Ball, Grosvenor House, London.
	21	Present at fashion show arranged by the European Commission for the Promotion of Silk, Guildhall, London.
		Attended Bob Hope British Classic Golf Tournament, Grosvenor House Hotel.
	22	Attended reception given by 4th International Migraine Symposium, Cunard International Hotel.
	23	Attended Press Club's Overseas Press Night Dinner, International Press Centre, London.
	30	Attended Royal Highland Fusiliers' luncheon, Belleisle Hotel, Ayr.
October	7	Attended Girl Guides Executive Committee meeting, Buckingham Palace Road.
	12	Visited Wakefield Cathedral and the Treacy Memorial Hall, Wakefield, Yorkshire.
		Opened Wakefield District College and visited Dunlop Sports Company Distribution Centre.
		Attended concert in aid of St John Council, Huddersfield, West Yorkshire.
	13	Duties as Counsellor of State, Buckingham Palace.
	15	Visited St Christopher's Nursery School, North London.
	18	Duties as Counsellor of State, Buckingham Palace.
	21	Visited Lichfield exhibition of pictures, Kodak Library, High Holborn, London.
	27	Duties as Counsellor of State, Clarence House.
	28	Attended the Cartier Gala Dinner, Grosvenor House Hotel, London.
	29	Duties as Counsellor of State, Buckingham Palace.
November	2	Visited Princess Margaret Hospital for nurses and midwives prizegiving ceremony, Swindon, Wiltshire.
	3	Attended the State Opening of Parliament, Palace of Westminster.
	10	Attended Queen Alexandra's Royal Army Nursing Corps Reception, Royal Hospital, Chelsea.
	11	Opened 1982 Caravan Camping Holiday Show, Earl's Court, London.
	15	Attended the Memorial Service for Lord Rupert Nevill, St Margaret's Church, Westminster.
	16	Attended welcoming ceremonies for Queen Beatrix and Prince Claus of the Netherlands, Westminster Pier.
		Attended the State Banquet for Queen Beatrix and Prince Claus at Buckingham Palace.
	18	Attended a State Banquet given by Queen Beatrix of the Netherlands, Hampton Court Palace.
	22	Attended a charity performance of *Camelot*, Apollo Victoria Theatre, London.
	23	Attended Annual General Meeting of the Friends of the Elderly and Gentlefolks Help, Merchant Taylors' Hall, London.
	25	Opened the International Prosthodontic Symposium, Royal Lancaster Hotel.
	30	Re-opened Theatre Royal, Bath.
		Attended gala performance of *A Midsummer Night's Dream*, Theatre Royal, Bath.
December	1	Visited Sainsbury's supermarket, Green Park Station, Bath.
		Visited Willenhall Social Club, and Hagard Youth Centre, Coventry.
		Attended Silver Jubilee service of St John the Divine Church, Willenhall.
	2	Attended gala performance of ballet, Royal Opera House, Covent Garden.
	9	Attended Carol Service for Haberdashers' Aske's Hatcham Schools, Greenwich.
January	19	Attended the British Film Institute's film show, National Film Theatre, London.
	30	Attended a concert given by the Halle Orchestra, Manchester.

Engagements of **PRINCESS MARGARET**
August 1982-July 1983 *(continued)*

March **16** Attended the premiere of *Marilyn*, Adelphi Theatre, London.

           22 Attended the welcoming ceremonies for President Kaunda of Zambia, Victoria Station.

                   Attended the State banquet for President Kaunda of Zambia at Buckingham Palace.

           23 Opened new extensions to Royal College of Nursing Headquarters at Ty Maeth, Cardiff.

           30 Attended the re-dedication ceremony of *HMS Illustrious*, Portsmouth.

April **7** Presided at the Annual General Meeting of the Scottish Children's League, City Chambers, Glasgow.

                   Presided at the Annual General Meeting of the Royal Scottish Society for Prevention of Cruelty to Children, City Chambers, Glasgow.

           11 Visited the Victoria League students' hostel, Leinster Square, London.

           13 Visited RAF Lyneham, Wiltshire.

           14 Attended the service of the Royal Victorian Order, St George's Chapel, Windsor.

           19 Attended the centenary annual meeting of the NSPCC, Liverpool.

                   Attended a reception given by the Lord Mayor of Liverpool, Town Hall, Liverpool.

                   Visited the workshops of Gostins Ltd, Halewood, Liverpool.

           20 Visited the factory of Bryant and May, Garston, Lancashire.

                   Attended a concert for the National Art Collections Fund, Barbican Centre, London.

           26 Visited Perrins House, Malvern, and the Friends of the Elderly and Gentlefolks' Help, Davenham.

May **5** Attended a reception given by the Prime Minister, 10 Downing Street.

           10 Attended a concert at Sutton Place, Guildford, Surrey.

           12 Visited the Haberdashers' Monmouth Schools, Gwent.

           13 Inspected renovations to the fort at Tilbury, Essex.

           15 Opened the Leicestershire Headquarters of the Girl Guides Association, Victoria Park, Leicester.

                   Attended a gala performance for St John Ambulance, De Montfort Hall, Leicester.

           16 Attended the Royal Caledonian Ball, Grosvenor House, Park Lane, London.

           18 Undertook engagements as Chancellor of the University of Keele, Staffordshire.

           19 Undertook further engagements as Chancellor of Keele University.

           20 Attended a gala concert for St John Ambulance Association, Barbican Centre, London.

           22 Attended a concert for the National Art Collections Fund, Eastleach, Gloucestershire.

           23 Attended the Chelsea Flower Show, London.

           25 Attended an International Federation of Newspaper Publishers' reception, Guildhall, London.

           26 Visited the headquarters of the Royal Scottish Society for the Prevention of Cruelty to Children, Edinburgh.

                   Visited the Princess Margaret Rose Orthopaedic Hospital, Edinburgh.

June **1** Visited the Suffolk Agricultural Association Show, Ipswich.

           2 Visited the Pro Corda Trust, Leiston Abbey House.

                   Visited the craft workshops and young people's camp, Thornham Magna.

           3 Visited Bury St Edmunds Cathedral, and Theatre Royal.

           6 Attended the annual general meeting of the Girl Guides Association, Merchant Taylors' Hall, London.

           20 Opened the Oliver Messel exhibition, Victoria and Albert Museum.

           21 Opened the *Light Dimensions* exhibition, Royal Photographic Society's Centre, Bath.

           22 Attended the State Opening of Parliament, Palace of Westminster.

Engagements of **PRINCESS MARGARET**
August 1982-July 1983 *(continued)*

June	**28**	Presided at a degree congregation, University of Keele, Stoke-on-Trent.
	29	Attended the annual council meeting of the NSPCC, Euston Road, London.
		Received Prince Naruhito of Japan, Kensington Palace.
	30	Visited the Haberdashers' Aske's Boys' School, Elstree, Herts., and opened the preparatory department.
July	**4**	Attended a Victoria League for Commonwealth Friendship reception, Carpenters' Hall, London.
	5	Attended a Royal Ballet School performance, Sadler's Wells Theatre, London.
	8	Represented Queen Elizabeth the Queen Mother at the Memorial Service for the Rev Dr Eric Abbott, Westminster Abbey.
	20	Attended the Royal International Horse Show, White City, London.
	21	Attended a performance of the Royal Tournament, Earl's Court.
	25	Attended a performance of the Royal Ballet, Royal Opera House, Covent Garden.
	26	Visited the Duchess of Kent's Military Hospital, Catterick, Yorkshire.
	28	Visited the International Camp of the Girl Guides Association, Coedarhydyglyn, South Glamorgan.

Engagements of **PRINCESS ALICE**
August 1982-July 1983

October	1	Attended Pearly Kings and Queens Annual Charity Ball, County Hall, London.
	11	Attended Gilbert and Sullivan gala, Royal Albert Hall, London.
	15	Attended meeting of St John Opthalmic Hospital Ladies' Guild, London.
	19	Presented Brighter Kensington and Chelsea Scheme awards for 1982, Chelsea Town Hall.
November	2	Visited East Park Home for Infirm Children, Glasgow.
		Attended charity musical extravaganza, Kelvin Hall, Glasgow.
	3	Opened Mitchell Library Extension and Theatre, Glasgow.
	13	Attended Festival of Remembrance, Royal Albert Hall, London.
	14	Attended Remembrance Day service, Cenotaph, London.
	16	Attended the State banquet for Queen Beatrix and Prince Claus of the Netherlands at Buckingham Palace.
	17	Attended Queen's Nursing Institute Annual Meeting, Portland Place, London.
	23	Attended the East African Women's League General Meeting, Brompton Road.
	25	Attended Service of Thanksgiving for Help the Aged, Westminster Abbey.
		Visited London House for Overseas Graduates, Mecklenburgh Square.
December	1	Attended reception given by Royal Green Jackets' Ladies' Guild, Tower of London.
	2	Visited Park Lane Fair, London.
	15	Attended a concert in aid of St John Hospitals Centenary Celebration, Smith Square, London.
March	17	Visited Derby Lonsdale's College of Higher Education, Derby.
	22	Attended the State banquet given for President Kaunda of Zambia, Buckingham Palace.
April	9	Attended the centenary of 7-a-side rugby, the Greenyards, Melrose, Scotland.
	14	Attended the service of the Royal Victorian Order, St George's Chapel, Windsor.
	24	Attended a concert in aid of St John Musical Society, Barbican Centre, London.
May	17	Visited the North London Collegiate School, Edgware, and opened the McLauchlan Theatre.
	21	Attended the dedication of a window, Grafton Underwood Parish Church, Northants.
	23	Visited the Chelsea Flower Show, London.
June	10	Opened a flower and art festival, Church of the Holy Sepulchre, Northampton.
	11	Attended the Queen's Birthday Parade, Horse Guards' Parade, London.
	13	Attended the Officers Club reception of the King's Own Scottish Borderers, Army and Navy Club, London.
	19	Attended the Royal Leicestershire Regiment's annual parade service, Leicester Cathedral.
July	5	Visited the Royal Agricultural Society Show, Stoneleigh, Warwickshire.
	14	Presented awards for the Royal Academy of Music, London.
	15	Attended a *Fete champetre*, Wherwell Priory, Andover.
	21	Visited the East of England Show, Peterborough.
	27	Attended a garden party at Buckingham Palace.
	28	Attended a performance of the Royal Tournament, Earl's Court.

Engagements of **THE DUKE AND DUCHESS OF GLOUCESTER**
August 1982-July 1983

September	2	The Duke visited Quincentenary Festival of Berwick-on-Tweed.
	17	The Duchess opened Flower and Craft Festival, Botanical Gardens, Birmingham.
	22	The Duke attended East of England Agricultural Society's exhibition, Newport Pagnall, Buckinghamshire.
		The Duke opened Peterborough Volunteer Fire Brigade Station.
	25	The Duchess attended re-dedication service and Investiture for the Order of St John, St David's Cathedral, Wales.
		The Duchess attended Omnibus' Dinner/Dance, Royal Lancaster Hotel.
	29	The Duchess visited five children's homes and clubs in Gloucestershire.
	30	The Duke visited four schools and colleges in West Sussex.
October	2	The Duke left London to visit India as President of the British Consultants' Bureau, and in Cyprus, to visit the 1st Battalion Gloucestershire Regiment.
		The Duchess visited National Association for Gifted Children Explorers Club, Kilburn, London.
	5	The Duchess visited British Library of Tape Recordings, London.
	7	The Duchess visited Franklyn Community Support Unit.
		The Duchess opened Civil Service Sports Council Clubhouse, Exeter.
	10	The Duchess present at a charity Ballet Gala, Sadler's Wells Theatre, London.
	11	The Duchess left London to visit Royal Army Educational Corps Schools and Units in Cyprus.
	16	The Duke and Duchess returned to London from Cyprus.
	18	The Duke launched Boys' Clubs Club Week, Guildhall, London.
	19	The Duke attended a Medical Congress Dinner, St Bartholomew's Hospital, London.
	20	The Duke visited the Motor Show, Birmingham.
		The Duke opened Parkway Hospital, Solihull.
	21	The Duke visited the European Commission, Brussels.
	26	The Duke opened Spencer House, for British Foundation for Age Research, Richmond, Surrey.
	27	The Duke visited Boys' Clubs in Berkshire.
		The Duke visited Gillette UK Ltd, Reading.
		The Duke attended reception, Shire Hall, Reading.
	28	The Duke presided at British Consultants' Bureau Annual General Meeting, Piccadilly, London.
	29	The Duke attended 1982 Oyster Feast, Colchester, Essex.
		The Duke visited Oxley Parker School, Colchester.
		The Duke visited offices of LEPRA and opened new insurance company headquarters, Colchester.
November	1	The Duke opened *Living with Energy* exhibition, Edinburgh.
	2	The Duke and Duchess visited Southampton where the Duchess launched *HMS Gloucester*, Woolston Shipyard.
	3	The Duke and Duchess attended the State Opening of Parliament, Palace of Westminster.
		The Duke presented Professional Portfolio Awards 1982, Glaziers' Hall, London.
	4	The Duchess visited National Association of Gifted Children Headquarters, London.
	6	The Duchess attended finals of the Wightman Cup, Royal Albert Hall, London.
	9	The Duchess opened "Women and Tourism" conference, Inn on the Park, London.
	10	The Duke attended Institute of Advanced Motorists Luncheon, Pall Mall, London.
		The Duchess attended Royal Danish Orchestra concert, Royal Festival Hall, London.
	11	The Duke was admitted as a Royal Fellow of the Society of Antiquaries of London, .pa Burlington House, Piccadilly.

Engagements of THE DUKE AND DUCHESS OF GLOUCESTER
August 1982-July 1983 *(continued)*

November **13** The Duke and Duchess attended Festival of Remembrance, Royal Albert Hall, London.
 14 The Duke and Duchess attended Remembrance Day Service, Cenotaph, London.
 14 The Duke attended a Festival of India concert, London Coliseum.
 15 The Duke attended a reception at the Banqueting House, Whitehall, London.
 16 The Duke and Duchess attended welcoming ceremonies for Queen Beatrix and Prince Claus of the Netherlands, Westminster Pier.
 The Duke and Duchess attended the State banquet for Queen Beatrix and Prince Claus at Buckingham Palace.
 18 The Duke opened Blue Circle Cement Industries Depot, Carlisle, Cumbria.
 The Duke visited Abbot Hall Art Gallery and the Museum of Lakeland Life and Industry, Kendal, Cumbria.
 The Duke opened Abberfield Society's Crossfield House home, Arnside, Cumbria.
 The Duke and Duchess attended the State banquet given by Queen Beatrix of the Netherlands, Hampton Court Palace.
 23 The Duke attended Gala concert in aid of MENCAP, Royal Festival Hall.

December **2** The Duke inaugurated new premises of the German Historical Institute and attended a lecture there, Bloomsbury Square, London.
 7 The Duke and Duchess attended the Anglo-Danish Society Dinner Dance, Royal Garden Hotel, London.
 8 The Duchess attended the St John Royal Ball, Hotel Intercontinental, London.
 13 The Duke visited National Coal Board Mining Research and Development Centre, Bretby, Derbyshire.
 The Duchess attended lecture at Westfield College, London.

January **12** The Duke attended a luncheon given by the Pattenmakers' Company, Pewterers' Hall, London.
 The Duke opened the Victorian Society Silver Jubilee Exhibition, Heinz Gallery, London.
 13 The Duke and Duchess attended the opening by Queen Sophie of Spain of the Murillo Exhibition, Royal Academy of Arts, London.
 18 The Duke opened Equitable Life Assurance Company's Headquarters, Aylesbury, Buckinghamshire.
 20 The Duke attended the council meeting and luncheon of the Royal Smithfield Club, Butchers' Hall, London.
 21 The Duke attended the Royal Engineers briefing for Honorary Colonels, Brompton Barracks, Chatham, Kent.
 25 The Duke attended a reception of the Heritage of London Trust, Mansion House, London.
 27 The Duke visited *HMS Illustrious*, Portsmouth, Hampshire.

February **2** The Duke opened a new audio visual aids centre, Little Ann Street, Bristol.
 The Duke visited Bristol United Press offices, and saw the restoration of Brunel's Temple Meads Terminus.
 24 The Duke attended a reception to mark the 25th anniversary of the Victorian Society, St James's Palace.

March **2** The Duchess attended a performance by the English National Opera, London Coliseum.
 3 The Duke attended a dinner given by the British-Mexican Society, Naval and Military Club, Piccadilly, London.
 8 The Duke and Duchess began a three-day visit to Paris where the Duke toured an agricultural show.

Engagements of **THE DUKE AND DUCHESS OF GLOUCESTER**
August 1982-July 1983 *(continued)*

March	**15**	The Duke opened information technology centre, Hanley.
	16	The Duke visited Messrs Widnell and Trollope, Wilton Road, London.
		The Duchess attended annual general meeting of the Women Caring Trust, Church House, Westminster.
	17	The Duke attended the conference of the World Council for Education in World Citizenship, and presented awards, Logan Hall, London.
	18	The Duchess attended the Festival of Queens, York University.
	22	The Duke and Duchess welcomed President Kaunda of Zambia at Gatwick Airport at the beginning of his State visit to Britain.
		The Duke and Duchess attended the State banquet for President Kaunda at Buckingham Palace.
	23	The Duke attended a concert given by Leicestershire Schools Symphony Orchestra, Banqueting Hall, Whitehall.
	24	The Duke and Duchess attended a State banquet given by President Kaunda at Claridges.
	25	The Duke attended the luncheon of the Sino-British Trade Council, Dorchester Hotel, London.
April	**11**	The Duke attended a dinner given by the Chancellor of the Priory of the Order of St John of Scotland, Edinburgh.
	12	The Duke attended the installation of the Prior of the Order of St John of Scotland, St Andrews and St George Church, Edinburgh.
	13	The Duke addressed the Business in the Community national conference, Goldsmiths' Hall, London.
	14	The Duke attended the service of the Royal Victorian Order, St George's Chapel, Windsor.
	19	The Duchess visited the Royal Army Educational Corps, Aldershot, Hampshire.
	20	The Duke opened new civic offices, Woking, Surrey.
	21	The Duchess opened the Greater Manchester Police Headquarters, Manchester.
		The Duchess visited Princess Christian College, Manchester.
		The Duchess opened Wallness Gamma Camera Unit, Royal Manchester Children's Hospital, Pendlebury.
	22	The Duchess attended the annual council dinner of the Medical Women's Federation, York.
	26	The Duke opened a play park for disabled children, Birmingham.
		The Duke opened a warden service central control room, Bush House, Birmingham.
		The Duke visited Bells Farm Community Centre, Druids Heath, Birmingham.
		The Duke opened Compton Grange Housing Scheme, Cradley Heath, Birmingham.
	28	The Duke visited Robert Burns Cottage and Museum, Alloway.
		The Duke visited Ayr Agricultural show, Scotland.
		The Duchess opened Dorton House School for the Blind, Sevenoaks, Kent.
May	**3**	The Duke attended a Royal Geographical Society reception, Kensington Gore, London.
	4	The Duke unveiled commemorative tablet to Princess Alice of Athlone, Kensington Town Hall.
	5	The Duke opened the Building Conservation Trust's Care of Buildings Exhibition, Hampton Court, Middlesex.
	8	The Duchess left London to visit the USA in connection with *Britain Salutes New York* and the Victorian Society of America.
	11	The Duke attended a dinner to mark the quincentenary of Richard III's accession, Guildhall, London.
	12	The Duke opened the Fitzwilliam Hospital, Peterborough.

Engagements of THE DUKE AND DUCHESS OF GLOUCESTER
August 1982-July 1983 *(continued)*

May 15   The Duke left London to visit Korea in connection with the centenary of Anglo-Korean diplomatic relations.

16   The Duchess presented the Radio Times awards, Langham Gallery, London.

17   The Duchess visited RAF Sealand, Clwyd.

18   The Duchess attended a charity dress show, India House, London.

23   The Duchess visited the Chelsea Flower Show, London.

24   The Duke opened Deringate Centre for Information and Technology, Northampton.

25   The Duke opened Royal Hospital School, Holbrook, Suffolk.
The Duke opened Harwich Day Hospital, Essex.
The Duchess attended the Annual General Meeting of Counsel and Care for the Elderly, Plaisterers' Hall, London.

26   The Duke visited boys' clubs in South and West Yorkshire.
The Duchess attended a charity gala concert, Royal Albert Hall, London.

31   The Duke unveiled a walkway indicator, Trafalgar Square, London.
The Duke attended a reception and luncheon given by the Canadian High Commissioner, Canada House.

June 3   The Duke left RAF Northolt to visit Ottawa in connection with St John's Ambulance.
The Duchess opened the Nordoff Robbins Music Therapy Centre, Leighton Place, London.
The Duchess attended a Royal Army Educational Corps Ladies' Dinner, Beaconsfield, Bucks.

5   The Duchess attended Dame Ninette de Valois' 85th birthday ballet gala, Sadler's Wells, London.

6   The Duke returned to London from Ottawa.

7   The Duke attended a briefing for Nuffield Farming Scholars, Wye, Kent.

8   The Duke and Duchess attended a massed bands display by the Prince of Wales' Division, Horse Guards' Parade.

11   The Duke and Duchess attended the Queen's Birthday Parade, Horse Guards' Parade.

12   The Duchess attended the finals of the Stella Artois Grass Court Championships, Queen's Club.

13   The Duke attended the NAC Housing Association Ltd conference and opened old people's bungalows, Hadnall.
The Duke opened the Court and Parade and visited Pride Hill pedestrianisation scheme, Shrewsbury.

15   The Duchess attended a WRVS meeting, Bromley, Kent.

16   The Duchess attended a concert for the London Suzuki Group, Fishmongers' Hall, London.

20   The Duke opened a new laboratory at the Institute of Cancer Research, Sutton, Surrey.

21   The Duke visited boys' clubs in Kent.
The Duke attended a boys' clubs reception, County Hall, Maidstone, Kent.

22   The Duke and Duchess attended the State Opening of Parliament, Palace of Westminster.

23   The Duke visited RAF Honington, Suffolk.

25   The Duchess attended the Lawn Tennis Association Ball, London Hilton Hotel.

28   The Duke carried out engagements in Yorkshire to mark the quincentenary of the accession of King Richard III.

29   The Duke attended the Grand Priors' Advisory Council of the Order of St John, Clerkenwell, London.
The Duke and Duchess attended a Royal College of Art gala fashion show, Kensington.

30   The Duchess attended the Lawn Tennis Championships, Wimbledon, London.
The Duke attended the Master's Dinner of the Company of Guilders, Guildhall, London.

Engagements of **THE DUKE AND DUCHESS OF GLOUCESTER**
August 1982-July 1983 *(continued)*

July 7   The Duke visited the Royal Agricultural Society Show, Stoneleigh, Warwickshire.
The Duchess attended a Baby Life Support Systems seminar, Chandos House, London.

8   The Duke opened new extensions to County Hall, Beverley.
The Duke visited Beverley Priory and Minster.

9   The Duchess attended the annual commemoration service for the Order of St John, Cardiff.
The Duchess attended the Hospitallers' Club of Wales' banquet, City Hall, Cardiff.

12   The Duke opened the new headquarters of the Institute of Advanced Motorists, Chiswick, London.

14   The Duke presided at the Annual General Meeting of the Cancer Research Campaign, St James's Palace.
The Duke and Duchess attended a Victorian Extravaganza, Claremont Landscape Garden, Esher, Surrey.

15   The Duke attended the Annual General Meeting and luncheon of the National Association of Boys Clubs, Saddlers' Hall, London.

18   The Duke carried out engagements as President of the East Midlands Tourist Board, in Derbyshire, Nottinghamshire and Lincolnshire.

19   The Duke and Duchess visited the East of England Show, Peterborough.

22   The Duchess visited the Army Apprentices' College, Chepstow.

23   The Duke and Duchess attended a performance of the Royal Tournament, Earl's Court.

25   The Duke opened the International Council of Museums Conference, Barbican Hall, London.

26   The Duchess presented the London in Bloom 1983 prizes, Bedford College, Regent's Park.

27   The Duke and Duchess attended a garden party, Buckingham Palace.
The Duke presented awards to Australian Science scholars, Royal Institution, London.
The Duchess visited Explorers Unlimited residential course, Shrewsbury.

Engagements of **THE DUKE AND DUCHESS OF KENT**
August 1982-July 1983

August	10	The Duke welcomed 2nd Battalion Scots Guards from the Falkland Islands, RAF Brize Norton.
	30	The Duke attended reception for Commonwealth Finance Ministers, Tower of London.
September	5	The Duke attended Air Day, Duxford, Cambridgeshire.
	7	The Duke opened a Computer exhibition "ICCC '82", Barbican Centre, London.
		The Duke visited exhibition given by the Industrial Society, Bryanston Square.
	9	The Duke visited Farnborough Air Show.
		The Duke attended Computer Communications Banquet, Guildhall, London.
	20	The Duke named new lifeboat, Aldeburgh, Suffolk.
		The Duchess opened Scanner Unit, Ipswich Hospital.
		The Duchess opened Resin Plant, ICI, Stowmarket, Suffolk.
	21	The Duchess opened Myton Hamlet Hospice, Warwick and attended a service of thanksgiving in Coventry Cathedral.
	28	The Duke visited factories at Hull and Marfleet, Humberside.
	29	The Duke visited 2nd Battalion, Scots Guards, Chelsea Barracks.
		The Duke attended reception for the retiring Director of the Imperial War Museum, London.
October	4	The Duke attended rehearsal of London Philharmonic Orchestra, Henry Wood Hall, London.
		The Duchess attended reception to mark 1982 Appeal, National Society for Cancer Relief, Stock Exchange, London.
	5	The Duchess opened Boots' Consumer Products Development Laboratory.
		The Duchess opened central Headquarters building of Rushcliffe Borough Council.
	6	The Duke attended Commonwealth Study Conference Luncheon, London.
		The Duke attended Council Meeting, King Edward VII's Hospital for Officers, London.
		The Duchess presented awards for the Kent County Playing Fields Association.
	7	The Duke attended World Scout luncheon, Grosvenor House Hotel, London.
		The Duke attended London Philharmonic Orchestra's 50th Anniversary concert, Royal Festival Hall.
		The Duchess visited Boosey & Hawkes Ltd musical instrument factory, Edgware, Middlesex.
	8	The Duchess visited Norwich and Norfolk Triennial Festival, attending its opening concert at Norwich Cathedral.
	13	The Duchess opened Earl Mountbatten House, Fairlee Hospital, and visited The Family Centre, Newport, Isle of Wight.
	13	The Duchess visited Isle of Wight College of Arts, Newport.
		The Duchess visited Yarmouth Lifeboat Station, Isle of Wight.
	14	The Duke was inaugurated President of the British Computer Society. Queen Elizabeth Hall, London.
		The Duke presided at British Computer Society's Silver Jubilee dinner, Dorchester Hotel, London.
		The Duchess attended YMCA Women's Auxiliary Annual General Meeting, London.
	15	The Duke left London for private visits to Australia and New Zealand and an official visit to Hong Kong.
	16	The Duchess attended Annual General Meeting of the Spastics Society, Royal College of Surgeons, London.
	19	The Duchess opened new buildings at Bessels Leigh School, Abingdon, Oxfordshire.
	24	The Duchess left London to visit Hong Kong.
November	2	The Duke and Duchess arrived back in London from Hong Kong.
	3	The Duke and Duchess attended the State Opening of Parliament, Palace of Westminster.

Engagements of **THE DUKE AND DUCHESS OF KENT**
August 1982-July 1983 *(continued)*

November 9   The Duke presented Torch Trophy Trust Awards, Simpson's, Piccadilly, London.
                 The Duchess opened Continuing Care Unit, Compton Hall Macmillan Home, Wolverhampton.
          10   The Duke presided at Technical Education Council's award ceremony, London.
          11   The Duke attended Automobile Association Committee Meeting, Fanum House, Basingstoke, Hampshire.
                 The Duchess attended the Ivor Spencer Ball, London Hilton Hotel.
          12   The Duke attended a Scots Guards Memorial Service, St Giles' Cathedral, Edinburgh.
          13   The Duke and Duchess attended Festival of Remembrance, Royal Albert Hall, London.
          14   The Duke laid a wreath at the Cenotaph, for Remembrance Day. The Duchess attended the service.
          15   The Duke and Duchess attended the Memorial Service for Lord Rupert Nevill, St Margaret's Church, Westminster.
          16   The Duke and Duchess attended the State Banquet for Queen Beatrix and Prince Claus of the Netherlands, Buckingham Palace.
          17   The Duke visited the University of Surrey, Guildford.
          18   The Duke visited RAF Chivenor, North Devon.
                 The Duke and Duchess attended the State Banquet given by Queen Beatrix of the Netherlands, Hampton Court Palace.
          23   The Duke presented the Society for Historical Research Templar Medal, National Army Museum.
                 The Duke and Duchess attended a concert by the Royal Northern College of Music, St James's Palace.
          25   The Duke visited Fairey Engineering Ltd, Stockport.
                 The Duke attended Scots Guards Association Dinner, Ukrainian Club, Manchester.
                 The Duchess attended Royal Dragoon Guards Regimental Dinner, Piccadilly.
          28   The Duke attended performance of Mahler's 8th Symphony by the Bach Choir and the Royal College of Music, Royal Albert Hall.
          29   The Duke attended United Grand Lodge Masonic meeting, Freemasons' Hall.
                 The Duke attended Fellowship of Engineering lecture, Birdcage Walk.
                 The Duchess presided at Leeds University Degree Ceremony.
          30   The Duke opened Product Test Centre, MK Electric Ltd, Brunswick Park, London.
                 The Duchess opened Helen House Hospice, Oxford.
                 The Duchess presented prizes, Nuffield Orthopaedic Centre, Headington, Oxford.

December 1   The Duke presented South Atlantic Medals to members of the Household Division, Buckingham Palace.
            2   The Duke chaired committee meeting for European Music Year 1985, Arts Council, London.
            3   The Duke presided at University of Surrey Degree ceremony, Guildford.
                The Duchess opened Burns Unit, St Andrews Hospital, Billericay, Essex.
                The Duchess visited Basildon Corporation Headquarters.
                The Duchess visited Marconi Avionics Ltd, Basildon, Essex.
            5   The Duke and Duchess attended a charity gala performance at the Theatre Royal, Norwich.
            8   The Duke opened Sterile Products building, May & Baker, Dagenham, Essex.
            9   The Duke attended Variety Club luncheon, Hilton Hotel, London.
                The Duchess presided at Awards ceremony and a concert, Royal Northern College of Music, Manchester.
           10   The Duchess visited Cheetham's School of Music, Manchester.
                The Duchess visited the Christie Hospital and Holt Radium Institute, Manchester.

Engagements of **THE DUKE AND DUCHESS OF KENT**
August 1982-July 1983 *(continued)*

December	10	The Duchess attended Students' Christmas Ball, Royal Northern College of Music.
	14	The Duchess attended the Not Forgotten Association Christmas Party, Royal Mews.
	16	The Duchess attended International Show Jumping Championships, Olympia.
January	19	The Duke chaired a council meeting for the British Computer Society, London.
	20	The Duke left London to attend the Kandahar/Martini Skiing competitions, Sestriere, Northern Italy.
February	2	The Duchess left RAF Northolt to carry out engagements in Germany.
	3	The Duke and Duchess visited the International Sweets and Biscuits Fair, Cologne, Germany.
	4	The Duchess opened new courthouse, Leeds.
		The Duchess visited the department of Chinese Studies, Leeds University.
	6	The Duke and Duchess attended the Edward Boyle Memorial Trust concert, Royal Opera House, Covent Garden.
	10	Duke attended a concert by the London Philharmonic Orchestra, Royal Festival Hall.
	14	The Duchess attended BBC's exhibition to mark the 60th anniversary of children's programmes, Langham Gallery, London.
		The Duke visited the Men's and Boys' Wear exhibition, Olympia.
		The Duke attended a pre-conference dinner of the British Overseas Trade Board, Holiday Inn, Plymouth.
	15	The Duke presided at the British Overseas Trade Board Conference, Plymouth.
	16	The Duke chaired a presidential luncheon of the Modern Language Association, Royal Festival Hall, London.
	18	The Duke chaired the annual general meeting of Endeavour Training, Butchers' Hall, London.
	24	The Duke presented the Television Journalism Awards, Dorchester Hotel, London.
March	1	The Duchess opened the department of Rheumatology and Rehabilitation, Haywood Hospital, Stoke-on-Trent.
	2	The Duke visited the new headquarters of Wang (UK), Isleworth.
	3	The Duke visited Williams Grand Prix Engineers, Didcot, Oxfordshire.
		The Duke visited the National Environmental Research Council, Swindon, Wiltshire.
		The Duchess visited York House youth clubs, Milton Keynes, Buckinghamshire.
		The Duchess visited the factory of Steinberg and Son, Milton Keynes.
		The Duchess visited the Neath Hill Spastic Society Workshop, Bucks.
	4	The Duke and Duchess attended the opening concert of the Toronto Symphony Orchestra, Royal Festival Hall.
	8	The Duke attended the *Autopartec '83* Exhibition, Barbican Centre, London.
		The Duke and Duchess were entertained to dinner by the Jordanian Ambassador to London, Belgrave Place.
	9	The Duke attended the quarterly communication of Grand Lodge, Freemasons' Hall, London.
		The Duke attended the memorial service for Queen Helen of Roumania, St Sophia's Greek Cathedral, Bayswater.
	10	The Duke visited the Central Electricity Generating Board's nuclear installation, Heysham, Lancashire.
	11	The Duke installed as High Steward of the Borough Council of King's Lynn and West Norfolk, King's Court, King's Lynn.
	16	The Duke and Duchess left Heathrow Airport to visit Saudia Arabia and Jordan.
	25	The Duke and Duchess returned to London.

Engagements of **THE DUKE AND DUCHESS OF KENT**
August 1982-July 1983 *(continued)*

March	**29**	The Duke visited the Edinburgh branch of the British Computer Society.
April	**5**	The Duchess visited the Samaritans Centre, King's Lynn, Norfolk.
	12	The Duchess opened the Jan de Winter Clinic for cancer prevention advice, Brighton. The Duchess visited Copper Cliff Hospice, Brighton.
	14	The Duke and Duchess attended the service of the Royal Victorian Order, St George's Chapel, Windsor. The Duke visited the Wellcome Foundation, and the YMCA, Dartford, Kent. The Duke attended a performance of *Don Giovanni* given by the Kent Opera, Dartford. The Duke and Duchess attended the requiem mass for ex-King Umberto of Italy, Westminster Cathedral.
	18	The Duke attended the European Music Year 1985 committee meeting, Arts Council, Piccadilly, London.
	19	The Duke chaired a general committee meeting of the National Electronics Council, London. The Duke visited the All Electronic Show, City Hall, London.
	21	The Duke opened the Royal Masonic Benevolent Institution Home, Zetland Court, Bournemouth, Hampshire. The Duke visited Quest Automation, Ferndown, Hampshire.
	27	The Duke visited five RNLI stations in Lancashire and Cumbria.
	28	The Duke attended a Masonic convocation and investiture, Freemasons' Hall, London.
May	**12**	The Duke attended the Duke of Edinburgh's Commonwealth Study conference meeting, Wellbeck Way, London.
	15	The Duke attended a gala performance of *Rigoletto*, London Coliseum.
	16	The Duke opened the British Robot Association exhibition, *Automan '83*, Birmingham.
	17	The Duke presided at the annual presentation of RNLI awards, Royal Festival Hall. The Duke attended a council meeting of the RAF Benevolent Fund, Portland Place, London.
	19	The Duke attended the 80th anniversary reception of King Edward VII's Hospital for Officers, St James's Palace.
	22	The Duchess visited the Lawn Tennis Association's National Training Centre, Bisham Abbey.
	27	The Duke returned to Heathrow Airport from Egypt.
June	**1**	The Duke left RAF Northolt to visit 3rd Battalion, Royal Regiment of Fusiliers, West Berlin.
	2	The Duke took the salute at the Queen's Birthday Parade, Berlin.
	3	The Duke visited the 2nd Battalion, The Royal Regiment of Fusiliers, Berlin. The Duke returned to RAF Northolt, and attended the *Alliance Francaise* anniversary dinner, Royal Garden Hotel, London.
	8	The Duke visited Courage's brewery and the Digital Equipment Company in Reading. The Duke opened Reading Information Technology centre, Berkshire.
	11	The Duke attended the Queen's Birthday Parade, Horse Guards' Parade, London.
	12	The Duke attended a thanksgiving service for the Royal Northern College of Music, Manchester Cathedral. The Duke attended a Royal Northern College of Music gala concert, Manchester.
	14	The Duke visited British Aerospace plc, Dunsfold. The Duke attended charity concert, Lakeside Country Club, Frimley, Surrey.
	15	The Duke visited Huddersfield Technical College. The Duke visited factories in Huddersfield.
	20	The Duke attended the opening day of the Wimbledon Tennis Championships.

Engagements of **THE DUKE AND DUCHESS OF KENT**
August 1982-July 1983 *(continued)*

June **22** The Duke visited the Proof and Experimental Establishment, Eskmeals, Cumbria.
24 The Duke laid a wreath to honour Simon Bolivar, Belgrave Square, London.
28 The Duke entertained at dinner by the Saudi Arabian Ambassador, Kensington Palace Gardens, London.
30 The Duke attended a reception given by the Prime Minister, 10 Downing Street.

July **1** The Duke visited the Polytechnic at Wolverhampton, West Midlands.
3 The Duke attended the Tennis Championship meeting at Wimbledon, and presented trophies to the winners.
6 The Duke attended the Royal Agricultural Society Show, Stoneleigh, Warwicks.
8 The Duke attended the North of England Study Conference, Salford University.
12 The Duke opened BICC-Vero Packaging Ltd factory, Hedge End, Hampshire.
The Duke visited Fairey Allday Marine Ltd, Southampton.
The Duke opened new Fairey Allday boatyard, Cowes, Isle of Wight.
13 The Duke presented prizes at the Jubilee Schools project competition, Lanchester Polytechnic, Coventry.
14 The Duke attended a performance of the Royal Tournament, Earl's Court.
15 The Duke presided at a degrees ceremony, University of Surrey.
The Duke visited the Guildford Festival, Guildhall, Guildford.
16 The Duke attended the British Grand Prix, Silverstone.
18 The Duke named the new Penlee Lifeboat, and attended a service of thanksgiving, Newlyn, Cornwall.
19 The Duke attended the annual service of the Order of St Michael and St George, St Paul's Cathedral.
20 The Duke opened the new wing of the Royal Armoured Corps Tank Museum, and attended its Annual General Meeting, Bovington Camp, Dorset.
22 The Duke attended the opening concert of the 1983 Kings Lynn Festival.
27 The Duke attended the Norfolk International Jamboree camp, Royal Norfolk Show Ground, Norwich.
29 The Duke hosted a luncheon party for the President of the Ivory Coast, Lancaster House, London.

Engagements of **PRINCESS ALEXANDRA**
August 1982-July 1983

August 24 Presented prizes for 1982 Cutty Sark Tall Ships Race, Southampton.
26 Attended Charity Film Premiere, Odeon Cinema, Leicester Square, London.

September 1 Opened St Nicholas House residential community for children, Enfield.
20 Attended a gala performance, Perth Theatre.

October 4 Attended reception and presentation of New Zealand Red Cross Society awards, New Zealand High Commission, London.
5 Opened an Elizabeth Fitzroy Home for the mentally handicapped, Richmond, Surrey.
6 Opened new flats of the Royal British Legion Housing Association, Southsea, Hampshire.
7 Attended reception to mark 125th anniversary of Freeman Fox & Partners, London.
12 Attended meeting of British Red Cross Council, London.
13 Left London for Thailand for the Rattanakosin Bicentennial celebrations.
24 Returned to London from Thailand.
27 Attended Julio Iglesias concert, Royal Albert Hall, London.
28 Inspected preparations for International Festival of Fruits of the Earth, Westminster Abbey.
30 Attended inauguration ceremony of the Shrine Hall of Buddhapadipa Temple, Wimbledon.

November 2 Visited Queen Victoria Seamen's Rest Mission and opened the Princess Marina Medical Suite, Poplar, London.
Attended Anglo-Hellenic League reception, Hellenic College of London.
Presented at Falkland Islands Ball, Grosvenor House, London.
3 Visited the District Services Centre, Maudsley Hospital, Denmark Hill, London.
4 Left London for West Germany to visit regiments in Berlin and Munster.
6 Returned to London from West Germany.
8 Accompanied the Queen Mother to the Royal Variety Performance, Theatre Royal, Drury Lane, London.
9 Visited United Westminster Almshouses, London.
11 Attended a meeting of the Town and Country Members of Caxton Hall, London
12 Present at the Requiem Mass for Princess Grace of Monaco, Church of the Immaculate Conception, Farm Street, London.
13 Attended the Festival of Remembrance, Royal Albert Hall, London.
14 Attended Remembrance Day service, Cenotaph, London.
16 Attended State Banquet for Queen Beatrix and Prince Claus of the Netherlands, Buckingham Palace.
17 Attended Banquet given by the Lord Mayor of London for Queen Beatrix and Prince Claus, Guildhall.
18 Attended the State Banquet given by Queen Beatrix of the Netherlands, Hampton Court Palace.
22 Attended a Musical Evening given by the Purcell School of Harrow-on-the-Hill, Fishmongers' Hall, London.
23 Opened Elizabeth Newcommen House for doctors and nurses, Guy's Hospital, London.
Attended celebration of the Guardee Committee of the Jewish Welfare Board, Royal Opera House, Covent Garden.
25 Visited children's cancer unit, Kensington Ward, and opened a centre for clinical research, St Bartholomew's Hospital, London.
30 Opened Fairley House for dyslexic children, Princes Gate, London.
Attended Reception for the Diplomatic Corps, Buckingham Palace.

Engagements of **PRINCESS ALEXANDRA**
August 1982-July 1983 *(continued)*

December	1	Opened the 3rd World Travel Market, Olympia.
	2	Attended the 1982 Charles Carter Lectures, Lancaster University and was present at a dinner for Honorary Graduates.
	3	Opened The Sugar House, Lancaster University's campus social centre.
	15	Attended Mental Health Foundation Carol concert, Guildhall, London.
	16	Visited St Christopher's Hospice, Sydenham, Kent.
	19	Attended the International Show Jumping Championships, Olympia.
	20	Attended a Carol service, HM Remand Centre, Latchmere House, Richmond, Surrey.
January	12	Visited the Queen's Flight, RAF Benson, Oxfordshire.
	25	Attended rehearsals of the English National Opera at Lilian Baylis House, Hampstead, North London.
February	2	Attended a concert in aid of charity, Lambeth Palace, London.
	3	Attended the premiere of *Heat and Dust*, Curzon Cinema, London.
	19	Attended a concert arranged by the Anglo-Austrian Society, Royal Festival Hall.
March	22	Attended the State banquet for President Kaunda of Zambia, Buckingham Palace.
	24	Attended the State banquet given by President Kaunda of Zambia, Claridges Hotel, London.
	30	Attended a reception and film in association with Earthlife, Britannic House, City of London.
April	14	Attended the service of the Royal Victorian Order, St George's Chapel, Windsor.
		Attended the requiem mass for ex-King Umberto of Italy, Westminster Cathedral.
	16	Left London for Washington, to attend the dedication of the Ditchley Bells.
	20	Returned to London from Washington.
	21	Attended a recital given by the Royal College of Music for the Sultan of Oman, St James's Palace.
	23	Attended a thanksgiving service for the 200th anniversary of St George's Hospital, Westminster Abbey.
	27	Visited Queen's Road Estate, Richmond, Surrey.
	28	Attended an appeals committee luncheon for the Women's National Cancer Control Campaign, Grosvenor House, London.
	29	Opened the new control room, West Sussex County Fire Brigade Headquarters, Chichester.
		Opened the Concern for Life Mothers' Unit, St Richard's District General Hospital, Chichester.
		Opened a new municipal swimming pool, Littlehampton.
		Attended receptions to mark the Golden Jubilee of the Guild for Voluntary Service, Worthing.
May	4	Visited the annual holiday for the handicapped, Pontin's, Lytham St Annes, Lancashire.
		Opened a new guide dog training centre, Middlesborough.
	5	Laid the foundation stone of Emanuels School, Battersea Rise.
	10	Opened the West of England Antiques Fair, Bath.
		Visited the Temple Precinct excavations, Roman Baths, Bath.
	12	Opened a public park at Walkerburn, Scotland.
		Opened Hay Lodge Hospital and Health Centre, Peebles.
	19	Attended the 80th anniversary reception of King Edward VII's Hospital for Officers, St James's Palace.

Engagements of PRINCESS ALEXANDRA
August 1982-July 1983 *(continued)*

May 23   Attended Royal Academy of Arts dinner, Burlington House, London.

24   Attended a gala performance of *South Pacific*, Logan Hall, London University.

26   Attended St Mary-le-Bow Restoration service and a reception, Grocers' Hall, London.
Attended a London Contemporary Dance Theatre gala performance, Sadler's Wells, London.

June 1   Attended the England v Scotland Championship match, Wembley.

2   Attended the annual meeting of governors of King Edward's Hospital Fund for London, Paddington.
Attended reception and presented awards for the Cystic Fibrosis Research Trust, Savoy Hotel.

6   Attended a reception celebrating the twinning of Bond Street and Fifth Avenue, Intercontinental Hotel, London.

8   Visited the Royle Group of Companies Headquarters, North London.

11   Attended the Queen's Birthday Parade, Horse Guards' Parade, London.

14   Attended a River Thames Ship Towage reception, Fishmongers' Hall.

17   Attended the sounding of retreat by the Light Infantry, Raby Castle, Durham.

21   Visited University College Hospital, London.

22   Received Prince Naruhito of Japan, Thatched House Lodge.

23   Opened Alexandra House residential home, Southport, Merseyside.
Opened Crawshaw Court housing scheme, Huyton, Lancashire.

29   Visited the Central School of Speech and Drama, Embassy Theatre, London.

30   Named *HMS Peacock*, Royal Navy Patrol Craft, Aberdeen.
Attended a concert given by the Light Infantry and the Royal Green Jackets, Royal Albert Hall.

July 4   Presided at two degree ceremonies, University of Lancaster.

5   Presided at two degree ceremonies, University of Lancaster.
Opened a new therapeutic swimming pool, Mayfield School, Chorley, Lancs.

6   Presided at two degree ceremonies, University of Lancaster.
Opened the Trust House Forte Post House, Lancaster.

7   Entertained to dinner by the Wardens of the Goldsmiths' Company, Goldsmiths' Hall, London.

8   Attended the Memorial Service for Dr Eric Abbott, Westminster Abbey.

12   Visited Winn and Coales (Denso) Ltd, West Norwood, London.

14   Opened the new Breakwater Pier, Douglas Harbour, Isle of Man.
Opened Sulby Reservoir, Isle of Man.
Visited Ramsey, and Peel, Isle of Man.

15   Visited Port Erin, Port St Mary, and Castletown, Isle of Man.

21   Took the Salute at the Royal Tournament, Earl's Court.

22   Opened the new Parish Centre, All Saints Church, Tooting, London.
Attended the Royal International Horse Show, White City, London.

25   Opened the Cheshire Home, Jersey.

26   Carried out engagements in Jersey.
Attended a reception of the Royal Yacht Squadron, Cowes, Isle of Wight.

Engagements of **PRINCE AND PRINCESS MICHAEL OF KENT**
August 1982–July 1983

September 5 Prince and Princess Michael attended Charity Day at Amaretto Country Club, Northolt.
                7 Prince Michael attended the Farnborough International Air Show, 1982.
                10 Prince and Princess Michael presented trophies at the World Championships in Sports Acrobatics, Wembley Arena.
                14 Prince Michael visited Westland plc, Yeovil, Somerset.
                15 Prince Michael attended the SSAFA "Christmas Market" Reception, New Zealand House.
                16 Prince Michael visited Britten Norman and the British Hovercraft Corporation, Isle of Wight.
                17 Prince Michael attended the British Bobsleigh Association cocktail party, Royal Hospital, Chelsea.

October 7 Prince and Princess Michael attended the official opening of the Exhibition *Treasures from the Tower of London*, Cincinnati Art Museum, Ohio, USA.
             8 Prince and Princess Michael visited Kent State University, Ohio.
Prince and Princess Michael attended an Inaugural Gala in Cleveland, Ohio, to celebrate the establishment of an Arts College and Museum at Kent State University.
             15 Princess Michael visited Columbus, Ohio in connection with the British Store Promotion *Doorways to a Great Britain*.
Prince Michael addressed the Annual Luncheon of the Fellowship of the Motor Industry, Connaught Rooms, London.
             20 Prince Michael attended a meeting of the Trustees of the National Motor Museum, Beaulieu, Hants.
             21 Prince Michael visited the 1982 Motor Show, National Exhibition Centre, Birmingham.
             22 Prince and Princess Michael attended the official opening of the Teviotdale Leisure Centre, Hawick, Roxburghshire.
             25 Princess Michael attended the Women of the Year Luncheon, Savoy Hotel, London.
             26 Prince Michael attended the Motor Agents Association Annual Dinner, Dorchester Hotel.
             28 Princess Michael opened Rosser & Russell's new building development, Queen's Wharf, London.
             29 Prince and Princess Michael attended a Gala Dinner in aid of the Stars' Organisation for Spastics, Europa Hotel, London.

November 3 Prince Michael attended the Annual General Meeting of the Institute of the Motor Industry, London.
                5 Prince Michael attended the Yeomanry Dinner at Whitbread Porter Tun, City of London.
                7 Prince Michael took part in the 1982 RAC London to Brighton Veteran Car Run.
                10 Prince Michael attended a meeting and lunch at the Institute of the Motor Industry, Fanshaws, Brickendon, Herts.
                12 Prince and Princess Michael attended "An Evening with the Royal Philharmonic Orchestra", Banqueting Hall, Whitehall.
                13 Prince and Princess Michael attended the Royal British Legion Festival of Remembrance, Royal Albert Hall.
                14 Prince and Princess Michael attended the Service of Remembrance, Cenotaph.
                18 Prince Michael opened the new Engine Test Facility at the Motor Industry Research Association in Nuneaton.
                24 Prince Michael attended the Castrol Institute of the Motor Industry Gold Medal lunch, Savoy Hotel, London.
                25 Prince Michael attended the Annual General Meeting and luncheon of the Motor Industry Research Association, Hotel Europa.

November	30	Prince Michael attended the Presentation of the Ferodo Trophy, Dorchester Hotel.
December	1	Prince Michael attended a Council Meeting of the Royal Life Saving Society, New Zealand House.
		Prince and Princess Michael attended the British American Ball, Grosvenor House.
	17	Prince and Princess Michael attended the Breast Cancer Research Trust Ball, Sutton Place, Guildford, Surrey.
January	11	Princess Michael opened additional buildings to the Junior Section of Redland High School, Bristol.
	21	Princess Michael visited Beeches Green Catholic Youth Club, Stroud, Gloucestershire.
February	3	Princess Michael visited the Society of Women Artists Exhibition, Mall Galleries, London.
March	1	Prince Michael presented the Castrol/IMI Gold Medal, RAC Club London.
	4	Princess Michael presented the Dettol Midwifery Care Award at BBC Pebble Mill at One Studio, Birmingham.
	7	Princess Michael opened the Daily Mail Ideal Home Exhibition, Earl's Court.
	17	Prince Michael attended the London Transport Golden Jubilee Gala Concert, Royal Festival Hall.
	24	Princess Michael opened the new wing of the Garden Hospital, Hendon.
	28	Prince and Princess Michael attended a concert in aid of the Mental Health Foundation, Royal Albert Hall.
	29	Princess Michael presented Tufty Club/Woman's Realm Competition prizes for children, The Old Library, Guildhall.
		Prince and Princess Michael attended the Ulster Defence Regiment banquet, Mansion House, London.
	30	Prince and Princess Michael attended the naming ceremony of *Victory '83*, Fairey Allday Marine, Hamble, Hants.
	31	Prince Michael attended the meeting of National Motor Museum, Grafton Street, London.
April	19	Princess Michael attended the British Digestive Foundation reception, Lettsom House, Chandos Street, London.
	20	Princess Michael presented the Sony Radio Award trophies, Hilton International Hotel.
	21	Prince Michael attended the Honourable Artillery Company Annual St George's Dinner, Armoury House, London.
	22	Prince Michael attended Standard Telephone and Cables Annual General Meeting, London.
	23	Prince Michael attended Standard Telephone and Cables Management Information Meeting, Barbican Centre.
		Prince and Princess Michael attended Burma Star Association Reunion, Royal Albert Hall.
	26	Prince Michael visited Jaguar Cars, Coventry.
	27	Princess Michael attended the Ski Ball, Dorchester Hotel.
	28	Prince Michael visited Lotus Cars at Norwich.
	29	Prince Michael visited JCB at Rochester, Uttoxeter.
	30	Princess Michael visited Colt Car Amberley Horse Show and Country Fair, Cirencester Park, Gloucestershire.
May	7	Prince and Princess Michael attended the Kentucky Derby, Louisville, Kentucky, USA.
	11	Prince Michael attended the ITT Stockholders' Meeting, the Barbican.

Engagements of **PRINCE AND PRINCESS MICHAEL OF KENT**
August 1982-July 1983 *(continued)*

May	17	Prince Michael visited Talbot Motors at Coventry.
	18	Prince Michael visited Henlys at Hendon and Coventry.
	19	Prince and Princess Michael attended the presentation by the Queen of new standards to the Regiments of Household Cavalry, Horse Guards' Parade. Prince Michael attended the Army Air Corps Centre Guest Night Dinner, Middle Wallop, Hampshire.
	20	Prince Michael visited Marshall Limited at Cambridge.
	22	Princess Michael attended a charity auction, Littlecote, Wiltshire.
	23	Prince and Princess Michael visited the Chelsea Flower Show. Prince Michael attended an STC Communications Lecture, Savoy Hotel.
	25	Prince Michael visited SSAFA Units in West Germany. Prince and Princess Michael attended the FA Cup Final replay, Wembley, and Princess Michael presented the Cup.

June	1	Prince and Princess Michael attended the Beating Retreat, Horse Guards' Parade.
	2	Prince Michael opened Security Centre's office in Manchester. Prince Michael visited the factory of HJ Quick, Manchester. Princess Michael opened the Americas Cup Exhibition, Aquascutum, Regent Street, London.
	3	Prince and Princess Michael attended Eton College Combined Cadet Force Trooping the Colour, Eton College.
	5	Prince and Princess Michael attended a performance of *Medea*, Barbican Centre, London.
	6	Prince Michael visited Standard Telephones and Cables at Paignton.
	8	Prince Michael attended a luncheon with the Institute of Highway Engineers, and received the Honorary Fellowship of the Institution, Hyde Park Hotel.
	11	Prince and Princess Michael attended the Queen's Birthday Parade.
	14	Prince Michael visited Bristol Cars, Filton, Bristol.
	15	Prince Michael visited the Battersea Power Station. Prince Michael visited Hoopers Coachworks, Willesden.
	16	Prince and Princess Michael attended Ascot Races. Princess Michael attended the Royal Ascot Ball, Cafe Royal, Regent Street.
	18	Prince and Princess Michael left London Heathrow to attend a special performance of *Turandot*, Royal Opera House, Vienna.
	20	Prince and Princess Michael attended the Renaissance Ball in aid of charity, Sutton Place, Guildford.
	22	Prince Michael presented the Institute of Administrative Management "Office of the Year Award", Ironmongers' Hall, London.
	23	Princess Michael attended luncheon and presented the Silver Clef Award, in aid of the Nordorff-Robbins Music Therapy Centre, Intercontinental Hotel.
	25	Prince Michael attended a garden party at the Royal Life-Saving Society Headquarters, Mountbatten House, Studley, Warwickshire.
	28	Prince Michael visited Scammell Assembly Plant, Watford, Herts.
	29	Princess Michael attended a hair fashion show, Rainbow Room, Kensington High Street.
	30	Prince Michael attended the Society of Genealogists Annual General Meeting, Royal Overseas League, London.
	30	Princess Michael attended the David Bowie Gala Performance, Hammersmith Odeon.

July	3	Prince and Princess Michael attended the Finals of the Lawn Tennis Championships, Wimbledon.
	5	Princess Michael opened St George's Shopping Centre, Gravesend.

Engagements of **PRINCE AND PRINCESS MICHAEL OF KENT**
August 1982-July 1983 *(continued)*

July   **7**   Princess Michael attended the AGM of the British Digestive Foundation, Lettsom House, Chandos Street, London.

      12   Prince Michael attended the Worshipful Company of Scientific Instrument Makers' Election Court lunch, London.

      13   Prince Michael attended the AGM of the Royal Patriotic Fund, Royal Chelsea Hospital. Prince and Princess Michael attended a Garden Party at Buckingham Palace.

      16   Prince Michael attended the British Grand Prix, Silverstone.

      17   Prince Michael attended Badminton Air Day, Gloucestershire.

      20   Prince and Princess Michael attended the Royal Tournament, Earl's Court.

      21   Prince and Princess Michael attended the Royal International Horse Show, White City.

      23   Prince Michael attended the RAF Benevolent Fund Air Tattoo, Greenham Common, Berkshire.

      31   Prince and Princess Michael opened their garden at Nether Lypiatt Manor, in aid of the British Red Cross Society.